CREATION

RESTORING THE CREATION MANDATE

HEALING for People, Pets, Plants, and the Planet

by

DR. ROGER DE HAAN

RESTORING THE CREATION MANDATE: Creation Doesn't Die, We Kill It—*Healing for People, Pets, Plants, and the Planet*

ISBN: 978-0-924748-80-6

UPC: 88571300050-5

Printed in the United States of America

Milestones International Publishers
140 Danika Dr. NW
Huntsville, AL 35806
(256) 830-0362; Fax (256) 830-9206
www.milestonesintl.com

1 2 3 4 5 6 7 8 9 10 / 10 09 08 07

DISCLAIMER

The information and procedures contained in this book are based upon the research and the personal and professional experiences of the author. They are not intended as a substitute for consultation with your physician or other health care provider. The publisher and author are not responsible for any adverse effects or consequences resulting from the use of any of the suggestions, preparations or procedures discussed in this book. All matters pertaining to your physical health should be supervised by a health care professional. It is also a sign of wisdom, not weakness, to seek a second or third opinion.

DEDICATION

I dedicate this volume to my children and grandchildren. They are the promise of the future. With the passing of years, I am better able today to share what I wish to instill in my family. So, I say to Reuben, Andy, Paul and to their precious wives, thank you for not settling for a trifling 8-5 existence of work or falling into contemporary traps that rob time but produce nothing of excellence. Your talents and creativity are alive and well. Thank you for dedicating yourself to searching out your creative purpose in life. We live in a day when it is great to be alive!

ENDORSEMENTS

Dr. Roger De Haan sheds a profound and insightful light on creation as well as on the true power of "man's dominion."

We are in control. Out choices determine the outcome in all aspects of life. If your desire is to live a long, healthy, meaningful life, as well as to secure a foundation of health and nutrition both physically and spiritually for your family and friends, and yes…even bring healing to Planet Earth, then this book is for you. Learn how your choices can make a difference in your world.

—James B. Richards, President and Founder, Impact Ministries, Huntsville, Alabama; Bestselling author of *Breaking the Cycle* and *How to Stop the Pain*

I am thankful that Roger De Haan has taken the time to write a wake-up call regarding our stewardship of God's creation—and the resulting lack thereof. I can speak with compassion when I say that we, as a nation, and as the body of Christ, are missing out on the daily reminders of God's eternal power, never mind the benefits, of healthful practices, by no longer interacting with His creation as part of our lifestyle.

Beginning at age 19, I spent the next 17 years immersed in the outdoor life of Montana's Rocky Mountains. Living a life of organic farming, animal husbandry, home births and natural health care practices showed me God's power and natural principles. Over the past several years of suburban life in the Boston area, it has been heartbreaking to me to see that disconnection with the creation is a common ailment for which we are paying the price of poor health and spiritual impotency.

In his book, *Creation Mandate*, Dr. De Haan reminds us that we are designed to be stewards of God's creation for our benefit and for His glory. What pleasure it must have given God to see Adam, the first man, interact with His animals and eat the fruit of His plants and trees (Gen. 1:24-31; 2:7-9, 15-20a). As Dr, De Haan explains, our choosing to live connected to creation delights God (Gen. 1-2), helps us see God (Rom. 1:20), and keeps us healthy.

Once you grasp the principles that Dr. De Haan elaborately outlines in *Creation Mandate*, the practical applications will make sense. If you are willing, you will find ways to implement them into your life and make a difference for your generation and the next.

—Jackie Bell, Certified Health Practitioner, MA

May 2007

Dr. Roger is a progressive and powerful crusader for the natural health cause. He is a leader in all aspects of the journey that man is privileged to undertake in God's kingdom. Never before in the history of man has the statement, "Your fruit shall be your food *and* your medicine," been more apropos than it is in our world today. Our entire world is in the throes of a health crisis of unprecedented magnitude. We truly are dying by the fork!

I am blessed and honored to call Dr. De Haan a friend and fellow crusader. This book contains powerful and common sense knowledge. Putting into action the ideas set forth in his series of books will lead readers to great wisdom, which will result in increased knowledge, better health and a more enjoyable quality life. I highly recommend both books!

—Jay P. Vanden Heuvel PhD

Board Certified Holistic Health Practitioner

Roger's book strikes close to home in my own heart and mind. For years God has been growing within me a vision for reconnecting with the earth—the land and soil that we are formed from. It all began with a word study of the various Hebrew and Greek words for land, earth, soil, etc. I continue to be amazed at the central and pivotal role that the land plays in God's scheme of things, a role tragically missed by the vast majority of Christians today.

Fortunately, Roger is not alone in this call to remember our Creation Mandate, but the voices are still too few and far between. The time has come to once and for all throw off those vestiges of gnosticism that have colored the Church's view of our relationship to this earth that God called "very good."

It is common knowledge that the identity and destiny of God's original chosen people, the Hebrews, was intrinsically interwoven with the land. Acts 17:26-27 clues us in to the fact that it wasn't only Israel who was given this kind of connection to the land. Every people group on the face of the earth has its own unique "boundaries" that have been given by God for the purpose of exploring and seeking out God's purposes for them on that geographical spot.

The Lord told the founder of a recently established ministry that he should build what can last for a thousand years. A major paradigm shift is upon us. We can either keep our heads buried in the sand, or we can become a part of that army that recognizes the Great Commission as a call not only to all nations but also to "all creation" (Mark 16:15). The Church has been part of the problem long enough! Roger's book can help many begin to turn the tide of indifference and ignorance and stimulate a repentance that will result in action, not mere lip service.

—Bruce Jones

This remarkable book gives encouragement to those of us who know that we have a God-ordained mandate to take responsibility for all parts of creation. It is one of the great features of this book. We all need more of this kind of inspiration to push ahead, try harder, and really accept our calling—especially when the call we receive is not one that is generally accepted by most people, including many Christians. Here is a touching challenge to do more for the glory of God, now, while we still have the opportunity. If we all accept the challenge, with God leading us, we can truly be used to do more than we can think or imagine.

Growing up in the same family with Roger on an organic farm was part of our unique educational experience. We realized early the problem poisons were causing to our health and the environment. I learned early that bug sprays killed "good" bugs, made farmers sick, and gave many people allergic reactions from the chemical-laden foods. Our dad made a first-rate start, with our commercial organic farm, in teaching us to care for our world.

After Roger came back from the jungle and started learning and sharing his experiences with better nutrition, herbal remedies, and holistic health care, I discovered that he had many fascinating and helpful solutions that I could put to the test. Applying the results of these natural approaches, we were able to resolve family difficulties such as chronic ear infections in two of my young children and difficult chronic fatigue issues of my own. We now have a much greater appreciation of how important it is to learn all we can about health care, and that we can often improve or prevent illness in ourselves, in our animals and in the plants gracing our gardens.

—Sherry Brummel B.A., N.C.H.P.
(Natural Certified Health Professional), Michigan

Creation Mandate, by Dr. De Haan, presents ideas and opportunities too large and important to ignore. Sometimes the scope and meaning of our lives and purposes are lost in the rush and rashness of modern culture. This book begins the process whereby the scope and meaning of our lives can be regained, understood, and responsibly acted upon. It meets a deep need for believers who are interested in the questions and answers they will face when they meet their Creator.

Mankind's stewardship was never meant to be an impotent or powerless thing, but was, in truth, a powerful and genuine *trust* the Creator endowed His creation with, manifesting His great wisdom and faith in His Creation. Yahweh trusts *us* to fulfill His mandate for creation's benefit. We could probably say, "He trusts us more than we trust Him," and not be stretching the truth.

Most believers that we meet are committed to obedience, but many times they are unsure of the tasks required of them. They want to get beyond profession and confession into real action. You only believe what activates you into action.

Creation Mandate is an excellent textbook for all believers who truly seek to walk in obedience and make a real difference in this world. The truth is *everyone can do something*—something good for this world. We are delighted to endorse Roger De Haan's powerful book. We will never again be the same—in a good way!

—Rev. Qaumaniq Suuqiina and Dr. Suuqiina.
(Dr. Suuqiina is the author of: *Can You Feel the Mountains Tremble—A Healing the Land Handbook.* See the Suggested Reading List.)

"Mankind has always had the tendency to swing the pendulum from one extreme to the other. The great debate between physical and spiritual truth has had convincing advocates on both sides. Unfortunately, this unbalanced approach has left multitudes in the doldrums, unable to reach their prescribed destiny—fulfilling their *Creation Mandate.* Roger DeHaan has sought to catch the wind of balance for the marriage between life in the Spirit and its practical application in the physical realm. Roger has effectively sounded a trumpet to awaken us to the realities of the laws of sowing and reaping, laws which apply to the spirit, as well as the soul *and* body. Can we expect to put water in the gas tank of our car, pray over it, and hope for the best? Can't put inappropriate fuel into the body either, and expect the best results! Thank you, Roger, for igniting the spark of challenge to dress and keep the garden of God."

—Garry Snow, Minister,
2004 Body for Life Grand Champion, Arkansas

Dear Roger: I agree with what you wrote. I believe that the redemption of the body, soul and spirit is what God wants. God is after an eternal work of redemption. I can get excited about how God works creatively through man whom He redeems. The most important part of this subject is that man must come under the covering of the Spirit of God. As we look back on the major discoveries in science, medicine and other areas of creativity, all came from inspiration—and inspiration comes from God. He quickens an idea, followed by an unrelenting desire to know more. I know your book will be a blessing to all who read it.

—Susan Lin: Missionary to the Orient

"Everyone wants to know what I think about taking vitamins, or super greens, or something, because they want the ok that that's all they have to do. If I eat some salad, not too much junk food and take a vitamin or super food and then I'm healthy, right? Meanwhile, they are absolutely clueless about health as a lifestyle, about the common cold being a natural cure for the body, that our intestinal flora is part of our immune system, and so on. I want them to understand and use Biblical principles in their daily health practices, such as sowing and reaping, and repentance and cleansing. I want them to see the sins of idolatry, slothfulness and pride in the way we eat and practice health (or practice disease!). So keep writing! Spell it out for us."

—Jackie Bell, Health Practitioner

I met Dr. Roger DeHaan while living as a missionary in Costa Rica, where I was also a principal member of an Environmental Foundation and Consulting firm. What a rare blessing it has been to associate with one who has such a clear vision and understanding of the Creation Mandate that God has given to all mankind. We live in a day and age where this aspect of the Gospel has all but been overlooked, to our harm and shame. Dr. DeHaan sounds a clear call to all of us that says, "God has commanded His children everywhere to care for His creation—every human soul—as well as the earth that these souls must live in." I count it a privilege to be associated with such a Biblical Visionary!

—Paul H. Cleath, Fundacion Oro Verde, San Jose, Costa Rica

Roger: I would agree with your thesis. It is clear that the church has a mandate to deliver the earth from its present state of corruption. It is not easy to express heavenly mysteries in earthly language. What you so clearly express is only possible in Christ.

—Rev. Arthur Jehle

In our world today, there is a great divide between much of what is considered to be science and Christianity. Many espouse the belief that if you believe in Christianity, you cannot be considered a scientist. Roger DeHaan is like the scientists of two hundred years ago who made discoveries in science because they saw clues in the Bible that stirred their scientific imaginations. Roger also sees the joining of science with God's Word (the Bible) as the ultimate in scientific investigation. The greatest scientific discoveries came from this approach, and it is still the strongest way to conduct experimentation. The relationship between the Creator and His creation is still there, just as it was with Adam in the beginning.

The church today has left unchallenged those who hold to the view that science and Christianity cannot be mixed. It is encouraging to see Roger challenge this misconception. It is my hope that others will be encouraged by his book to follow in his footsteps.

—Rev. Bob Sprinkle, Temple Presbyterian Church, SC

Dr. Roger DeHaan's first book, *We Don't Die, We Kill Ourselves,* clearly illustrates the correlation between optimal health and physical, emotional, and spiritual well being. This, his new book, *Creation Doesn't Die, We Kill It,* reinforces and builds on those principles and puts us on a path clearly outlined by the Creator Himself. I love the illustrations and the simplicity with which he puts forth these truths. I love the challenges placed before us that *if* we are willing to persist in our pursuit of health and blessing, they are there waiting for us. Naturally, changes need to be made, sometimes massive changes, but this book explains those changes and opens up a path of hope and revelation. Why not try it? Start by reading this dissertation on how we can reverse a curse in our lives and everything else on this planet. It is time to obtain vitality in body, soul and spirit as never before!

—Terry Kelly, missionary and professor, Georgia

I have known Dr. De Haan for over 35 years. If I were to describe him, one thing for certain I would say is that he is a paradigm-buster. If you are up for challenge and adventure, I highly recommend that you read his book, *Creation Doesn't Die, We Kill It.* Dr. De Haan clearly reveals that our physical bodies and our physical life and the environment around us are all part of God's plan. As he so well states: "God so loved the 'cosmos.'"

From a Christian standpoint, as a word of caution, I think it is important that nobody should take any of these wonderful principles and practices of life and turn them into law. If that became the case, it would only become another legalistic practice where those who can follow it well would feel self righteous and those who cannot would feel condemned. What Dr. De Haan has written, as I see it, is essentially a guidebook that shows us a route to a more healthy, enjoyable, and rewarding lifestyle...all to the glory of God.

I want to encourage everyone to read this inspiring book, for it will impart a much bigger picture of the heart of God. All of creation has sprung from the inspiration of God and is worthy of nurture and stewardship. If the creation and the created human are in balance, as intended by God, then abundant life will flourish. It is not a matter or worry of worshiping the creation more than the Creator, as some might be tempted to conclude; rather, it is discovering the perfect balance and harmony where God is magnified in all that He is. But to get there is a long road, and if the readers of this book would only take a few of the valuable points and incorporate them into their lives, they would take a huge step toward joining with the heart of God on this exciting journey called life.

—Mary Savard, NC, health enthusiast, nature lover, wife and mother.

QUICK REFERENCE GUIDE

Three compelling and urgent reasons for reading this book.
Introduction

The Miracle of Black-Eyed Peas in the jungle.
Read Chapter 1

The Miracle of 100-fold melons—seeing is believing.
Read Chapter 2

Challenges of a Jungle Doctor, against all odds.
Read Chapter 3

Dr. Pottenger's Cat studies—we must change course NOW!
Read Chapter 4

Should the church "ecclesia" engage in a health ministry?
Read Chapter 5

Can animals and plants actually talk and make sense?
Read Chapter 6

Four Principles of Basic Nutrition you can use Today.
Read Chapter 9

Clean or Unclean meats, does it even matter?
Read Chapter 10

Seven powerful guidelines to a healthier & happier diet
Read Chapter 10

Your DNA (genes) can be harmed or healed by your foods!
Read Chapter 11

Hip Dysplasia in dogs is nutritional, definitely *not* genetic!
Read Chapter 11

Five scary lessons in genetic manipulation—be aware!
Read Chapter 11

Vaccinations are Controversial, get educated!
Read Chapter 12

The mystery, power and safety of home foliar spraying.
Read Chapter 12

A proposed worldwide network of Training Facilities.
Read Chapter 12
A doctor cured himself of cancer—but why not his wife?
Read Chapter 14
YOU *can* Hear God's Voice! Four powerful guidelines.
Read Chapter 14
Here's how to tame an angry tiger cat.
Read Chapter 15
Red, Yellow, Black and White—our cultural challenge.
Read Chapter 18
A Creation Mandate "Word Picture" you must understand!
Read Chapter 19
A powerful concluding prayer of dedication & purpose.
Read Chapter 20
Answering a pastor's three powerful accusations.
Appendix 1
Answering an agnostic's probing questions.
Appendix 2
Answering the question of the "Origins" and "First Use."
Appendix 3
77 more Scriptures that challenge us to ACTION.
Appendix 4

TABLE OF CONTENTS

	Dedication v
	Preface xix
	Introduction xxiii
	Three Reasons for Writing This Book
Chapter One	**Calling All Dreamers!** 1
	Our Connection with the Earth; One Couple's Dream;Where Have All the Dreamers Gone?
Chapter Two	**It's Time to Reconnect** 13
	Overflowing Abundance; The Law of the Continuum; Health Care is Ministry Too!; Man: Machine or Spirit Being?
Chapter Three	**A Long and Winding Road** 25
	Out of the Box and into the Jungle; From Veterinarian to Medic and Dentist; An Alternate Route; Holistic Health Care
Chapter Four	**Dietary and Emotional Factors of Disease** 37
	The Pottenger Cat Study; Garbage In, Garbage Out; Nutrition: The Forgotten Element
Chapter Five	**Spiritual and Scriptural Insights into Husbandry of the Earth** 47
	The Image of God in Animals; Reconciliation is On the Way!; We Are Called to Be Salt and Light; The Body-Mind Connection; Blessings and Cursings
Chapter Six	**Animal Husbandry is Part of Our Mandate** 61
	Animal Nutrition? Go Natural!; Let's Learn from the Animals; Can We Communicate with Animals?
Chapter Seven	**Mega-Shift** 71
	Thirty Characteristics that Typify an Expanding Group of the Stressed World Population
Chapter Eight	**Ten Steps to Healing Your Individual Creation** 81
	1. Hear; 2. See; 3. Touch; 4. Believe; 5. Empower Others; 6. Seek Counsel; 7. Be Patient; 8. Experiment;

9. Follow the Plan; 10. Never Never Give Up; 11. (Bonus) Be a Well-Grounded Dreamer

Chapter Nine **Take Care of Your Temple** 91
Basic Nutrition; Retrain Your Eating Habits; Exercise, Rest and Sleep

Chapter Ten **Clean or Unclean—Does It Matter?** 103
Are the Dietary and Hygienic Laws of Moses Still Applicable Today?; Why "Clean" and "Unclean"?; Defining Clean and Unclean Animals; What, Then, Should We Eat?; Seven Guidelines Toward a Truly Healthy Diet; Scriptures Relating to Creation Law Dietary Guidelines

Chapter Eleven **Nutrition and Genetics Mystery Solved** 115
Five Scary Lessons in Genetic Manipulation that are Preventable!; We Have a Creative Opportunity to be Guardians of the Future!; Canine Hip Dysplasia is NOT Genetic; It is Time to Jump Off the Merry-Go-Round and into the Answer Apparatus!

Chapter Twelve **Healing Yourself and Your Environment: Additional Tips** 127
Vaccinations; Foliar Sprays; The Treasure of Good Soil; "Soil Is Better Than Gold"—Article by Dr. Robert Rodale; My Dream: A Worldwide Network of Training Facilities

Chapter Thirteen **Intuitive and Spiritual Tips for Healing the Creation** 139
The Anointing; Common Sense; Be A Lighthouse; Use Professional Guidance; Prayer

Chapter Fourteen **Learning to Listen to God** 147
A True Story; Preparing Our Hearts to Hear; "You Can Hear God's Voice!"—Article by Dr. Mark Virkler

Chapter Fifteen **Taming the Tiger!** 159
(Winning the Trust of Animals)—Step #1: Nutrition; Step #2: Natural Flower Essences; Step #3: Be Non-threatening; Step #4: Let the animal make the first move; Step #5: Use a neutral object to build trust; Step #6: Understand and use non-verbal communication; Become Like Children

Chapter Sixteen **Can a Hopelessly Damaged Eye Be Restored? 167**
1. MSM (methylsulfonylmethane); 2. Magnetic therapy; 3. Nutrition; 4. Frequency, sound, music, laser and Rife hertz treatments; 5. Laying on of hands; 6. See; 7. Speak; 8. Believe

Chapter Seventeen **Lyme Disease: The Unrecognized Epidemic 175**
All in Your Head?; A Tricky Invader; Understanding Your Enemy by Searching Outside the Box; Cutting-Edge Lyme Disease Treatments to Consider; Nutritional Support; Commit to Positive Change to Achieve Your Miracle; Balance is Another Key to Your Miracle; Find a Qualified Health Coach

Chapter Eighteen **The Joys and Benefits of Diverse Cultures Working Together 189**
The Judge was Shocked!; A Hopi Indian Prophecy Concerning the Oneness of the Human Race; Great Shakings and Imperialistic Empires Have Built Walls Rather than Bridges; God Moves in All the Nations and People Groups of the Earth; Color Blind and Culture Blind; A Massive Shift is about to Break Forth; A Missionary Incentive for All Cultures; Twelve Personal Points to Ponder in Moving Toward Oneness

Chapter Nineteen **Spokes and Wheels: A Stunning Word-Picture of Our Creative Calling in Christ 205**
Agriculture; Animal Husbandry; Nutrition; Geography; History; Government; Religion and spirituality; Arts & Music; Science; Language Skills; Mathematics; Social Skills

Chapter Twenty **Creation Mandate: Concluding Thoughts 213**
Creation Mandate: A Worldview Worth Considering; Do You and I Have the Authority Required to Restore and Replenish the Earth?; Application; Model Prayer of Repentance

Appendix One **Response to a Pastor in Maine 223**

Appendix Two **A Response to a Challenge Regarding the Legitimacy of Homeopathy 241**

Appendix Three **A Response to a Question Concerning "Origins" or "First Use" 247**
The Origin of Things, Their Proper Use and Significance

Appendix Four **Creation Mandate Scriptures 253**

Appendix Five **Creation Mandate Definitions** 263

Suggested Reading and Website Resources 267
Various Resources for Basic Animal, Human, and Soil Information; Creation Mandate Suggested Reading and References; Websites

Endnotes 271

About the Author 275

Contact Information 275

PREFACE

This book, my second published by MileStones International Publishers, is Volume 2 of a planned three-volume series that challenges the status quo of small thinking with regard to the health and welfare of the earth and its inhabitants. The first book in this series, *We Don't Die, We Kill Ourselves: Our Foods are Killing Us,*" could be said to be the *body and bones* of my message, the natural and necessary foundation for everything that follows. This second volume, then, is the *heart and soul* of my message, the center of what I have always sought to be and to share. It digs into the very reason we were created as a human race and, therefore, delves deeper into our purpose on this planet than did the first volume.

We humans have a calling from our Creator to stewardship of the total creation: people, pets and plants, as well as the planet itself. He created, chose and empowered us to *heal the wounds* of the creation that are manifested daily in hurting people, in dysfunctional pets, in diseased plants, in nations in conflict and crisis, and in everything else on our planet that groans. We have a destiny to fulfill and a dream to realize. This book reveals what holds us back and lays out principles and strategies for achieving the breakthroughs that are necessary for the healing of our planet.

As caretakers are we too late to heal a planet so out of balance? Is there still time to discover and apply answers for the traumas of "Mother Earth"? Any workable solutions will call for great creativity. Fortunately, creative caretaking perfectly fits our job description. Being a caretaker does not necessarily mean that you must live with soil between your toes and labor with a hoe. We are all so different from one another. Our callings and talents are different. One thing we all have in common, however, is that we share the same sick, troubled planet. The time for complacency is past. What we need to do now is to get off our duffs and do something proactive for ourselves and all we share the planet with. Plant some flowers, walk the dog, stop to feel the wind blowing in our faces—and ask God for the spirit of revelation to propel us into the realm of invention and innovative answers!

By joining our hearts, working together in harmony, sharing our creative talents and speaking life into this planet, we can still carry out our job of caretaking and do it with excellence! But it calls for radical thinking, radical faith, and radical decisions while at the same time remaining humble, teachable and accountable to God and to each other as we pursue genuine answers together.

Even a casual observer would acknowledge that our world is getting worse and worse every day. And where is the body of Christ—the *ecclesia*—in all of this? There are many in the church who are complacent about the problem, expecting that the church will be "rescued" at any moment, at the sounding of the last trumpet! Our true calling as believers, however, is to saturate the nations with the gospel of the Kingdom of Heaven. The gospel is more than just a message on how to be forgiven of our sins and receive eternal life. The gospel of the Kingdom contains answers to all sorts of problems; solutions for the "groan" in every cell of this planet, not just in people but also in pets, wildlife, plants, soil, rocks, hills, mountains, oceans and rivers of our beautiful globe.

This book contains practical steps that every believer can take in regard to hearing, seeing, speaking, dreaming, and creating for the betterment of the earth and everyone and everything on it. You and I have real answers for this generation because the Kingdom of God is within us. It is time for the Kingdom of God in us to show itself in nitty and gritty ways at every level of life and need.

One defining characteristic of the Kingdom of God is *creativity.* The spirit of revelation belongs to the Kingdom. The heavens are open to those who believe. Inventions are within us. *Creativity is a necessary component of the Kingdom.* The answers are there waiting to be uncovered. How the world needs to hear the answers from the perspective of the Kingdom of God!

In college during the 1960s, my faith was sharply challenged by the claims of humanistic evolution, which was widely touted to hold the answers to all the world's problems. At the same time, the radical movement of "free love," drugs and rebellion swept through much of my generation. There was a saying on my campus, "Don't go walking through the bushes at night, as they are very active and might kick you!" This was just before dorms went co-ed. How did I survive this onslaught of worldly morals and philosophy?

I survived because I was tuned to a different drummer. Today I thank God for the stable faith of my parents, a faith that for me resulted in a solid grounding in biblical thinking. Thank God for the large church library where I checked out books on history, apologetics, science and religion. Thank God that I was beginning to know the Creator in a very personal way. Thank God for high school youth groups, Intervarsity Christian Fellowship in college, and other fine examples that helped build foundations that did not crumble.

Armed with these fundamentals, I withstood the challenges of university "scientific" analysis and pompous atheistic professors of philosophy. Somehow I was able to consider alternate ideas and theories and yet grow more solid in my own beliefs. You will find some of those beliefs in this book.

I also have always loved to read and do research. Thank God for dictionaries, concordances, and writers of previous centuries who seemed wiser than many of our present day academic but humanistic scientists and theologians, many of whom seem to have lost "The Path." It was Isaac Newton who said, "If I have seen farther it is because I have stood on the shoulders of giants!" In this book you will find some of the wisdom and stellar accomplishments of some of those giants, believers who laid solid foundations for us to build on.

Therefore, I now salute the various scientists, astronomers, geologists, biologists, apologists, healers, writers, theologians, fathers, instructors, friends and fellow travelers who held to the light even when it was very, very dark. We stand because they stood. We see farther in our hour because they were faithful in their hour.

Isaac Newton also said, "I find more sure marks of authenticity in the Bible than in any profane history whatsoever." I read some of the touted authors of the 19th and 20th centuries, profane agnostics such as Robert Ingersoll, David Hume, Thomas Huxley, Bertrand Russell and Charles Darwin. In the end, theirs proved to be philosophies of sinking sand. Some of them actually repented on their death beds. Others, filled with fear, approached death with curses, foaming at the mouth and screaming. Death without inner faith and peace is a scary way to depart life.

Amazingly, I was able to see through their smoke screen. My own faith increased as I progressively perceived the empty arguments of writers and professors who uttered pompous pronouncements from their pedestals but whose lives displayed gaps in integrity and character. Modern humanism, hedonism, gnosticism and time-honored Greek philosophy are crumbling around us. It is evident from the decaying nature of societies, governments, health systems and stuffy religions based on those philosophies.

We have the honor of living at a time in history when our lives can make a dramatic difference in the outcome of world events. Our assignment is to live as though nothing were impossible. The command to disciple the nations is not figurative. It is a literal command. But what does the making of disciples include? Read on! The destiny of nations hangs in the balance. Our words have creative force. We are capable of all sorts of things. But we must first maintain stewardship of our own hearts!

Let us also be faithful to pave the way for the next generation for the sake of our children, grandchildren and great grandchildren! A brighter day lies ahead. Light is always stronger than darkness. Darkness is merely the absence of light. May this book strengthen your own candle of true creativity into a flaming blaze, a torch that lights up the way for future generations!

—Dr. Roger L. De Haan

INTRODUCTION

Ours is a world in crisis.

Even aside from political, social and moral upheaval, both the human species and the physical world we live in are in the midst of a health crisis unprecedented in history. We have poisoned ourselves and our environment and the deadly consequences to our bodies and to our planet have reached pandemic proportions. Almost everyone agrees that something is desperately wrong but there is little common agreement on the exact nature of the problem—or the solution. That is the reason for this book.

Three Reasons for Writing This Book

My purpose in writing this book is threefold. First, I intend to demonstrate the intimate and inseparable relationship between the *natural* and the *spiritual* realms of creation. This essential relationship has been marginalized by a humanistic and naturalistic philosophy that is totally unbiblical because it dismisses the spiritual dimension of creation as either nonexistent or, at most, irrelevant. This book will show that the key to healing our planet and ourselves is found in restoring this vital relationship. You hold in your hands a guidebook for natural and spiritual healing.

Secondly, I propose to provide a Scriptural foundation for the title of the book. You and I are not here by accident! We are part of an orderly, purposeful universe. God created us for a reason. He has given us a *CREATION MANDATE*:

> [27]*So God created man in His own image; in the image of God He created him; male and female He created them.* [28]*Then God blessed them, and God said to them, "Be fruitful and multiply; fill the earth and subdue it; have dominion over the fish of the sea, over the birds of the air, and over every living thing that moves on the earth"* (Genesis 1:27-28).

King David, the "sweet psalmist" of Israel, echoed this same awareness of man's purpose:

> [4]*What is man that You are mindful of him, And the son of man that You visit him?* [5]*For You have made him a little lower than the angels* (Heb. *elohim*, lit., "God" or "gods") *And You have crowned him with glory and honor.* [6]*You have made him to have dominion over the works of Your hands; You have put all things under his feet,* [7]*All sheep and oxen—Even the beasts of the field,* [8]*The birds of the air, And the fish of the sea that pass through the paths of the seas* (Psalm 8:4-8).

Essentially, God created us to exercise dominion over the rest of His created order; to care for the land and the environment and all the creatures that inhabit the earth. Frankly, man's overall track record in this regard is dismal. Instead of embracing our dominion with the gentleness of a caretaker, we have manhandled it with the brutality of a dictator. We have raped the land, polluted the water and poisoned the air. And with most of the people in the industrialized world living in the glass, metal and concrete mazes of the cities, the majority of humans on the earth have lost touch with the *husbandman within*; we have lost our connection to our creation mandate.

Instead of embracing our dominion with the gentleness of a caretaker, we have manhandled it with the brutality of a dictator.

One uniquely gifted preacher of the 1960s and 1970s who had a powerful message of "restoration," said, "God's farmer will have wisdom and knowledge. He will not take from the land and not restore again. He will not uproot and then not replenish. God had sovereignly commanded Adam and Noah 'to replenish the earth': to build up that which had been removed. IF they were faithful to do this—then the land would respond abundantly."

Children generally have the same characteristics as their parents. Do you have "farmer" blood in you? You should; God is your Father, and He planted the first beautiful garden! You and I have been crowned and equipped to take care of our earthly dominion. So far, we humans have done a pretty poor job fulfilling our mandate. It falls to us—everyone alive today—to change the trend and record of the past. We have a great work before us to reverse the mess we have inherited from previous generations. If we don't do it, who will?

My third purpose is to *show how this can be done!* By weaving together science, technology and theology and by adding personal history and experiences, I will speak specifically about how we can learn to dream again—how we can learn to hear God speaking specific words of direction via dreams and visions into the crevices of our intuition and our hearts as we tune to His flow. This book, therefore, is the fruit of my learning, labor and life experiences over a period of more than 50 years. In a very real way it is the summation of my personal journey.

Our creation mandate is to exercise our God-given dominion over the created order. This means accepting our responsibility of stewardship over the earth and its resources. *Stewardship, however, includes a lot more than dirt! It includes having authority over the arts! It means drawing music out of the heavenly realm and planting it on earth! Stewardship involves controlling wind and fire for tasks that make the human life enjoyable! It means inventions, conversation, creativity, writing, teaching and working with purpose! And finally, stewardship means fulfilling our divine calling on earth, driven with purpose and a zeal for excellence!*

A new paradigm is on the horizon. In the pages that follow I will present an "apologetic" for a truly scientific philosophy of health—but with a twist. In our investigation the Holy Bible as well as the "book of nature"—the natural world of God's creation—will be our guide. To the skeptics out there who resist "religion" and the traditions of the past and who even may question the existence of God, let me challenge you to suspend your doubts for a time and open your heart. The philosophies and ideas of man have failed. It's time to try something else. The only way to heal our planet and ourselves is to return to God's original design and plan. We must sift through all the disinformation and uncover the hidden truth of the ancient ways. It will be an exciting, even stunning journey that just may change your life forever!

It is my hope and prayer that this book will inspire you to a renewed and growing love for the land, for agriculture, for the animals, for the arts, for invention and for your fellow human beings with whom you share this planet—persons of all colors, cultures and curious beliefs. And I hope it will challenge you to nurture that love. Everything begins and ends with love because God *is* love. This love, however, must encompass more than it has in the sterile historical past. May it enlarge us and enliven us as together we take up the challenge to stretch our boundaries to encompass new dimensions of life and dominion!

Roger L. De Haan
May 2007

Summary

1. We have poisoned both ourselves and our environment and the deadly consequences to our bodies and to our planet have reached pandemic proportions.
2. There is an intimate and inseparable relationship between the *natural* and the *spiritual* realms of creation.
3. The key to healing our planet and ourselves is found in restoring this vital relationship.
4. God created us to exercise dominion over the rest of His created order; to care for the land and the environment and all the creatures that inhabit the earth.
5. Instead of embracing our dominion with the gentleness of a caretaker, we have manhandled it with the brutality of a dictator.
6. It falls to us—everyone alive today—to change the trend and record of the past.

ENDORSEMENTS FOR CHAPTER ONE

"I believe you've GOT IT. The heart of the Father for His people, and a vision for where we are headed. I see the same things as you do all around (good and bad) and my wife and I have had experiences walking in some of it. We have experienced what Bruce and Becky (chapter one) long for, to a small degree.

Your book should be an overwhelming success because it will "strike a chord" with the hearts of many believers today. We see God doing the very things in the hearts of people all over today, which you describe, that is, beginning to dream of what is possible "in God."

—Rev. Ben Konkle, California

"What happened to you with black-eyed peas (chapter one) happened to me with Mexican white-corn, Cacahuazintle. In Mexico, these corn stalks never grow much above 6 1/2 feet; in Canada the corn stalks grew above 9 feet! We did not have the patience or knowledge to watch as you did in Colombia, but your message is clear!

The seed, the soil, the weather and amount of light have relevance, but mainly it is the Lord who gives increase!" 1 Cor.3:6; Col 2:19.

—Prof. Raul Cardenas, Mexico

Chapter One

CALLING ALL DREAMERS!

I had just prepared a garden plot in the steamy jungle of Colombia, in South America. It was the 1970's. I had never planted black-eyed peas before. It was a southern pea and I was a northern boy! My teacher and mentor had flown in from the States for a series of teachings. Black-eyed peas were among his favorites and he asked if he could plant them. "Sure," I replied. "Need any help?"

"Nope; I would just as soon do it alone," which he then proceeded to do. As I watched from a distance I saw nothing spooky, nothing abnormal. Nothing, that is, until those peas began to grow—and *grow* and **grow** and **GROW**!!! Those plants produced like nothing I had ever seen before: baskets and baskets full of black-eyed peas!

How tall and proliferate are these peas, I wondered? My southern friends told me they normally grow about 16 inches high. These were over 5 feet tall! Wow, I thought, this is an answer to food in the jungle! But never again did a crop of peas grow over 16 inches tall.

I was puzzled. What secret lay in the hands of that man, my mentor? Did he talk to the seeds? Did he say some kind of prayer that I did not hear? Did he have an intimate connection with the earth that brought forth such fruitfulness; an ancient connection like that at Eden, a connection that most of the rest of humanity has lost? How did this miracle happen? And, more importantly, could it happen again?

Our Connection with the Earth

Each of us bears a personal responsibility for the creation. Without exception, every one of us as human beings—and especially those of us who are believers—has a *creation mandate* from our Creator; a mandate that connects us inseparably to the land—the very soil of this planet Earth that is our home. God has entrusted us with an important job to complete. He has a specific purpose on earth for each and every one of us. This means that life is worth living! It also means that He has endowed each of us with the specific gifts and talents we need to fulfill our purpose. Otherwise we would miss both our calling and our specific inheritance here on this earth.

Our creation mandate has been in effect ever since Adam, newly created by God, took his first breath as a living being. From the moment he was created, Adam had a special deal. God had prepared a beautiful and magnificent garden in Eden and He placed Adam there to dress it and keep it. Adam's "job" was to exercise dominion over the physical creation on earth: to rule over the plants and animals and birds and fish—all the flora and fauna of the earth. His assignment involved more than simple care-taking and maintenance, however. Adam was to be creative, turning something that was already good into some greater design. By doing so he would reflect the creativity of the God in whose image he had been created. He was to complete the job God started.

Adam was to be creative, turning something that was already good into some greater design. By doing so he would reflect the creativity of the God in whose image he had been created. He was to complete the job God started.

Isn't that what a caretaker and husbandman does, especially one created in the very image and likeness of his Creator? By God's design, Adam knew exactly what to do! Genesis 2:19 tells us that Adam gave names to all the animals. I believe personally that he also talked to the animals and to the plants as well. Whatever the case, wonderful things began to happen in that garden under Adam's care. Fruitfulness to a magnitude unmatched and probably unimagined by any gardeners or farmers anywhere during the ages since. No sweat, no tiredness, no weeds (although weeds are merely plants out of place), no arduous labor trying to coax a crop out of reluctant and resistant soil. Overflowing abundance was everywhere!

Nothing has been the same since the day Adam and Eve, the original farmers/gardeners, were evicted from Eden for disobeying their mandate. In Romans 8:21-22, Paul says: "*The creation itself also will be delivered from the of corruption into the glorious liberty of the children of God. For we know that the whole creation groans and labors with birth pangs together until now.*" Sin affected *all* of creation, not just Adam and Eve! Many people overlook this fact, and doing so generally leads to a myopic view of life.

All of creation groans with "birth pangs" for liberation back into God's original design. Those groans include humans but go beyond humanity into the very heart and womb of every created thing. This understanding is foundational to the theme of this book.

Our first responsibility as Christians is to reach and touch the people of the world with the gospel of Jesus Christ—to "make disciples of all the nations" (Mt. 28:19). But our responsibility does not end there. Our creation mandate includes touching and restoring *health care* for people *and* pets *and* livestock *and* the soil *and* the entire creation! At no time has our creation mandate from God been changed or rescinded. John Milton wrote a great classic called "Paradise Lost." In Romans 8 Paul here is talking about "Paradise regained!" That is the challenge that is before us! What an inspiring and challenging mission! Wow! Are you beginning to get the bigger picture?

In his recently published book, *The Heart's Code*, cardiac researcher Dr. Paul Pearsall writes: "Simple physics tells us that energy and information leave the body and go out into space. It reaches our loved ones and our PETS and PLANTS."[1] In other words, whether we know it or not, whether we intend it or not, and even whether we believe it or not, every one of us "broadcasts" into the creation 24 hours a day!

Whether we know it or not, whether we intend it or not, and even whether we believe it or not, every one of us "broadcasts" into the creation 24 hours a day!

Each of us is endowed with something extremely powerful and unique to speak into the creation. We have a message of freedom to and for the "lesser creatures" and it is *our responsibility to liberate them also!* Many pets in my practice have been "rescued" from homes where they were being abused or abandoned. They carry in their cells gut-wrenching issues of fear, of abandonment, and many have physical scars. They come to me for answers. That is part of my job!

Although most people today (especially those who live in the cities) have little or no sense of their fundamental connection to the soil and to the creation as a whole, mankind's original creation mandate has never been rescinded. I believe that if we are to have any hope of healing our planet as well as ourselves, we must return to our original mandate. We must reconnect with our God-given bent for working the soil and unleashing marvelous creativity in our world. Learning to work with our hands and with our creative minds is what this book is all about.

I have worked with plants and animals since childhood. At first it was just a job, working under the direction of my father. As I grew older, my vision also grew. I came to understand that I had two fathers, one natural and one spiritual. Through relationship with God, my spiritual Father and the highest authority in my life, I recognized that I was called to tend the larger creation—to restore what had become damaged goods and to bring out the best in that which was less than average. As I grow older I am gripped more and more with an increasing sense of what this all means. It is awesome to be called to be creative, to grow, to learn and to have the opportunity to leave creation better than I found it!

As I grew older, my vision also grew. I came to understand that I had two fathers, one natural and one spiritual.

As beings created in the image of a creative God, every one of us was born with the innate ability to be a creative genius. God designed us to be innovative in nature; to become enterprising pioneers! And pioneers dare to experiment. Pioneers live at the edges of truth! Pioneers go where others fear to tread. Pioneers dare to take calculated risks. Pioneers don't fear making mistakes because they understand that failure is a part of learning. And while all of us are creative by nature, we are each unique, equipped to make a singular contribution to the world that no one else can make.

As beings created in the image of a creative God, every one of us was born with the innate ability to be a creative genius.

A hundred years ago, most people still lived on and worked the land, even in the industrialized nations. Today, only 3% of the population tends to the soil and that number is fading fast. No wonder most of us have become disconnected from our original mandate! Over the last century farming has changed rapidly from a family-supported business to an industry owned and run by huge corporate conglomerates. And yet within the hearts of many—and their number is growing—something still resonates: the distant memory of their calling to the soil.

The nature of a husbandman to the earth still stirs within. The connection is still there, however faint. My purpose with this book is to reawaken our vision and reeducate us to our need to reclaim our original creation mandate and to reconnect with the land!

Few Christians in the west today would regard such an "earthy" vision as having any real connection to a "spiritual" life or a meaningful ministry. We are too thoroughly caught up in our modern high-tech, fast-paced, consumer-driven society to think of a life lived close to the land as anything more than a quaint and sentimental reminder of a simpler past that is gone forever. Or is it? Gradually, more and more people are waking up to a dream for a simpler, less stressful life.

One Couple's Dream

Bruce and Becky, a Christian couple who are friends of mine, have just such a dream. Bruce, who currently is a painter, was born and raised in a third-world country to missionary parents. Although he has no practical farming experience, he dreams of getting back to the land. And Bruce and Becky both confess to having difficulty explaining their dream in a way that their friends and acquaintances understand. Bruce says:

Most Christians get a glazed-over look in their eyes whenever we've tried to explain our vision to them; it just doesn't fit with what the Church has defined as a valid "spiritual" vision or "ministry". Actually, we don't want to define this as a "ministry," but more as a lifestyle that brings together the spiritual and the physical into a harmonious relationship. This disconnect seems to predominate in the world and, unfortunately, in the Church as well.

Our vision focuses more on "the land," which to us means moving away from cash dependency to being increasingly self-sustainable on a piece of land. Personally, we find close connections with such things as eating organically and taking a holistic approach to health. Our interest in Israel and Hebraic roots dovetails in a rather interesting way, because Israel's destiny has always been tied up intricately with the land. If you separate Israel from "the land", you've separated her from her destiny.

I see that as a microcosm of this larger picture—that the Church has substituted Gnostic tendencies, where knowledge has been substituted for practicality. We too, as the people of God, will miss our destiny if we think we can continue living disjointedly from the earth.

And Becky adds:

All I know is that:

1) I want to raise our children in the country.
2) I want to have chickens and goats.
3) I've never felt like I fit in the city or urban setting although we've lived in the city for 15 out of our 24 yrs of marriage.
4) I waited 40 years to dance, having that desire for that long a time. Hebraic dance came along (for free and right down the street), so I jumped at the opportunity. It's always been my desire to do folk dancing....I've wanted to have a building or barn where there could be live music and people enjoy square or folk dance on a regular basis.
5) Eating healthy is important to me too...raising some of our own produce, and joining a food co-op.
6) If I ever grow up—I thought I'd like to be a naturopath! (a person who eschews drugs and surgery for disease treatment in favor of natural treatments such as air, water and sunshine)

Somewhere deep inside me I feel like whenever we get property, that land will minister to us and we will minister to it. I can't say that to just anyone because, as Bruce said, people's eyes just glaze over.

Where Have All the Dreamers Gone?

What about you? What is *your* dream? What ignites and excites your creative spirit? Are you alive and bubbling with ideas, plans and dreams? Or has your creative flame been snuffed out by the "practical realities" of life or, perhaps, by the demands of a dogmatic religion that regards any emphasis on "nature" and the physical land as "unspiritual"?

It is no secret that young children generally are highly creative, especially during their preschool years. Studies reveal, however, that around the age of six 90% of the creative part of their brain shuts down. Why? They get boxed in by regimented training and a "one-size-fits-all" approach to education. Their creative spirit is suppressed and submerged under social standardization until they become pasteurized, "canned" copies of cultural conformity.

One morning during church I looked around me and was shocked to notice that at least 60% of the people in attendance were overweight. Out of that group I knew that, statistically, 2 out of 5 would be diabetic and another 2 out of 5 eventually would die of cancer. The more I reflected on these numbers the more I wondered if they were symptomatic of a deeper truth; a reflection of something in the spiritual realm. Did our current epidemic of obesity say something about the *spiritual* state of modern humanity? Even worse, did it expose the spiritually lukewarm status of contemporary culture and especially modern Christianity? *Something* certainly was amiss!

Upon further thought I realized that modern man *as a race* was sick; one of the telltale symptoms was that *our creative instincts were nearly dead.* People were sick and tired and also were sick and tired of being sick and tired! Who would wake us up? Could sick people dream? Could people who were nearly dead be brought back from the brink.

I realized that modern man as a race *was sick; one of the telltale symptoms was that* our creative instincts were nearly dead.

That's when it became *personal.* What could *I* do to sound the alarm? I am not a radical person by nature, but a radical thought occurred to me that I needed to do something to rock the boat. If we Christians are called to help restore creation, we have not done a very good job. Our own bodies are falling apart! Only radical answers would serve to reverse our downward slide. Recovery and restoration would be a demanding uphill journey.

We spend so much time and energy nourishing and strengthening our inner spiritual man while our physical bodies, our health and our creativity are squandered. Does this make any sense? Why have we let ourselves get fat through poor diet, camping under only one or two trees when *all* the trees of the garden are calling out to us with their delectable fruit? Why have we allowed ourselves to become fat and lazy mentally by camping around one or two favorite doctrines or ideas when a whole world of discovery is available to us? How have we become so sedentary that we are no longer exploring, building, working and redeeming? Why has our lust gone to our belly rather than our passion into powerful creative building, nurturing families brimming with hope, ideas and joy?

Press the limits? No way! Take sides? Not unless it is the "safe" side, usually the politically correct side. Most of us do our best never to rustle any feathers. We try not to make any waves. We rarely take any risks. And we rarely accomplish anything! More often than not, religion dampens our dreams rather than inspiring us to enlist in God's army to "take the kingdom."

I predict that unless we turn the tide, an enormous tragedy is coming on the earth. It will roll in like a tsunami, sweeping away all in its path. Will we get off that path now, or will we ignore the danger and end up flattened by its power, pressed into gingerbread men with no ability to express ourselves? It is time to sound the trumpet and awake the sleeping! The grim reaper is swinging his sickle. I do not want to be counted among the dead! Do you?

Who could deny, observing the state of our world today, that the creation is badly out of order? Who has dominion over the earthly realm: the mosquitoes...or us? Cancer...or us? Seventy diseases for which there is currently no treatment or cure...or us? Science has failed us. Cancer research has failed us. Billions of research dollars have failed us. The armies of the world have failed us. Today we are no closer to elusive answers than we were 100 or even 1000 years ago. Yet we have far more knowledge...and far more problems! We now possess the means to destroy the earth and all life on it. But it seems that we are farther away from the answers to life's critical questions than we were when the so-called "scientific revolution" began! Don't get me wrong; I am not against science. But I am in favor of using science the way it was intended to be used: to illuminate and elucidate the glories of God's creation!

Who has dominion over the earthly realm: the mosquitoes...or us? Cancer...or us? Seventy diseases for which there is currently no treatment or cure...or us?

Are the answers out there that we need? Yes indeed! The key to unlocking those answers lies with every true follower of Christ, because each and every one of us has breathtaking potential! We must discover *who we are*, what our calling is and how to walk daily in that calling! Answering these questions is the objective of this book.

I have a dream that is based on principles and promises that are clearly presented in the Word of God for this present age. Our generation stands on the precipice between two ages: the failed practices of the past and the limitless potential of the future. Trust me; there *are* real answers for the problems of this present creation! Reversing and healing our present condition, however, is stalled until we find those answers. As the "Bride of Christ," the church is called to "make herself ready." The Scriptures tell us how to do that!

Our generation stands on the precipice between two ages: the failed practices of the past and the limitless potential of the future.

Miracles abound all around us if we will but look to see them. Yet even with those miracles you and I have tasted only a tiny portion of what the Scriptures call the "in part" realm. Real answers wait for a more complete fulfillment...for a people *committed to finding answers for the here and now!*

Those liberating answers are way beyond the grasp of any one person or group of persons. For the answers to mankind's problems to unfold, our search for truth must reach a critical mass worldwide in the hearts and minds of millions of individuals. Currently, global population exceeds six billion individuals. It may be that no more than one or two in a thousand will have any desire to look beyond their own noses for answers. But those one or two, multiplied on a worldwide scale, could be enough to unleash answers that will sweep the globe. And *that* is our purpose for being born!

It may be that no more than one or two in a thousand will have any desire to look beyond their own noses for answers.

Where have all the dreamers gone; the creative geniuses; the folks who refuse to settle for the status quo? Consider some of the "dreamers" of the Bible: Abraham, Moses, David, Elijah, John the Baptist, Jesus, Paul. In their own ways, radical "wild men" and risk-takers every one! These were men who lived life on the edge—and changed their world. Can such energy, zeal and world-changing creativity be restored in our generation? My answer is *yes*! Absolutely!

Today, despite the critical nature of the crisis, there is much reason for hope. In the background, a fresh wind is stirring. Over the last 5-10 years a shift of perception has begun to occur. More and more people, and young people especially, are becoming fed up with the status quo. They are tired of empty, meaningless tradition and hunger for something fresh and new. The answer for the new is to return to the old: the creation mandate that God established in the beginning and still holds out to each of us today. The hour is late but there is still time to change. But it will require of us a whole new paradigm of life and health and science and faith. Are you a dreamer? Are you hungry? Are you ready? Are you up to the challenge?

More and more people, and young people especially, are becoming fed up with the status quo.

Summary

1. Each of us bears a personal responsibility for the creation, a *creation mandate* from our Creator; a mandate that connects us inseparably to the land.
2. Our first responsibility as Christians is to reach and touch the people of the world with the gospel of Jesus Christ—to "make disciples of all the nations" (Mt. 28:19). But our responsibility does not end there. Our creation mandate includes touching and restoring *health care* for people *and* pets *and* livestock *and* the soil *and* the entire creation!
3. We must reconnect with our God-given bent for working the soil and unleashing marvelous creativity in our world.
4. As beings created in the image of a creative God, every one of us was born with the innate ability to be a creative genius.
5. We must discover *who we are*, what our calling is and how to walk daily in that calling!

ENDORSEMENT FOR CHAPTER TWO

"I loved reading the chapters you wrote. When I was a child we raised most of what we ate. We had chickens, cattle, a huge garden and an orchard. As children we worked in the garden, put up hay, worked with cattle and did many other things. Most kids today would not even begin to know what that kind of life was like. We worked very hard but I never felt bad for working hard. I can't say that I was fond of it always as a kid but I look back now and cherish what I did as a kid. One of the first times Dave (my husband) came to see me, my sister and I were throwing hay from a wagon into the hay loft and stacking it. We as girls worked like guys."

—Diann Burton, NC

Chapter Two

IT'S TIME TO RECONNECT

Several years ago, when I was living in Frazee, Minnesota, Heidi, my next-door neighbor, purchased several plants at a local nursery. The nursery also offered her their last 3 end-of-the-season spindly cantaloupe melon plants, just to get rid of them. They were the left over rejects from a flat nobody wanted. Heidi took them, but having no room in her garden for melons she thoughtfully brought them over and asked if I wanted to plant them in my garden.

"Sure," I replied. "I don't have any melons planted. It will be nice to enjoy some home grown melons." I accepted the melon plants gratefully and immediately planted them in my garden. However, even though mine was an entirely organic garden with no chemical fertilizers or no toxic sprays, those poor plants still got off to a rough start. Stunted and spindly to begin with, they didn't respond well at first. Deciding after a couple of weeks that they were planted in the wrong location, I transplanted them to another spot. To make matters worse, one afternoon during a roto-tiller weeding session, one of the melon hills was accidentally cut in half by the rotating power blade, and barely survived.

Because I care intensely about my gardens, I was already applying my green thumb. I foliar sprayed homeopathic and plant nutrients on the plant foliage, carefully observed the plant growth, put down straw mulch and performed other "fatherly" actions. Finally, the melon plants began to grow. Beautiful yellow blossoms sprouted everywhere—thousands of them! However, by the end of July, as I carefully parted the leaves, longing for baby melons, I could not find a single blossom that had turned into a melon.

What was wrong? This was highly abnormal. I did not understand why those plants were not producing any melons. As I pondered the problem I thought of the remarkable George Washington Carver, who was characterized as "the scientist who talked to flowers." Anyone familiar with Carver's work knows of the amazing things he did with plants.

But talking to flowers? Please understand that I am of a strict and somewhat stoical theological heritage and, in addition, was born and nurtured as somewhat of an introvert. Talking to *people* was enough of a challenge for me, to say nothing of talking to plants! That seemed downright illogical! It simply was not *my nature*. But since it seemed to work for Carver, I decided to try it. I decided to talk to those melon plants; to speak softly and encouragingly to those yellow blossoms; to try to coax them into giving me some sweet, juicy melons because producing melons was *their nature*. It was only fair and reasonable, I thought, to "ask" these plants to provide delicious fruit. After all, that was their "job" on earth, wasn't it?

It was only fair and reasonable, I thought, to "ask" these plants to provide delicious fruit. After all, that was their "job" on earth, wasn't it?

Thirty melons seemed a reasonable request, I thought. A little high perhaps, but then again, look at the hundreds of beautiful blossoms! So in my mind I "asked" them to produce 30 melons for our family and for our neighbor Heidi and her family. Even as I made my request I pictured those melons in my mind. Being also a believer in prayer, I asked God to bless those plants with abundance.

As I continued mulling over my melon situation I remembered from a course I had taken several years earlier that the *mineral sulfur was a key to triggering flowers into fruit bearing mode.* Quickly I hunted down my powdered sulfur and added it carefully to my foliar spray solution. I decided that homeopathic sulfur would be a good idea also, so I added some to affect the energetic part of the plant. I also have a unique way of preparing a solution so that it is "balanced." Since there are several ways to do that, I chose a way that was easy and the most convenient for that moment.

Then, remembering that it had not rained for several weeks, I had another thought: since melons are mostly water, was it reasonable of me to ask them to produce 30 melons if I did not provide them with sufficient water? Hastily I rigged up a hose and sprinkler, which I used to soak the ground with water twice a week. I also diligently applied my foliar spray concoction on a weekly basis in the evenings, just before sundown. Now the only thing I could do was wait to see what would happen.

Overflowing Abundance

About two weeks later I noticed that baby melons had begun to form. Beginning as fuzzy little stumps, they grew very rapidly to one and two inches in length. I was quite pleased with the initial results. My interest in this little project intensified as I perceived that my experiment was actually working!

Meanwhile, the melon plants themselves were also growing vigorously. They sprawled over and through the fence and shot out in every direction. I was amazed at the lush growth. Never before had I seen that many blossoms, that many melons and that many runners. I could almost taste those melons!

Frazee is located in northwestern Minnesota about an hour from Fargo, North Dakota. I postulated that the town name must have originated from the word "freezer" but, although I asked around, I never found anyone who knew for sure. During our first winter after moving there, the temperature plummeted to 56 degrees *below zero*! And the temperature stayed below zero for more than 30 days that winter! Early-September brought a killer frost. This was the same fall of my melon experiment! We had already eaten a few melons but I had no idea of the treasure that lay hidden on those hills until that early killer frost decimated the leaves.

We had already eaten a few melons but I had no idea of the treasure that lay hidden on those hills until that early killer frost decimated the leaves.

As the leaves shriveled and turned brown, I could not believe my eyes. I stood in shocked amazement and counted melons by the hundreds! They were lying on the ground, hanging on the fence and over and through the fence. I took out my camera and shot numerous pictures as witness to this special miracle. As further witness, I brought several friends over to see my garden, and especially this highly unusual production of melons. I counted 30…60…90…100…and kept counting. I finally *stopped* counting at 300 and there were still many melons to go! Those three scraggly, spindly, reject melon plants had produced over 300 melons! Melons were lying on top of melons. And all of this in a total area approximately 8x18 feet square! I had never seen so many melons hugging each other—except in the back of a truck or on a fruit stand.

Those three scraggly, spindly, reject melon plants had produced over 300 melons! Melons were lying on top of melons.

How could three hills of melon plants even *sustain* that number of melons? It would appear scientifically impossible and yet there they were. Seeing is believing. A horticultural miracle had taken place! What is a miracle? A miracle is something that takes place that is outside the norm, beyond our understanding and which cannot be explained by our everyday experience. This melon experience was *way* over the top!

What was the key, I wondered, to such phenomenal growth? Was it merely the plants' response to my petition? Had God answered my prayer? Was it the foliar spray and the added sulfur at just the right time? Was it a combination of good soil and water? Was it the heart of the husbandman, seeking 30-fold but being blessed with 100-fold production? Personally, I am convinced that it was *all of the above*! How else could I account for this miracle of "multiplication"? Can we dissect out any single ingredient when it was the combination of all these factors that led to success? There was no one single "silver bullet" but a *series of keys* that each did their part to help unlock the potential of those plants to produce this kind of harvest.

Can I guarantee that I could reproduce that experiment? Probably not. But this amazing melon production was a *lesson* to me and for me, which I gladly share with you. I hope that this story of my experience will stir something inside of you, whether you are a gardener or not; a Holy Spirit desire to duplicate this same kind of experience—overflowing abundance—in your own life! There are great blessings in the earth just waiting to be manifested on behalf of those who can "catch the vision" and who are willing to walk this road of expectation and faith.

There are great blessings in the earth just waiting to be manifested on behalf of those who can "catch the vision" and who are willing to walk this road of expectation and faith.

The Law of the Continuum

At this point some of you may be thinking, "So what? Your 'bumper crop' of melons is an interesting, maybe even fascinating story, but what does it have to do with me? Why is it so important? I'm not into gardening or farming, so why should I care?" Good questions. As I said in the Introduction, most people today have lost the sense of closeness to nature and the land that once was almost second nature to humans—a closeness built into us by our Creator.

My story of the abundant melons is important because of what I call *the law of the continuum.* All living things on earth, including the living soil, all the plants, all the insects, all the animals on the land, in the sea and in the air, and all of mankind as well, are intimately related and interconnected on the biological, emotional and spiritual levels. This interrelationship is hard for many of us to understand, distant from the land as we are because of our city-dwelling ways and high-tech lifestyles.

In using the word "continuum" I mean that everything in nature is directly connected to everything else. It is so convenient to divide life into neat compartments that never get connected, but this does not accurately reflect reality. Just as there is a close connection between our natural body, our soul and our human spirit, all unified into one person, there is also a direct connection between the *natural* and the *spiritual.* At the same time, a *direct connection* exists between mankind and the rest of the creation!

For example, many major health problems and diseases that frequent the human body have been found also in trees and in just about every other form of life. As another instance of this continuum, humans and plants both have a circulatory system. Blood flows through ours while sap flows through theirs. The difference between human and plant blood is quite small. Human blood is red because of the mineral cobalt. Plants substitute the mineral magnesium, which is why plant "blood" is green. And just as we humans use our lungs to exchange carbon dioxide for oxygen to nourish our blood, plants also have a form of respiration where they take in carbon dioxide and release oxygen. In an even more startling example of this direct connection, numerous experiments have demonstrated that every form of life, including plants, is capable of some degree of emotional feeling and response![2]

The difference between human and plant blood is quite small. Human blood is red because of the mineral cobalt. Plants substitute the mineral magnesium, which is why plant "blood" is green.

On the emotional level, there are various hertz and electromagnetic frequencies (love, peace, fear, anger, etc.), which are inherently present and can affect every form and level of life. This means that the very herb, nutrient, homeopathic remedy or medical remedy that helps you may likewise be beneficial for your animals and crops. The law of the continuum applies universally. We are all intimately and directly connected to each other and to all other life on this planet. To a significant degree, our future and the future of our planet depend on our rediscovering and reclaiming this vital link!

For decades there has been in America, as well as in Europe, a serious disconnect between theology and stewardship of the earth. Stewardship (or environmentalism, as some call it) has been regarded as a "liberal" issue and therefore many conservatives, including conservative Christians, have resisted buying into it. Until very recent years, responsibility toward the creation has not been a high priority generally among conservatives. I contend that stewardship of the land is neither a liberal nor a conservative idea. We've got to get off the kick of joining one or the other opposing parties and remember that from the first day man walked the face of the earth stewardship was a *God idea*!

I contend that stewardship of the land is neither a liberal nor a conservative idea. We've got to get off the kick of joining one or the other opposing parties and remember that from the first day man walked the face of the earth stewardship was a ***God idea!***

But there is hope. Today, at all levels of society, we are noticing a resurgence of interest in stewardship and conservation of the creation. People from all walks of life are becoming concerned. Our mismanagement of the creation has become so evident that we can no longer afford to hide our faces in the sand.

Today a great "power shift" is taking place in the hearts and minds of people around the globe. Everywhere people are crying that we must *do something*! The problem is that so many of us have lost touch with the creation that we don't know what to do. Fortunately that "touch" can be redeveloped at every level. This is why my melon story is so important; it reveals not only our *need* to reconnect with the land but also that such a reconnection is *possible* even in our advanced technical age. So let me ask you: are you willing to be a part of this current wave of interest, this resurgence of liberal ideas that are neither liberal nor conservative—but biblical?

Health Care is Ministry Too!

So often in our churches today the focus of our attention is given almost exclusively to addressing the spiritual needs of people by proclaiming the gospel of Jesus Christ and leading them to profess faith in Him. And as I stated in the Introduction, this certainly is our first and highest priority. I also stated, however, that we have a "creation mandate" from our Creator that has never been rescinded—a mandate that *includes* restoring health care in every area of creation: people, animals, plants and even the very soil itself. So stewardship of the land and all life on it is just as biblical a concept for us as is the proclamation of the gospel, and one for which God will hold us accountable.

Many years ago I was asked to contribute a chapter for a book that my eldest son, Reuben, co-authored. Although a groundbreaking book, *Restoring Health Care as a Ministry* focused primarily on the human element. The chapter I wrote addressed the book's theme from my perspective as both a veterinarian as well as a Christian minister. The unique thesis of the book was that *health care wrongly has been relegated to the secular part of society.* The church by and large has abdicated its legitimate and proper role in health care education and assistance. As a result, virtually all health care information and counsel today is presented from a secular rather than a biblical perspective. And much of it is simply *bogus*!

*Virtually all health care information and counsel today is presented from a secular rather than a biblical perspective. And much of it is simply **bogus**!*

Under the terms of the first covenant, as laid out in the Old Testament of the Bible, the priest was the designated official who not only represented the people before God but also looked after the physical health of the overall Israelite community. Of the 613 laws and statutes that fell under their jurisdiction, *213, or a little more than one-third, had to do with health, nutrition, hygiene, sanitation and diet*!

With the coming of the new covenant in Christ as revealed n the New Testament, a significant change of office took place. The priestly and health ministries were transferred to every citizen of the kingdom of God because as believers we are *all* "kings and priests" in Christ (Rev. 1:6). This is truth of great significance that often is overlooked. We tend to look to others for answers when we should look more and more within!

As the vision for this book developed, I found myself challenged both intellectually and scripturally to expand the health care ministry beyond mankind to include the animals, the plants, the living soil itself—the whole of created order. This all-inclusive approach is necessary because of the indisputable and intimate interrelationship that exists between each "kingdom" of life. The connection with plants and animals seems obvious, but what about the soil? Many people are unaware that every shovelful of soil contains billions of active living microbes that are absolutely critical for the proper functioning of the life cycle of nature. And the health and vitality of those microbes depend on how we as stewards manage the soil.

Many people are unaware that every shovelful of soil contains billions of active living microbes that are absolutely critical for the proper functioning of the life cycle of nature. And the health and vitality of those microbes depend on how we as stewards manage the soil.

In every generation there have always been caring people who are gifted in the area of health care. This includes not only highly trained professionals but also "lay" health care practitioners from every conceivable background and talent. For instance, all of us are familiar with the image of the "old school" grandmother who was wise in the ways of natural healing: "Here, drink this herbal tea, it will relieve your congestion!" She would minister to children, grand children and neighbors alike.

I personally know several Amish farmers who have attained enormous success as natural healers. People travel hundreds of miles, even from surrounding states, to benefit from their gifts and knowledge. Although these healers have a natural gift in the areas of nutrition and healing, each one also has developed his gift diligently through research, study and training. Over time each has become recognized as a healer, successfully prescribing herbs, poultices, nutritional counseling and, of course, prayer. Their success has been astounding!

Recognizing the need for natural centers of teaching and healing, the authors of *Restoring Health Care as a Ministry* proposed visionary steps to establish "Christian Lifestyle Centers" that would be under the government of the local church and community. The purpose of these centers would be to teach and minister effectively to local health needs at *all levels of discomfort*: spiritual, mental and physical. Because all three levels are intimately interrelated, healing unavoidably must become a combination ministry at all three levels of need!

Just as the roots, trunk and branches of a tree all must be healthy for the tree to be healthy, so too must a person's body, mind and spirit all be healthy if he or she is to enjoy true and full health. Unless we recognize this interconnectedness of healthy parts as critical to producing a healthy unified whole, we will not make much headway in solving the endemic health care problem of our day.

Just as the roots, trunk and branches of a tree all must be healthy for the tree to be healthy, so too must a person's body, mind and spirit all be healthy if he or she is to enjoy true and full health.

In frontier America it was common for clerics also to be ministers of the health of their congregations. After all, they normally were the most highly-educated people in the community and often were quite knowledgeable in multiple disciplines. They were the educated ones in the community, and multidisciplinary in their education. In addition to preaching and teaching the gospel and conducting prayer meetings, these brave folks also visited the sick, dispensed herbs and taught health and the basic principles of sanitation and hygiene.

Dr. Benjamin Rush, a prominent medical doctor and one of the signers of the Constitution, stated clearly that if the medical profession ever got a monopoly on healing, it would destroy the health of the nation. We got off to a good start but somewhere along the line the balance shifted heavily in favor of professional medicine. The medical profession has made and continues to make important breakthroughs and renders valuable care and treatment, but the best solution for our day and age is to restore the original balance between professional and natural healing. It's time to get health care back into the hands of the people!

Dr. Benjamin Rush, a prominent medical doctor and one of the signers of the Constitution, stated clearly that if the medical profession ever got a monopoly on healing, it would destroy the health of the nation.

It's time to get health care back into the hands of the people!

Man: Machine or Spirit Being?

Let's focus on the *hidden root* of our health care system. Increasingly larger numbers of people in our society are becoming sick and unproductive. Disease is clearly on its deadly march. Many experts agree that the next global pandemic is just around the corner.

No matter how you cut it, the 20th century "mechanistic" approach to health has failed us. The mechanistic approach thinks of man as basically as a marvelous machine that can be "repaired" through drugs and surgery. Did something break down? Bombard it with drugs and chemicals (so what if the drugs and chemicals are in their own way just as dangerous as the disease!) Cut the broken part out and replace it! Use microscopes, instruments, lab tests, X rays and the most cutting-edge inventions!

With all its wonders and expertise, the "mechanistic" view has almost totally eliminated the recognition of the spiritual needs of mankind. Man is a machine, nothing more. And under that philosophy, not only does the system fail, but other more appalling plans sometimes surface. For instance, Bertrand Russell, British philosopher and atheist, writing in *The Impact of Science on Society*, proposed some horrifying forms of population control as an answer to the world's problems:

> *I do not pretend that birth control is the only way in which population can be kept from increasing. There are others.... War...has hitherto been disappointing in this respect, but perhaps bacteriological war may prove more effective. If a Black Death could be spread throughout the world once in every generation survivors could procreate freely without making the world too full.*[3]

Others, providentially, propose a "vitalistic" approach to the health care problem. The vitalistic approach views man's body as infused with divine energy from Almighty God. Rather than being nothing more than a machine, man is a spiritual being with an underlying spiritual nature that guides and nurtures his physical development. In the DNA of every human dwells a life force that is uniquely human.

Recently I read a research book explaining that the DNA helix in the human chromosome has a unique sequential pattern based on the 4 letters of YHWH, the Hebrew name for Yahweh, or God. This understanding helps us recognize that inside every cell is a DNA code that connects us directly to a higher power, our Creator. This same energy is involved in the healing process. All truly effective treatments, therefore, should be based on this foundational understanding. Every healing modality ultimately must answer to God, our "Great Physician," or end up in the wastebasket of history.

Every healing modality ultimately must answer to God, our "Great Physician," or end up in the wastebasket of history.

Vitalistic treatments, therefore, must include live and vital foods, energetic herbs and spices, emotional and spiritual counseling, and life-giving prayer. Many other forms of treatments might qualify. Each and every vitalistic treatment, assuming it passes scriptural scrutiny, will be based on nurturing the vital flow, which those same scriptures call "life."

The Western mechanistic philosophy of life has infiltrated our medical system, our educational system and even our religious system. Many respectable books dismiss as "occult" or "quackery" any approach to health that differs from the current mechanistic medical model. One of my purposes in this book is to expose that false premise! Mechanistic methodology is not the only, nor even the best, approach to health care. Modern medicine is great, and even necessary, for some things, but for many others a naturopathic approach is the best. I hope this will become abundantly clear in the chapters that follow.

Summary

1. All living things on earth, including the living soil, all the plants, all the insects, all the animals on the land, in the sea and in the air, and all of mankind as well, are intimately related and interconnected on the biological, emotional and spiritual levels.
2. The law of the continuum applies universally. We are all intimately and directly connected to each other and to all other life on this planet.
3. Our mismanagement of the creation has become so evident that we can no longer afford to hide our faces in the sand.
4. Health care is ministry too!
5. No matter how you cut it, the 20th century "mechanistic" approach to health has failed us.

6. Every healing modality ultimately must answer to God, our "Great Physician," or end up in the wastebasket of history.
7. Vitalistic treatments must include live and vital foods, energetic herbs and spices, emotional and spiritual counseling, and life-giving prayer.

Chapter Three

A LONG AND WINDING ROAD

Whenever I talk about our creation mandate, the importance of getting back to the land, the value and effectiveness of naturopathic treatments and other types of natural or "alternative" approaches to health care, I am not speaking hypothetically. For me these things are more than mere theory. Everything I present in this book, every conclusion I draw, is based on more than 50 years of personal study, formal education and real life experiences in the field. I have come to where I am today by means of a long and winding road with many unexpected, but not unnatural, twists and turns.

Although I am a veterinarian by profession, farming is in my blood. I was born and raised on a large diversified farm in southern Michigan in the 1950s. Every acre of food we cultivated was raised 100% organically. We also raised and housed 1,000 chickens to provide eggs and meat for local customers. The commercial goat dairy we founded was home to some of the highest milk producers in the United States. And along with everything else, we operated a feed mill to grind and balance feed for farmers in the local area. My back still testifies to the level of work that all these projects demanded!

After some years in partnership with my father, I eventually decided to become a veterinarian. Because of my farming background, nutrition was one of my favorite subjects. Even then my desire and goal were to solve problems by preventing them.

Following my graduation from veterinary college, and in answer to a call into Christian ministry, I enrolled at Gordon/Conwell Theological Seminary in Massachusetts. Upon completing my course of study I spent the next 12 years serving in agricultural and Christian missions in the jungles of Colombia, South America, where I had ample opportunity to apply all three disciplines: farming, veterinary medicine and theological training. Through all of these and other related experiences my love and burden for the land grew deeper, along with my love and compassion for most classes of animals. (I draw the line at snakes, spiders and mosquitoes!).

Yet even today, some 60 years later, I still connect with my roots as a "farm boy." Occasionally I fall back on that as an excuse to my wife when I do something dumb like walking into the kitchen with mud on my shoes. I simply shrug my shoulders and say, "I'm just a simple farmer!" Admittedly, I have yet to impress her with that statement! Yet that is a side of me that I am thankful for because it defines my background, my sense of duty, and my connection with the land.

I believe God has a special love for farmers. Why? Because in the beginning He planted a garden! God Himself was the first farmer! My definition of a farmer is somebody who loves the land, loves the creation, and loves the God who strung it all out there in such a majestic and orderly way.[4] And then He told us to take care of it—that was our "job" as humans.

Today I find it remarkable that for the first half of my life I studied and practiced traditional disease care rather than health care. Treat the symptoms with drugs or surgery but with little attention given to cause or prevention. It didn't take me long, however, to realize that creation was in a crisis and seriously out of balance. This was evident by the types and frequency of diseases I saw in my animal patients. The more I observed, the more I understood that the human race as a whole, as well as the very land itself, was displaying the same out of balance symptoms. I also realized that very few physicians had permanent answers relating to the very *root causes* of chronic problems. Modern science seems to be focused on the leaves and branches, the externals of disease, rather than the root cause of disease. Therefore, when standard procedures like antibiotics, drugs and surgery fail, there are few alternatives.

Today I find it remarkable that for the first half of my life I studied and practiced traditional disease care rather than health care.

Eventually I concluded that white-coated scientists and black-suited theologians alike were not focused on the right areas to find permanent answers. A *wild* goose chase never catches the goose. How can you find the answer if you're not looking in the right place? How can you eliminate disease if you do not deal with the root causes of disease? To put it another way, why keep sweeping down spider webs, when we should be killing the spiders? If we never define the problem, how will we ever solve it?

Out of the Box and into the Jungle

Although my training in veterinary medicine was strictly traditional, my background of being raised on an organic farm gave me a heart and mind that resonated to the beat of a different drummer. Despite the formal training emphasis on treating disease with drugs, chemicals and surgery, I could not shake the importance of a good diet and nutrition. I'm not talking about the "ivory tower" nutrition of canned and pasteurized foods, but real live foods that still had enzymes and life vitality in every cell. Life begets life, right? It did not seem right that dead food could give the type of life that could keep people and pets healthy. Years later, when I ventured into the world of alternative medicine and health care, I learned that I was right on track!

Despite the traditional nature of my medical training, I was not destined to spend my life inside the box of tradition. Although it took many years for me to get completely out of the box, once out I never looked back and have never had any desire to return. My journey out of the box of tradition bore fruit in the jungles of Colombia.

My wife and I arrived in Colombia in 1971 and spent the next 12 years living in the rainforest 50 miles north of the equator. Those were very untraditional and exciting years! Have you ever had a yearning or "call" to break with the pack and live nontraditionally?

Our home in the Colombian rainforest had a bamboo floor and a palm leaf-thatched roof. And we loved it! The bamboo walls were only 4 feet high in the kitchen and living areas. Day and night the sights, sounds and smells of the rainforest surrounded us. Hour by hour we had front row viewing of the jungle plants, birds and animals. Our three sons were born in that jungle. Many people would regard life in such a place and under such primitive conditions as hell on earth. For us, however, it was a tropical paradise because we knew we were right where we were supposed to be.

Sharing our habitat with cockroaches, mosquitoes and iguanas was an everyday experience. Occasionally, scorpions, deadly snakes and giant poisonous spiders crossed our path. One day I was fumbling for something next to my bed when a 4-inch hairy-legged spider rushed toward me. I was the survivor of that encounter!

Our standard mode of travel was by foot along narrow jungle trails, but we also regularly traveled the swollen tropical rivers in hollowed dugout canoes

crafted by the local native carpenters. Fortunately for me, a non-swimmer, we had expert boatmen at our disposal who managed the outboard motors with great skill and adroitly maneuvered us around logs and other potentially hazardous jungle debris that floated in the rivers, especially at the height of the rainy season. On land we navigated the jungle trails in high rubber boots. This was necessary because of the heavy tropical rains, fallen trees and, especially, the ever-present mud. The boots also protected us from poisonous snakes.

There were no roads, no electricity, and no indoor plumbing. For washing clothes we used a metal scrub board and a large metal washtub. Even this was "advanced" however, compared to the method employed by the indigenous people of the jungle, who still washed their clothes over a large rock, with another rock as a washboard, just as their ancestors had done since prehistoric times.

We enterprising foreigners soon drove down well points for wash water and drinking water. On top of the two-inch pipe we placed a muscle-powered pitcher pump and soon had our own "running" water. This quickly caught on with the locals, and soon every house around had its own well point and pitcher pump.

For showers we built a three-sided bamboo shower stall, with a plastic curtain across the entrance. Water poured over us from a used tin can made for a cool, refreshing shower at the end of a sweaty day! A few enterprising folks rigged up a barrel overhead, pumped it full of water daily, connected a shower head with a shut off valve and then bragged about their "modern convenience!" Personally, our family stayed with the dip and pour method.

From Veterinarian to Medic and Dentist

Necessity is the mother of invention. In our jungle environment we had nurses and midwives, but I was the only "doctor." Although a veterinarian, I soon found it necessary to expand that medical knowledge to include treating people. I learned to clean and suture wounds and to dispense medicines. Occasionally, I even connected an IV drip directly into a patient's vein.

Much of our medical work involved emergency treatment. Accidental machete wounds were among the most common. I was called upon frequently to suture a newly inflicted wound. One morning, for example, we heard a loud commotion just before dawn. Several of the men had risen early to slaughter a fat pig. One of them, a hard-working young man named Hernando, had slipped in the sloppy rainforest mud and sliced open an artery in his forearm. We heard people praying passionately in the distance, but since no one called us, we figured everything was under control.

About an hour later, after the morning sun had dawned on the horizon, I asked about the reason for the commotion. Upon being informed of Hernando's deep machete wound, I quickly examined it and then sutured and properly dressed it. The wound healed uneventfully. When I asked why they had not sent for us when it happened, I discovered it was because of "pena," embarrassment. Surely prayer and faith would work, they reasoned, and decided it would not be proper to disturb a slumbering American. I urged them to call me immediately next time. Sometimes trained help is called for. It's okay to co-labor with the Creator!

On another occasion an American on a farm upriver accidentally cut 3 tendons on the back of his left hand due to a wild machete swing. It was an ugly cut, a three-inch, gaping wound that sliced through flesh, tendons and blood vessels, all the way to the bone. When they arrived by boat at our teaching farm for treatment, I was surprised to discover they had applied a poultice of old coffee grounds to the wound! This, I learned, was a local "secret" to stop life-threatening bleeding. It took me 30 minutes to pick out the several tablespoonfuls of coffee grounds on and in the wound before I could realign the tendons and suture the wound.

Had I left the coffee grounds in the wound, it would have festered and become infected. But what else can you do when you live in the jungle? Stop the bleeding first, save the life and then worry about what ever comes next when that moment arrives! It had worked, but this gave me an opportunity to teach them better emergency procedures, such as pressure packs and tourniquets. Most of the time my advice was well received by the locals because I had earned their respect. I learned early on that the way to gain an audience was not to overpower with argument, or to criticize, but slowly and patiently to live and demonstrate another option.

I learned early on that the way to gain an audience was not to overpower with argument, or to criticize, but slowly and patiently to live and demonstrate another option.

But they were not the only ones learning. As Americans we also benefited from their expertise in so many ways. The locals taught us many things necessary about living and surviving in the jungle. *There is so much you can learn when you are willing to embrace knowledge and wisdom wherever you find it!*

Then there was the "Exis Culebra", the poisonous snake whose concentrated venom can kill within hours. One morning, a young mother named Sue was hurrying along the jungle foot trail in comfortable flip-flop sandals. Because she was in a hurry, she was not watching closely where she was walking, and this deadly exis culebra struck, sinking its fangs deeply into her ankle. Fortunately, Sue was only 10 or 20 minutes from our jungle clinic, and soon we were using our snakebite kit on the wound. By that time the swelling had already begun. We used cold water to slow down the spread of the poison and administered some anti-inflammatory steroid drugs at the recommended levels. We also prayed.

Later that day, when a single-engine plane flew in to carry her out, we believed we were on top of the crisis situation. Sue was bedridden with a swollen leg for a few days, but slowly and uneventfully recovered. Today she is serving in Peru.

Those were the early days. Today I have other natural treatments at my disposal in case of a snakebite wound. It is not that I am against an anti-venom injection, but it is always wise to have a wide range of options in order to give the best advantage in any situation.

Eventually I also added human dentistry to my list of necessary skills. We purchased a foot-powered dental drill with a fancy system of pulleys and gears that turned the drill at a speed sufficient to drill and fill a cavity. Now I could drill and fill with confidence! I learned and practiced all forms of basic dentistry on people, including amalgam and porcelain fillings. I extracted hundreds of rotten teeth. I even learned how to perform root canals. After we returned to the U. S., the first dentist my wife visited said that the fillings I placed in her mouth were superior to any he had seen done by any of the city dentists! When necessity calls, you do what you have to do. You learn what you have to learn.

An Alternate Route

While we were in Colombia, my wife, Jinnie, became chronically and seriously ill. The physicians there were unable to supply any answers. Following a botched surgery, and despite many rounds of drug treatments, Jinnie's health continued its downward trend. Significantly, Jinnie had negative reactions to every drug that was prescribed for her. This in itself was an important factor in prompting us to undertake our own search for truth and an alternative path to healing.

We returned to the U. S. hoping to find the medical answers that eluded us in Colombia. Jinnie spent several days in the hospital, after which her physician concluded that she needed a new but experimental drug infused directly into her veins. Since Jinnie had already reacted negatively to a dozen or more other "approved" drugs, including two that this doctor had prescribed, we concluded that the wisest course was NOT to do another "experiment." It was time to branch out on our own and take responsibility for our own health!

The door soon opened for us to move to Dallas, Texas, where Jinnie began a series of alternative treatments, called "Metabolic Therapy," under the auspices of medical health researcher Dr. William Kelly. Dr. Kelly had cured himself of cancer and later cured his wife. During her illnesses he had been forced to recognize that they each required a different program from the vegetarian based program that cured his cancer. His wife required meat to get well. That sparked his interest. His research resulted in his identification of 10 different metabolic types in humans, each with different needs. His was not a "one size fits all" program. Each program was individualized to meet the unique needs of patients according to their specific metabolic type. Or stated in folk language: "What fits the gander does not always fit the goose!"

This insight of individual uniqueness (or individuality) remains a key mark of my own present philosophy of health care and treatment. Despite the obvious physical similarities, every human being and every animal on this planet is uniquely different from all others; as unique as each snowflake or fingerprint. *Creative growth demands that we burst out of the boxes that hinder us from recognizing these differences.* Consequently, every two years, on the average, I venture into some new area of healing and creativity. With every new advance, I am able to enlarge myself, and with every enlargement of my understanding I am able to offer a wider scope of answers. Whereas before I had only drugs and surgery in my bag, today I have a dozen or more possibilities at my disposal. Now I can choose the treatment to fit the need. It's a wonderful feeling!

During this same period of Jinnie's metabolic therapy, a circumstance transpired that shaped our entire future direction. One day in 1983, on her way home from visiting a highly recommended health practitioner, Jinnie inexplicably got lost somewhere between Fort Worth and Dallas. After three failed attempts to find the correct entrance to the highway, she turned with tears of frustration into an unknown health food store to ask for directions. The place seemed to beckon her. There she met a gentleman who became a turning point in our lives.

Bill Graves was a tough Texan who had learned much about alternative health practices because of his own health situation as a hemophiliac. Jinnie and I are convinced that this was a divine appointment because Bill only visited this particular store once every few months. Noticing the frustration and sense of helplessness on Jinnie's face, Bill asked if he could be of help.

"Yes," Jinnie replied. "I'm lost, and I need a restroom."

Bill quickly perceived that Jinnie's health and frustration level were at the breaking point, so when she returned from the restroom, he handed her his business card. Bill was a professional health practitioner specializing in alternative therapies and treatments. Jinnie was already unnerved from her visit to the other practitioner, who was openly and unapologetically involved in occult religious practices. Bill practiced some of the same healing modalities as the other practitioner but his entire manner seemed very different. As Bill handed Jinnie his business card he smiled, "If you ever need help, give me a call."

When Bill pointed out the way home for Jinnie, she saw that the route was clearly marked with signs. How had she missed them three times before? Was this a case of divine guidance to bring two families together who had a special need to meet? Was this odd set of circumstances engineered just for our benefit? Furthermore, could we practice these particular alternative healing modalities, yet use them scientifically and beneficially? We soon found out.

Could we practice these particular alternative healing modalities, yet use them scientifically and beneficially? We soon found out.

Over the next four months Bill regularly drove the long trek to our home to educate us in an alternate route to health. He gave us our first in-depth lessons in herbal medicine, holistic health, colonics, nutritional biofeedback testing and many other related modalities. The trip was a 45-minute drive for Bill, and we considered those personal teaching times way beyond the call of duty. In those sessions we received a personalized crash course that included a solid initiation into all forms of alternative and complementary medicine. A hemophiliac from birth, Bill had suffered much at the hands of doctors. One of his legs was permanently damaged because of inappropriate treatments. Although given a poor initial prognosis, Bill lived a vibrant and fulfilling life into his 80s! Bill was like an angel to us, arriving at the moment of our most desperate need.

Holistic Health Care

In the jungles of Colombia I discovered that the principles I learned in veterinary medicine were transferable to humans also. The physical body is essentially the same, regardless of species. Nutritionally and medically, what is effective on one species often is just as effective on the others also. I learned later that these same principles also transfer to plants. What an amazing world we live in! At some level, every aspect of life resonates to the same principles and divine plan!

Nutritionally and medically, what is effective on one species often is just as effective on the others also. I learned later that these same principles also transfer to plants.

As part of my expanding horizons, I took many advanced holistic courses in human health. What I learned about humans, I began to apply to our animal friends. And in speaking with other holistic veterinarians, I discovered that most of them currently practice holistic medicine on animals because someone in their family did not respond to orthodox medicine or drugs but was either helped or cured by some alternative treatment. Others intuitively took the same mental leap I did: "*Hmmm, if this works on people, I wonder if it will work on animals?" That significant seed-thought was my personal baptism into this new and exciting dimension of alternative medicine and healing.*

Most people do not realize that the basic principles of medicine and health work in both directions, and on different species. Of course, we veterinarians are already trained in treating different species, so the concept is not exactly revolutionary. What was revolutionary to my personal thinking was that the many varieties of plant life respond also, as do the soils of the earth, from which we all have our common origins. That discovery helped open to me doors for many other exciting discoveries.

In practice and by training, I now classify myself as a "holistic veterinarian". That means I use many other alternative and complementary modalities besides surgery, medicine and dentistry. I now incorporate chiropractic adjustments, osteopathic manipulation, neuro-muscular release, nutritional and medicinal herbs, whole-food diets, homeopathic remedies, glandular supplements, and energy medicine. I use "flower remedies" for complicated emotional dysfunctions. Every year or two I add something new! Every day I "believe" for good things to happen in my clinic, with my family, and in my garden!

When I first stepped into the maze of alternative medicine, I had to fight an oppressive internal fear. Back in the 1970s and 80s, medical doctors and veterinarians were losing their licenses just for practicing alternative medicine. Some even went to jail. Their medicine was unorthodox and "unapproved". A friend of mine had his license pulled for five years simply because of professional jealousy within his field. He was a top veterinary surgeon with a Masters Degree in Neurology. His troubles began after he started using osteopathic manipulations instead of surgery to cure crisis disc problems in dogs— a problem which often leaves animals paralyzed. He was so successful that cases began coming to him in large numbers, infuriating the veterinary surgeons in the area because they were losing business. Making matters worse, his osteopathic treatments cost only hundreds of dollars compared to the thousands of dollars for the traditional surgery. His angry, more traditional colleagues accused him of practicing "snake oil medicine."

Finally, they got him on totally unrelated charges. His technician was pressured into telling a client, over the phone, the results of a fecal exam test. The "client," who was actually an undercover "plant" by the local medical group, insisted on knowing the information immediately. Once the technician gave in and reported that the dog in question had hookworms, that was all they needed. In that state it was illegal for anyone but the doctor to diagnose a disease! So they had an airtight case. My friend lost his veterinary license for 5 years.

Now, about 20 years later, this same veterinarian has taught his technique to thousands of veterinarians. After a long legal battle, his technique was finally approved in his own state. The technique has been proven to be scientific, safe, and effective. In fact, I use the same technique nearly every day in my own practice. But simply the *fear* of losing one's license or reputation is enough to put the brakes on progress. Fear can both rule and ruin a life. It sure put a damper on mine for a while!

Fear can both rule and ruin a life. It sure put a damper on mine for a while!

Fortunately, I had developed a deep inner conviction in this area. I knew that what I was practicing was definitely in line with truth. It was slow going, and I was extremely cautious at first. After 10 years of battling that *nagging fear* I woke up one day and realized: "Hey, I am on the wave of the future. This 'unapproved' medicine really does work!" Clients were driving up to 5 hours to my clinic just to have these treatments given to their pets. Several local veterinarians were beginning to send their clients to me for "unresolved" and "hopeless" cases. And, in addition, I had not had one single complaint, not one instance of a threat to sue me, no letter sent to the veterinary board to report me.

I believe that my success is due, essentially, to three things. First and foremost is God's grace and covering. Secondly, I always try to use wisdom. James 1:5 says that wisdom comes from God. I always try to give my clients *all* the options. I answer their questions honestly and I never pressure them to follow my advice. I am the teacher; they are the learner, the student, the discerner of the ultimate decision. It was their animal and their decision, not mine. I am only responsible to give the insight and the options, and it is their choice to follow one or the other or neither.

Originally the word "physician" meant "teacher." My understanding and practice of that truth probably has kept me from a ton of trouble! It is the opposite of what many physicians practice today. In practice management courses there is an inherent pressure to enlarge the business and make more money. Sell every option you can, and especially recommend the one that will make you the most money, even if it also carries the greatest degree of risk—I reject that theory of practice! "Above all do no harm" was the oath I took when I graduated from the university. It is still my motto.

Thirdly, I frequently verbalize a prayer I learned from the pastor who married Jinnie and me: "Lord, please bring the ones I can help, and please keep the rest away!"

Today I am a convinced and unapologetic advocate and practitioner of alternative medicine because I have seen through training and personal experience how effective these healing modalities are. I favor alternative health care also because our modern system of disease care is broken. Over 70 major diseases have no known cause and no known cure. That, to me, is a blanket indictment against our present ivory-tower (white coat and black bag) medical system. Something is wrong with the foundation of the allopathic pharmaceutical model. I am convinced that the cracks in the system cannot be patched. A whole new system and approach are needed. That's what this book is all about.

Over 70 major diseases have no known cause and no known cure.

Summary

1. The more I observed, the more I understood that the human race as a whole, as well as the very land itself, was out of balance.
2. How can you eliminate disease if you do not deal with the root causes of disease?
3. My journey out of the box of tradition bore fruit in the jungles of Colombia.
4. There is so much you can learn when you are willing to embrace knowledge and wisdom wherever you find it!
5. The fact of individual uniqueness (or individuality) remains a key mark of my own present philosophy of health care and treatment.
6. In the jungles of Colombia I discovered that the principles I learned in veterinary medicine were transferable to humans also.
7. After 10 years of battling nagging fear I woke up one day and realized: "Hey, I am on the wave of the future. This 'unapproved' medicine really does work!"
8. Something is wrong with the foundation of the allopathic pharmaceutical model. I am convinced that the cracks in the system cannot be patched.

Chapter Four

DIETARY AND EMOTIONAL FACTORS OF DISEASE

Why is our current health care system broken? Why are there so many diseases that stubbornly defy treatment or cure despite all of our modern scientific and medical advances? The answer is really pretty simple. Traditional medicine with its drug/chemical/surgical approach to treatment virtually ignores the fact that *most diseases have a nutritional and/or an emotional or spiritual component.* Nutritional imbalances often produce emotional imbalances as well as inflamed bodily organs and tissues, making them susceptible to disease. In fact, literally dozens of modern diseases are unique to our industrial high stress and fast-track junk-food society.

Spina bifida, for example, long believed to be a congenital condition, is now known to result from a simple nutritional deficiency of the vitamin folic acid. Poor dietary habits and modern food processing methods both contribute to folic acid deficiency, with the result that thousands of babies are born with open spinal cords. *What a tragedy*, particularly considering the fact that spina bifida is not genetic but nutritional, and therefore preventable!

In another example, cleft palate was unknown in every aboriginal society. Research by the Price-Pottenger Foundation has revealed that in every society where cleft palate has appeared, it has shown up first in the first generation of offspring following the introduction of refined white sugar and white flour diets to that society. Although cleft palate has a definite nutritional cause, most textbooks still blame genetics.

Consider also the fact that many common ailments that plague both people and pets today—diabetes, cancer, arthritis, lupus and high cholesterol, to name just a few—are virtually unknown in the wild. They also are completely foreign to most primitive cultures. I believe this is highly significant! What is the difference between us and them? *Why are we in our modern and highly industrialized society sicker and less healthy than our more primitive and closer to nature counterparts?* Three things, essentially, are to blame:

1. Our highly refined diet
2. The chemicals in our food, water and medicines
3. The abnormally high stress level of modern culture.

Food refining processes may streamline production and may at times even make some foods more palatable, but they also strip away vitamins, minerals and other essential nutrients. Many chemical additives in our food, drink and medicines are actually toxic to the body. In small amounts they may seem harmless, but they can accumulate over time and many of them can cause inflammation or imbalance even in small doses. And regarding stress, we now know that fear, stress and anxiety are the root cause of many other major disease issues. According to current medical research, all allergies fall into this category.[5] Therefore, true healing also requires healing of the emotions as well as the healing of what Dr. Elden M. Chalmers calls the "broken brain."[6] The physical body was designed to be healthy! Something is messing up that design!

We are literally eating ourselves to death. Today 55-65% of all adults in America are overweight, with 25-30% classified as morbidly obese. The same goes for our pets and barnyard animals. We have falsely blamed genetics and slow metabolism when the real reason is poor nutrition, especially excessive snacking on rich foods, coupled with lack of exercise and emotional stress. All of these are *bad habit patterns*.

To most Americans these days, a "good diet" generally means iceberg lettuce, a low fat snack and an artificial "diet" drink. In reality, it should include instead more vegetables, nuts, fruits and quality water. In an effort to avoid fats we gulp down pasta, tortillas and hamburger buns and substitute hydrogenated margarine spreads for real butter. Over time, consistent consumption of all of these foods rob us of good health. Each of them have little more nutritional value than refined white sugar. They are a guaranteed prescription for disease.

Dr. Ross Hauser, MD, in an article titled, "Why Your Body Doesn't Heal," discusses ten reasons why healing does not take place. The very first item on his list *nutrition*! He says that despite the body's strong regenerative capabilities, many elements come into play in the healing process. One of the most overlooked of these is the nutrition factor. Many people with persistent health problems go from one doctor or other health care practitioner to another, and another, yet never improve. And in most of these cases, nutritional factors are never even considered either as a possible cause or a possible solution.

I once spoke with a nurse who was taking numerous prescription drugs daily for a persistent medical condition. She had missed work ever since being on those drugs, but rather than improving, she was getting progressively worse. Her physicians had told her that there were three possible diagnoses, but there was no way of confirming which one was correct. So they kept trying new drugs, and kept sending her to new specialists.

"Has a single doctor asked you about your nutritional status?" I asked.

"Not one", she replied.

As we discussed her situation further, I became convinced that her doctors were missing the basics. Even as a nurse she had not once considered nutrition as being relevant to her situation. Neither had her doctors. Why not?

For one thing, modern western medicine is dominated by the pharmaceutically-based approach to health care of treating every disease and symptom with drugs or, if necessary, surgery. Nutrition rarely, if ever, appears on the radar screen as a causative agent. Another related factor is that few physicians are trained in nutritional health, nor are they taught to think in nutritional terms when diagnosing disease. It is time for that to change!

The Pottenger Cat Study

Between the years of 1932 and 1942 Dr. Francis Pottenger, MD performed a historic feeding trial on cats.[7] As a surgeon and renowned medical researcher, Dr. Pottenger sought to understand the influence of nutrition on the genetic code. His interest in this subject had been aroused when he noticed the difference in organ tissue vitality when implanting organs from one animal into another. He noted that the difference seemed to depend on the type of diet the cats were fed.

The experiment he devised involved feeding one group of cats cooked, denatured food while feeding a second group of cats the same food in its raw, live form. The goal of the experiment was to determine the effects of heat on processed foods.

Dr. Pottenger's study was prompted in part by the high rate of mortality among his laboratory cats following surgery. The test group received cooked meat while the control group received only raw meat. Except for the cooking, the diets and husbandry of both groups were exactly the same.

In this carefully documented study, over a 10 year period and including over 900 cats, Dr. Pottenger observed both groups through many generations. The results were striking. The animals in the control group, those that received raw food, remained healthy at all stages of growth and reproduction. Results were quite different among the test group. Dr. Pottenger noted that as early as the *first generation* of offspring of the cats that received cooked meat, changes in skeletal structure began to appear, including narrowing of the facial bones and abnormal teeth and dental arches. In addition, these animals displayed more irritability than the other group. Within the *second generation,* heart problems, nearsightedness, under activity of the thyroid gland, arthritis, inflammation of the nervous system and other conditions began to appear. By the time the *third generation* was born, those cats were so physiologically bankrupt that few survived beyond the sixth month of life, thereby terminating the strain. A few, kept alive with antibiotics and drugs, were still unable to reproduce.

Another significant fact in the study was that if at any point a deficient cat was put back on a raw food diet (called now a "regenerative cat"), it still passed on its imperfections on to the next generation. Its DNA had been permanently damaged. Three to four generations on a raw diet were required to return the cats' genetics back to normal physical and psychological health!

In summarizing his findings, the study noted: "Improvement in resistance to disease is noted in the second generation regenerating cat, but allergic manifestations persist into the third generation. In the third generation, skeletal and soft tissue changes are still noticeable, but to a lesser degree; and by the forth, most of the severe deficiency signs and symptoms disappear...."

Dr. Pottenger postulated that humans on a 100% cooked/canned diet would probably manifest a similar degree of degeneration, worse in each progressive generation. *Degenerative foods create degenerative conditions in the animals and humans who eat those foods!*

Historically, we are now at the critical point between the 3rd and 4th generations of humans living primarily on high levels of cooked and processed foods. *Generally speaking, grandparents tend to be healthier than their children, and their grandchildren are the least healthy of all three generations. Fortunately, many people are rediscovering raw fruits and vegetables.* More and more nutritionists are advising people to shop around the periphery of the grocery store, where the *real* food is, and to avoid the center aisles, where all the canned, processed and preserved foods are stacked. Which aisles do you shop?

Similarly, it has been observed that domesticated pigs allowed to return into the wild follow a similar pattern. After only three or four generations, the pigs once again look and act like the old-time wild razor-back hogs. This same pattern of *regeneration* and *degeneration* has been noted with other plants, animals, and bacteria alike.

Not long ago I had the pleasure of getting to know Dr. E. Rentz, a trained biochemist and biophysicist, as well as a licensed osteopathic physician and holistic medical doctor. Dr. Rentz has noted that when raising plants or animals on foods of superior nutritional value, within three generations their DNA is so strengthened that neither the plants nor the animals raised on those plans get sick. In addition, insects will not bother them. This is another powerful indicator of the central role nutrition has in good health. *Every day it seems that more and more information comes to light to demonstrate beyond doubt the validity of Dr. Pottenger's findings from over sixty years ago.*

Garbage In, Garbage Out

As another sign of the seriousness of the modern health crisis, infertility in both humans and animals is nearing epidemic proportions. Our pets increasingly are suffering from the same diseases we do, the diseases of a prosperous but junk food society. *We are quantity rich but quality poor.* Pets and even barnyard animals are getting cancer, diabetes, lupus, and all of our stress-related and immune-related diseases. This is not primarily a spiritual problem but a direct result of our modern addiction to processed, refined and junk foods. *We are paying the price in ill health for our own stupidity. Folks, we have been deceived!*

Someone wrote, "Natures God will not interfere to preserve men from the consequences of violating nature's laws." That statement reflects the biblical law of sowing and reaping: "Do not be deceived, God is not mocked; for whatever a man sows, that he will also reap" (Gal. 6:7). The modern paraphrase of this Scripture would be, "Garbage in, garbage out."

Someone wrote, "Natures God will not interfere to preserve men from the consequences of violating nature's laws."

If we reap what we sow, why do we assume we can get away with violating universal nutritional laws? What makes us think we can "get around" these serious violations simply by "blessing the food"? And yet that is clearly the attitude among many. "If God blesses it, it's good for you," someone glibly said to me. Well, my question is, "*DID God bless it?*" Did God provide the food we ate—or is it instead a clear case of humans making *poor choices,* a subtle but absolute violation of basic eternal laws? The debate continues, while in the meantime cancer, diabetes, arthritis and every other subtle disease strikes both believer and unbeliever alike. Have we been deceived? Even worse, are we in rebellion and deceiving ourselves?

*Well, my question is, "DID God bless it?" Did God provide the food we ate—or is it instead a clear case of humans making **poor choices**, a subtle but absolute violation of basic eternal laws?*

Somehow we have turned proper nutritional principles upside down. Here's what I mean. The main ingredients of many of our carnivore pet foods are corn, wheat and soy rather than meat. Herbivore barnyard cattle and horses likewise are stuffed with high grain diets and sweet feeds, dried animal blood meal, and animal slaughter "by-products." These types of "foods" totally defy nature and natural law. They make no sense to anyone except highly paid salesmen! Whether designed for animals or people, every type of man-made diet seems to backfire, while disease continues its clear and exorable upswing.

Obesity, which is at epidemic levels in Western influenced societies, is a result of upside down nutrition. We are able to choose our diet and yet continually choose foods that feed obesity. What's wrong with this picture? *Is nutrition-based obesity of concern to God?*

I have some friends who reached that conclusion as the Lord spoke to their hearts and convicted them. They became convinced of the need to take authority over their eating habits and to start eating healthier foods. Most of them had already tried a dozen or more diets. Nothing worked until they were convicted enough to get to the *root* of the problem, which included self-indulgence, which is the sin of gluttony. The problem also often involves self-hatred because of a poor self-image, and insecurity in *who* they were as people. *This analysis probably fits at least 70% of the folks fighting obesity.*

My friends also began to recognize that overeating in *quantity*, no matter the quality of the food, clogs the living machine, thus hindering its function. Timothy Johnson, M.D., America's Family Doctor of "Good Morning America," says: "Take a guess at what the second biggest killer in America is (after smoking). It's obesity. The Surgeon General's office estimates that obesity is responsible for some 300,000 deaths per year!" In the animal population the statistics are similar. And obesity is, in part, malnutrition. The way we are eating is killing us!

Nutrition: The Forgotten Element

Pastor Henry Wright, in his book, A More Excellent Way: A Teaching on the Spiritual Roots of Disease, adds, "*All addictions are rooted in lack of self-esteem and insecurity and the need to be loved. The mouth, and whatever you put in it, is designed to try to bring the person to emotional security. Excessive eating is a direct result of not feeling good about your self.*"[8]

So if we ultimately are responsible for the proper care and nutrition of our bodies, which are temples of the Holy Spirit, guess who has the responsibility for our domestic pets and barnyard animals? We do. Many of them are on the same high-carb, low nutrition diets as their caretakers. As I said before, our animals share many of our diseases; the statistical ratio is about 50 percent. *The problem is not with the animals; this is a caretaker problem.*

"All addictions are rooted in lack of self-esteem and insecurity and the need to be loved."

And we caretakers are the ones with the answers. If the battle to bring our own indulgences under control is hard, it is doubly hard to stop indulging our pets because we transfer our bad habits to them. Many of us are in a co-dependency relationship with our pets! Out of pity, ignorance or simple indulgence, we keep stuffing food down their throats of a kind they don't need any more than we do! I suppose the truth hurts. But the truth rightly understood can also set us free!

Many of us are in a co-dependency relationship with our pets! Out of pity, ignorance or simple indulgence, we keep stuffing food down their throats of a kind they don't need any more than we do!

A 2003 National Institutes of Health survey of 20,000 adults who used alternative and complementary medicine revealed that 77% used prayer for themselves, for others, or in groups. This is good! Nineteen percent used one or more of the top five natural products: echinacea, ginseng, ginkgo biloba, garlic supplements and glucosamine. Eleven and a half percent used deep breathing and 25% used one form or another of chiropractic, massage, exercise or meditation. All of these are good! However, only 3½ % used diet. This is *not* good!

Somewhere we have lost sight of the age-old wisdom that says, "Let food be your medicine." Perhaps this helps explain why our society in general is overweight, overfed but under-nourished, and spends 14 to 15% of the national *gross* income on orthodox health care, hospitals, and pharmaceutically trained doctors. One seventh of our gross earnings go into disease care and yet we still are not disease free. That is an extremely poor return on our investment!

One seventh of our gross earnings go into disease care and yet we still are not disease free. That is an extremely poor return on our investment!

Modern western society is currently involved in a vast nutritional experiment. No one yet knows the full cost or long-term effects of synthetic chemicals in human and animal feeds, of hormones to stimulate growth and of pesticides for sanitation, of drug treatments for diagnosed and misdiagnosed nutritional problems. One thing is sure, however: no society that destroyed the foundation upon which it rested has ever survived for long afterwards. That is food for thought. Is that the ground shaking under our feet?

Summary

1. Traditional medicine with its drug/chemical/surgical approach to treatment virtually ignores the fact that *most diseases have a nutritional and/or an emotional or spiritual component.*
2. Many common ailments that plague both people and pets today—diabetes, cancer, arthritis, lupus and high cholesterol, to name just a few—are virtually unknown in the wild. They also are completely foreign to most primitive cultures.
3. The physical body was designed to be healthy!
4. Modern western medicine is dominated by the pharmaceutically-based approach to health care of treating every disease and symptom with drugs or, if necessary, surgery. Nutrition rarely, if ever, appears on the radar screen as a causative agent.
5. Degenerative foods create degenerative conditions in the animals and humans who eat those foods!

6. As another sign of the seriousness of the modern health crisis, infertility in both humans and animals is nearing epidemic proportions.
7. Obesity, which is at epidemic levels in Western influenced societies, is a result of upside down nutrition.
8. Overeating in *quantity*, no matter the quality of the food, clogs the living machine, thus hindering its function.
9. Somewhere we have lost sight of the age-old wisdom that says, "Let food be your medicine."

ENDORSEMENT FOR CHAPTER FIVE

Chapter 5 was great! It certainly does lay it out nicely. The body/mind connection is worth repeating again and again. I know most Christians think they know this, but most don't understand the outworking in lives and bodies—or perhaps just ignore it.

I remember that when I first started studying the KI method and attaching emotions etc. to the physical manifestations in the body, it made me a bit uncomfortable. Then as I learned the system/science I could see that every level of energy was attached to an emotion. I hated to tell people that if a problem showed up in one area that it also had a negative emotion attached to it. But I find they cannot be separated. They are so interconnected—someone who is angry has congested gallbladder/liver energy, and so on. Keep up the good work!

Blessings.

—Pam G., Texas

Chapter Five

SPIRITUAL AND SCRIPTURAL INSIGHTS INTO HUSBANDRY OF THE EARTH

One of the main reasons the health of man, beast and the earth itself is in such crisis today is that we, the designated caretakers, have forgotten our creation mandate and the principles behind it. Most of the people in the world neither truly acknowledge God nor follow His design and intent for the husbandry of the earth and its inhabitants. Yet these principles are presented clearly throughout God's Word, the Bible.

As we look into the Scriptures, we note *thousands* of references to agriculture. Soon after the beginning, Yahweh Elohim "planted a garden" (Gen. 2:8) and graced it with great varieties of delicious fruit-bearing trees, culinary and medicinal herbs, and multiplied species of animals. He then placed in charge of that garden the "crown" of His creation: mankind. A close communal, almost symbiotic relationship existed between God, man and the natural order over which man was made caretaker and general overseer. It was an awesome responsibility but one Adam was well suited for.

By creation and nature Adam was a husbandman, designed to manifest and move in harmony with his Creator's own creative nature. God charged Adam with a king/priest calling and endowed him with multiple talents to be His supreme ambassador to the creation. Enjoying perfect health himself, Adam's responsibility was to tend the garden in such a way that health and harmony would reign there also. *In the beginning, complete and perfect health was the standard of the day.*

Perfect health is still the standard and the perfect will of God for His creation. Scripture says, "Beloved, I pray that you may prosper in all things and be in health, just as your soul prospers" (3 John 2). The Greek verb for "be in health," *hugiaino* (from which our English word "hygiene" comes), literally means "to have sound health" and to "be well in body." There is *zero* evidence that this mandate has ever changed! But mankind, in his sinful rebellion against God, has failed to live up to the mandate, substituting his own ideas, methods and "wisdom" for those of God with regard to dominating and subduing the earth. The sickness of our soil, our plants, our animals, ourselves and our planet is stark testimony to our poor stewardship.

The sickness of our soil, our plants, our animals, ourselves and our planet is stark testimony to our poor stewardship.

The Image of God in Animals

When I was studying theology, my Master's Thesis was titled, "The Image of God in Animals." This was a rather challenging subject in a seminary staffed with professors of biblical studies who were experts in the subtleties of language and its meanings. But as a farmer/veterinarian, I had been around animals all my life, and I was curious.

One of my discoveries from my research was that animals, like humans, have very unique characteristics. For one thing, within their own beastly realm and in their own beastly way, animals also groan for the redemption of creation, for the "revealing of the sons of God" (Rom. 8:19). Scripture speaks of the animals "talking" to God: "*The beast of the field will honor (say "thank you") Me, the jackals and the ostriches...*" (Is. 43: 20); "*The young lions roar after their prey, and seek their food from God*" (Ps. 104:21). Those and similar Scriptures are too often overlooked.

The animals and man are all unique, but man is much more unique than any animal. As the "image bearer" of the Divine nature, and reflecting God's name and character, mankind was "inspired" by the life-giving breath of God in a way that makes him absolutely unique among all created life. Genesis 2:7 says that God "breathed into his nostrils the breath of life; and man became a living being." In Hebrew, the word for "living being" is *nephesh*, which means literally, "breathing creature." More than physical air is involved here, however. God actually "in-breathed" ("in-spired") His Spirit life into man so that Adam and all his descendents became living souls, spirit-beings in fleshly bodies, endowed with the capability to intimately interact with their Creator.

Although the animals were *created* and *made,* man was *formed* (*yatsar* in Hebrew). *Yatsar* means "to press or squeeze into shape" or "to mold" as a potter would. As such it denotes a workmanship of greater and grander design and exactness than the words used for the rest of creation. Man, as a vessel of clay and dust, was uniquely formed on the Great Potter's wheel for a very special purpose. Man had a higher level of reasoning and understanding than did the animals. He possessed a unique capacity for worship and intimate fellowship with God. *You and I, as inheritors of this plan, have an exclusive and pivotal role in God's ongoing plan for the entire created system!*

Reconciliation is On the Way!

Our responsibility in and to this world extends far beyond ourselves and our own personal well-being. God created us to harness the potential He built into the creation for the comfort and welfare of everything He created. And although we dwell in a creation that was subsequently corrupted by the sin of the first Adam, we are authorized to co-labor with the "Second Adam," Jesus Christ. In that covenanted relationship we also have the clear mandate to reverse that corruption. We should be inspired (God-breathed) daily to be a redemptive blessing to all the creation. How? By staying each day in covenant, in fellowship, in love, and in tune with our Creator. By following the constant recommendations of the Scriptures to "meditate, consider, harken, listen, ask, inquire, seek, and beseech." Those are relational terms, for we are relational beings designed to interact with each other and with a relational God.

Paul the apostle says in 2 Corinthians that all of us who are in Christ are ministers of reconciliation to the world:

> [18]*Now all things are of God, who has reconciled us to Himself through Jesus Christ, and has given* ***us*** *the ministry of reconciliation,* [19]*that is, that God was in Christ reconciling the world (cosmos) to Himself, not imputing their trespasses to them, and has committed to* ***us*** *the word of reconciliation* (2 Corinthians 5:18-19).

To reconcile means to call back, restore or return to friendship again. The Greek word for world, *cosmos,* takes in all of creation. God is in the business of reconciling the world to Himself through Christ, and He has committed that same ministry of reconciliation to *us!* Why? Because Adam, our genetic progenitor, failed in his mission. Instead of caring tenderly for the creation so it would become abundantly fruitful, he seeded corruption into the universe and we have willingly trudged along in his footsteps. We all share the same tragic results: frustration in work, weeds out-growing fruits, herbs and vegetables, struggles and heartaches in childbirth (including still-births, C-sections, deformities, and rebellious offspring), man against man, and fear, stress and anxiety between animals and between animals and man. How stupid and how tragic!

Adam, our genetic progenitor, failed in his mission. Instead of caring tenderly for the creation so it would become abundantly fruitful, he seeded corruption into the universe and we have willingly trudged along in his footsteps.

But the New Covenant in Christ is the story of *reconciliation*! It happened at the cross, where Christ paid the buy-back price so we could again be one with our Creator. That price was a one-time sinless blood sacrifice, substituting for our rebellion, resulting in "atonement". Atonement is at-one-ment. It means to unite or join. The English word "atonement" appears only once in the King James Version New Testament, in Romans 5:11: "And not only so, but we also joy in God through our Lord Jesus Christ, by whom we have now received the *atonement*." Here it translates the Greek word *katallage*, which is rendered "reconciliation" in its other uses. The New Testament Greek word which is the equivalent of the Hebrew word used in the Old Testament for "atonement" is the word *hilasterion*, which is translated in the King James Version as "mercy seat" or "propitiation."

Most interesting of all, however, is the Hebrew word *kaphar*, which is translated many times in the King James Version many times as "atonement." This same word is used in Genesis 6:14 to refer to the "pitch" or bitumen used to cover Noah's ark so that the waters of judgment could not destroy him and his family. The root of this Hebrew word means to "cover, " as in to cover sin, which is exactly what happens in the atonement of Christ. Our sins are covered and we are reconciled with God, which is what the word *kaphar* means.

The word atonement also carries a sense of meaning of being in harmony, as in sounding the same "tone" as God. A true tone is manifested when the *ecclesia* of called out ones (the church, the body of Christ) becomes one with God. That means we speak the same voice with the same liberating "tones". I am reminded of Paul's words to the Corinthians: "*Now I plead with you, brethren, by the name of our Lord Jesus Christ, that you all speak the same thing, and that there be no divisions among you, but that you be perfectly joined together in the same mind and in the same judgment*" (1 Cor. 1:10). Christ spoke only what He heard from His Father. At all times He was in perfect harmony (symphony, a uniting of tones, being "in tune") with His Father. And we, as the assembled *ecclesia*, have been invited to have a part in that ministry!

We Are Called to Be Salt and Light

Jesus said that we are "the salt of the earth" (Mt. 5:13) and "the light of the world" (Mt. 5:14). Does this mean that the church, the *ecclesia*, or "called-out ones," has the responsibility of ministering to all of creation and not just the spiritual needs of mankind? Salt seasons and preserves while light dispels darkness (including the darkness of ignorance and error). Although we are spirit-beings in essence, we inhabit physical bodies formed of the dust of the earth, and as such share an inseparable link with the rest of the created order. So I believe that the answer to the question above is *yes*. Our responsibility does extend to all of creation. I am also convinced personally that *we have abdicated virtually all of our creation mandate to secular institutions: healing to the medical profession, counseling to the psychologists, social engineering to the sociologists, education to the humanists, music and worship to the "professionals," leisure time to the television and Hollywood, and responsibility for the creation to the government! Ouch! This is huge! Do you get the impact of what I just shared?*

Ecclesia, the New Testament word for church, has an interesting history. Political in derivation, *ecclesia* originally referred to a legislative assembly, specifically, the lawful assembly of free Greek citizens gathered to transact public affairs. Therefore, the word "assembly" is closer to the core meaning than is the word "church".[9] Dennis Peacock says, "Ecclesia is a secular term adopted by the church as a body designated to govern society by leading society into the Kingdom message....we have the *responsibility* to affect the community around us!"[10] Of course, in much of western Christianity, "church" has come to mean a building, a physical structure with four walls and a roof, where singing, preaching and praying take place. To most people today, "church" is a religious word. These definitions are far off the mark of reality.

The church, or *ecclesia*, is a gathering of believers and followers of Christ. A gathering of the "assembly" consists of two or more believers who have come together in Christ's name, anticipating His presence and power, just as Jesus Himself said: "For where two or three are gathered together in My *name*, I am there in the midst of them" (Mt. 18:20). *To gather in Christ's name means to gather in His nature, because His name represents His nature.* And what is His nature? He is holy, righteous, loving, gracious, merciful, patient, powerful and infinitely creative. He is both King and Priest, both Judge and Healer. As the *ecclesia* of Christ, we are "called out" to a "Kingdom calling" to change the world by demonstrating the Kingdom of God on earth with creative and purposeful authority.

The opposite is also true. Any gathered assembly that substitutes its own human nature and agenda for those of Christ may *call* itself a church but it is not a true *ecclesia.* It is a counterfeit, and all such counterfeits manifest the nature not of God but of our enemy, either our flesh or Satan (as a master deceiver, a fallen angel of false light.)

Any gathered assembly that substitutes its own human nature and agenda for those of Christ may ***call*** *itself a church but it is not a true* ***ecclesia****. It is a counterfeit, and all such counterfeits manifest the nature not of God, but of our enemy, either our flesh or Satan.*

If that characterization sounds harsh, know too that it also conforms to the clear teachings of Scripture. Some of us need God to shake up our concepts of truth. It's time to get out of our mind and into His mind! As the *ecclesia* of Christ, we need to understand our *new name* so we also will understand our *new nature* in Christ.

Have we abdicated our role as Kingdom ambassadors and leaders and shapers of society? Has not society invaded the church, and has not the church, to a large degree, surrendered? Has our salt become tasteless and our light gone out? Where will we go from here?

The Body-Mind Connection

Because I have the unique situation of being a doctor with traditional training, a nutritionist, a holistic practitioner, a farmer, and a minister, perhaps I have a unique perspective on life. Having studied at a land-grant agricultural university, I had more nutrition courses than most veterinarians—and far more nutritional knowledge than most medical doctors. I remember, from both my studies and in our clinics, cases of animals that had nutritional diseases. Without exception, their brains, minds, emotions and attitudes were all negatively affected. Sadness, depression, confusion, anger and anxiety were the big ones. Also without fail, when we corrected the nutritional deficiency, the mental or emotional difficulty would totally disappear.

I remember, from both my studies and in our clinics, cases of animals that had nutritional diseases. Without exception, their brains, minds, emotions and attitudes were all negatively affected.

I remember talking to one internationally respected minister with whom I spoke about the intimate connection between diabetes and diet. Among American Indians, for instance, diabetes has become epidemic. In their earlier native culture diabetes was completely unknown. *The difference*? Instead of living off the land, they now subsisted on beer, junk food, a highly refined diet, and government handouts. Take two groups of animals and put them in the same dietary situation, with everything else being equal, and guess what happens? The junk food group will manifest high levels of diabetes in any susceptible population.

The perspective of the minister in question, however, was that all physical problems are a manifestation of emotional and spiritual problems. This is undoubtedly partly true. But *only* partly true. Emotionally, diabetes has been correlated to a "lack of sweetness in ones life". I can agree with that probability, not only for the American Indians but also for many others who have been displaced or stressed or are in some way live in broken situations—so they do not have much sweetness left in their life. It is also true that eating sugar is a *very* poor substitute for emotional and spiritual sweetness.

Eating sugar is a very poor substitute for emotional and spiritual sweetness.

At the same time, it is also true that emotional and spiritual problems can be a direct manifestation of physical problems. There is more than one way to look at things! There are two sides to this coin! Neither side has an absolute lock on the truth. This is a case that works in both directions, and if it works in both directions, it must be treated from both directions! We are connected at all levels! It is impossible to separate natural law from spiritual law.

Dr. Barbara Stitt, in her excellent book, *Food and Behavior: A Natural Connection*,[11] proved conclusively to the Ohio prison system that diet and crime were related. She found that the majority of those filling the jails were sugar-holics. Sodas, candy and fast foods were their mainstay diet. Dr. Stitt did a large study with prisoners on probation and parole. She found that if she could get them off sweets and junk and onto a balanced and healthy diet, hardly any of them returned to prison. They could now hold down good jobs and became productive citizens. They happily took control of their lives.

Depression, anger and roller coaster mood swings became a thing of the past. But those who refused to change their dietary habits ended up back in prison. They were confused and angry people who could not and would not adapt to an orderly society. Is that an emotional and a spiritual problem? Yes. Did the diet affect their health, their emotions, and their spiritual condition? Also yes!

In a recently released book, *Redeeming Your Mind*, authors Cort and Hackett open a chapter on "Mind Body Orchestration" with these words:

> In previous chapters we have seen how the mind affects the body. But we must not forget that the body also affects the mind to a greater degree than many realize. Modern medicine has turned up abundant evidence that the mind is vitally affected by food intake, by the abundance or lack of vitamins and minerals, and by certain chemicals in the body. Again we remind ourselves that man cannot be compartmentalized by treating one organ of the system without reckoning with its corresponding effect on other organs.[12]

Later, these same authors state:

> Under the influence of unhealthy foods, the conscience becomes stupefied, the mind is darkened, and its susceptibility to impressions is impaired. The relation of diet to intellectual development should be given far more attention than it has received. Mental confusion and dullness are often the result of errors in the diet."[13]

Twenty-three years ago I substitute taught a junior high health class for three *very* long months. One of the classes was called a "660 class" for challenged learners. The class consisted of two types of students: hyperactive youngsters, virtual busybodies who could not sit still or keep their minds focused; and lethargic, depressed kids with an "I don't care" attitude. This second group I could hardly keep awake long enough to listen to the lesson.

One day I took a written poll of the dietary habits of all of the students. The results were quite revealing! Both student types averaged 6-10 sugar and caffeine-loaded soft drinks a day. In addition, they ate for snacks a minimum of two large candy bars a day from the vending machine down the hall. From the candy and soft drink products alone they averaged 66 teaspoons of sugar daily! No wonder they were in the 660 class! And that calculation did not include the Twinkies, cookies, and sugary cereals they ate at home.

Later I learned the reason for this dual phenomena of opposite effects. I discovered that white refined sugar drives one's basic personality to an extreme. Persons with Type A extrovert personality will go up a wall—all the way into hyperactivity. Introverted Type B personality people, on the other hand, will be driven to the opposite extreme—and become depressed couch potatoes.

The State of California is in the process of removing soft drinks and candy bar machines from the halls of public schools. Several counties in New York State are also working on outlawing junk food machines in their schools. The Seattle School Board is another that has bucked the junk-food trend by banning the sales of sodas and junk food on the school campuses. But the Board went one step further. They also gave direction to the school meal program to offer fresh, *local,* organic, non-genetically modified, non-irradiated, unprocessed food, whenever feasible. Why? Because when the test schools complied with the rulings the students' grades went up dramatically, and for the exact reasons I am suggesting. *Would that every parent would be that wise.* Would that the students themselves would get the big picture! Nutrition makes a difference!

When the test schools complied with the rulings the students' grades went up dramatically.

Blessings and Cursings

Today we are reaping the bitter harvest of centuries of neglect and disobedience of the standards for health and prosperity that God laid down from the beginning. Blessings are contingent on our keeping our covenant with our Creator. The animals didn't blow it, we did. In a very real way we are cursing ourselves by our own behavior.

Shortly after the Israelites entered the Promised Land of Canaan, they carried out a command that Moses had given them before he died. As the Lord had directed, Joshua divided the people—perhaps as many as 2,000,000 men, women and children—with half standing on Mt. Gerizim, known as the "Mountain of Blessing," and the other half across the valley on Mount Ebal, the "Mountain of Cursing." There they recited in each others' hearing the blessings that would be theirs if they obeyed the Lord—and the curses that would afflict them if they disobeyed. The words themselves are recorded in the Book of Deuteronomy. They read, in part:

> [2]*And all these blessings shall come upon you and overtake you, because you obey the voice of the LORD your God:* [3]*"Blessed shall you be in the city, and blessed shall you be in the* country. [4]*"Blessed shall be the* fruit *of your body, the* produce *of your* ground *and the increase of your* herds, *the increase of your* cattle *and the offspring of your* flocks... [11]*And the LORD will grant you plenty of goods, in the* fruit of your body, *in the increase of your* livestock, *and in the* produce *of your* ground, *in the land of which the LORD swore to your fathers to give you* (Deuteronomy 28:3-4, 11 emphasis added).

The list of blessings for covenant-keeping was long, but the list of curses for disobedience was even longer. It included all the diseases and plagues that would follow as a result of violating the covenant, diseases that afflict the land and livestock as well as the people:

> [16]*"Cursed shall you be in the city, and cursed shall you be in the country...* [18]*"Cursed shall be the* fruit *of your* body *and the* produce *of your* land, *the increase of your* cattle *and the offspring of your* flocks... [21]*The LORD will make the* plague *cling to you until He has consumed you from the land which you are going to possess.* [22]*The LORD will strike you with* consumption, *with* fever, *with* inflammation, *with* severe burning fever, *with the sword, with* scorching, *and with* mildew; *they shall pursue you until you perish* (Deuteronomy 28:16, 18, 21-22 emphasis added).

This list sounds as if it could have been written specifically for our situation today! All of these curses—these maladies, injuries, and calamities—are the current experiences of the materially affluent but nutritionally poor western societies. The shoe fits!

The blessings are contingent on our being a covenant keeping people, walking in God's revealed precepts. It means breaking with selfish man-made traditions and ideas, recognizing the superiority of God's heart and God's methods. It also means keeping our side of the two-sided covenant agreement. Since we are God's creatures and creation, and He is our Father, does it not make sense that "Father knows best?"

Therefore we are challenged to walk in harmony with our Father, for our own good. Yahweh Elohim promises that if we keep His ways first in our lives, He will care for us. How desperately that promise is needed in the dangerous world we live in today!

The blessings are contingent on our being a covenant keeping people, walking in God's revealed precepts. It means breaking with selfish man-made traditions and ideas, recognizing the superiority of God's heart and God's methods.

Jesus said, "But seek first the kingdom of God and His righteousness, and all these things shall be added to you" (Mt. 6:33) As someone once said: "The main thing is to keep the main thing the main thing." Only then will true life begin to flow through us to bless the nations.

Summary

1. In the beginning, complete and perfect health was the standard of the day.
2. The sickness of our soil, our plants, our animals, ourselves and our planet is stark testimony to our poor stewardship.
3. Our responsibility in and to this world extends far beyond ourselves and our own personal well-being.
4. God is in the business of reconciling the world to Himself through Christ, and He has committed that same ministry of reconciliation to *us*!
5. We have abdicated virtually all of our creation mandate to secular institutions.
6. As the *ecclesia* of Christ, we are "called out" to a "Kingdom calling" to change the world by demonstrating the Kingdom of God on earth with creative and purposeful authority.
7. Physical problems often are a manifestation of emotional and spiritual problems.
8. Emotional and spiritual problems can be a direct manifestation of physical problems.
9. It is impossible to separate natural law from spiritual law.

10. Today we are reaping the bitter harvest of centuries of neglect and disobedience of the standards for health and prosperity that God laid down from the beginning.
11. The blessings are contingent on our being a covenant-keeping people, walking in God's revealed precepts.

ENDORSEMENTS FOR CHAPTER SIX

Roger,

Yes, chapter 6 is probably way out for the average Christian—but perhaps God will use this to awaken us all! I think it brings a great thought into the whole subject of redeeming creation. You are doing a good job of putting these thoughts into print.

What you write seems timely in light of all the Hollywood movies where lifelike (non animated) stories are being portrayed as *animals talking*, with lots of people characteristics, etc. The kingdom of darkness would like to pervert God's mandate and make animals like people.

Bless the works of your hands.

—Pam G., Texas (after reading chapter 6)

Roger,

"Thank you so much for letting me read this. Yes, I do resonate with this excellent chapter. (Chapter 6)

You know, I went to a prep high school here in the Boston area, graduated in top 5%, and went on the Cornell University's engineering college. By then I had been to France twice, the second time living for four months in Paris as a student, so I had been a bit humbled by the reality of mankind and was not as naïve and protected as most of my college friends. However, while in my freshman year, I would find myself gazing out of my dorm window into the beautiful scenery, thinking, "I have no idea who I am (no idea of my destiny) and I have no common sense." I knew I was disconnected from something but didn't know what. Well, I dropped out of college after my freshman year. I worked and lived in the Caribbean for a year and then headed to the Rocky Mountains of Montana. Roger, I didn't leave there for 17 years. It took me that long to get the common sense and the "connection" I knew I lacked. *It was as though I couldn't move on in my life until I had satisfied that void.* As you know, it was the immersion in the mountain life, living outdoors, organic farming and gardening, and experiencing animal husbandry, home births and health care practices that taught me common sense. *It was by watching the skies, the birds, the wildlife, my animals, the change of seasons, by wild-crafting and growing my food that I began to get grounded in God's principles.*

And now, talking with so many church folks, it's heartbreaking to see that really, in this area, most everyone is disconnected. And I agree that that's why our animals are as sick as we are.

This is a good message, one that will take repeating in order for the deaf ears to hear, but there's no time like now to get started. I am behind you on this one too, BIG TIME."

Blessings.

—Jackie Bell, Naturopathic and
RegulationThermography Therapist, MA.
(after reading chapter 6)

I just read chapter 6. I was fascinated by the horse who cured himself of cancer—and also the part of "alignment" with spirit, as I believe in energy alignment. It was fascinating to read about the wolf and St. Francis—whether or not that really happened—the point is getting to the truth; to me, that is what really matters. Knowing that animals—dogs in particular—basically take the path of least resistance, and that they seek to please, all that seems totally plausible. I loved your method of drawing the blood form the paw of the dog—and the training to get off the couch be "seeing" that accomplished.

I know this is a passion of yours, and I admire you for following it. I enjoyed this chapter. Thank you for allowing me to share it.

—Nancy S., President & CEO of an Animal Nutrition Company, NC.
(After reading chapter 6)

Chapter Six

ANIMAL HUSBANDRY IS PART OF OUR MANDATE

The blessings cited in Deuteronomy 28 include fruitfulness and prosperity of herds, cattle, flocks and livestock, as well as the produce of the ground. In other words, our faithfulness or unfaithfulness in covenant-keeping affects the health and welfare of our animals and our plants in addition to ourselves. This means, of course, that animal and plant husbandry are part of our creation mandate. Yet many Christians continue to overlook this dimension. *Traditional theology in general gives scant attention to the proper care of plants and animals as part of our overall ongoing calling as believers.*

In this chapter I want to address this issue, particularly as it concerns our pets and livestock.

Animal Nutrition? Go Natural!

A major limiting factor in health care progress with animals, from my standpoint, is our failure to understand an animal from the animal's perspective. When discussing with pet owners the diet requirements of their animals, the key point I stress is this: *What does the animal eat in* ***nature****?* What is the *natural* food for a dog or a cat or a cow or a sheep or a goat? In the wild, all animals will *by instinct* forage for miles to get their diet perfectly balanced. God put this innate ability into them when He created them.

We humans, in our *intellectual* "wisdom" and arrogance, assume that we can improve on nature, that we can go God one better. That kind of thinking has always gotten us into trouble and always will. We cook, preserve, denature, fractionate and adulterate, carefully subtracting living germ from our pet food. Confidently but ignorantly we add pharmaceutical, factory-synthesized vitamins, chemicals and salt minerals and then with pompous authority pronounce it "improved" and "100% complete." And our animals are becoming sickly as a result.

Here is a better approach. By astutely considering "the beasts" we would undoubtedly learn many major principles about nutrition and other key truths relating to ourselves as well. The innovative "Hoxy" herbal cancer formula is based on this foundation. Mr. Hoxy watched his dying horse totally recover from malignant cancer when turned out to pasture. Now insatiably curious, Hoxy carefully observed what the horse was eating. This was like Moses turning aside to watch the oddity of the burning bush that did not burn. "This I must understand!" Hoxy ruminated.

Free to roam the pasture, woods, creeks, hills and valleys, the horse was able to follow its own innate instinct. Mr. Hoxy himself harvested those same herbs, blended them with creative inspiration and used his formula to cure several of his friends of cancer. Out of this basic discovery eventually grew the Hoxy Cancer Clinic. The highly successful Hoxy Cancer formula was based not on pharmaceuticals but on *observation* plus *inspiration.*

Several years ago *National Geographic* magazine ran an article concerning the nutritional habits of monkeys in Africa. A group of scientists who studied local colonies of monkeys for years observed that the primates' diet changed specifically on a seasonal basis. Each spring the monkeys ate in abundance the leaves from a particular variety of tree. At no other time during the year did they eat these particular leaves. Eventually, the scientists discovered that these leaves possessed powerful anti-parasitic properties at that specific time of the year. By instinct, the monkeys purged themselves of parasites every spring.

Interestingly, herbal purging in the springtime has been the habit of many human cultures from time immemorial. It was practiced by the American Indians as well as by the early European colonists. Spring purging is also common among the indigenous peoples of South America and of many island cultures off the coasts of the major continents.

By instinct, the monkeys purged themselves of parasites every spring. Interestingly, herbal purging in the springtime has been the habit of many human cultures from time immemorial.

Let's Learn from the Animals

We need to lay aside our pride, humble ourselves and once more allow the animals to teach us:

> [11]*Who teaches us more than the beasts of the earth, And makes us wiser than the birds of heaven?* [12]*There they cry out, but He does not answer, Because of the* ***pride*** *of evil men* (Job 35:11-12, emphasis mine).

> [7]*But now ask the beasts, and they will teach you; And the birds of the air, and they will tell you;* [8]*Or speak to the earth, and it will teach you; And the fish of the sea will explain to you* (Job 12:7-8).

> [14]*For God may speak in one way, or in another, Yet man does not perceive it.* [15]*In a dream, in a vision of the night, When deep sleep falls upon men, While slumbering on their beds,* [16]*Then He opens the ears of men, And seals their instruction.* [17]*In order to turn man from his deed, And conceal* ***pride*** *from man...* (Job 33:14-17, emphasis mine).

I don't know about you, but these Scriptures tell me that we humans are not finding solutions that even the animals know and could teach us! The problem is quite simple: our pride, tradition and rebellion against God and His ways stand in the way of our understanding.

A common attitude among people is, "Animals are 'dumb.' What do they know?" However, anybody who has ever spent even a little time around animals recognizes the naiveté of that question. For example, when the terrible tsunami hit Asia in December, 2004, the elephants and other animals at the National Wildlife Refuge in Indonesia had already begun moving inland. In fact, their exodus away from the coast started two days *before* the tsunami hit! Dozens of people died on the National Reserve where the animals had been just 24-48 hours before—yet the humans perceived nothing different until the 30-foot waves hit, killing them and thousands of others along the Asian coast. In this case, who possessed wisdom and knowledge? The animals listened, acted and survived, while the oblivious humans partied on and died.

The animals listened, acted and survived, while the oblivious humans partied on and died.

Following this catastrophe, an acquaintance wrote to me how a friend of his had said the same thing—that the animals somehow sensed what was coming.

This acquaintance went on to say, "Our mixed-breed Pointer knows when a storm is coming hours and hours before there is any natural sign to confirm it. As for our adorable Boxer, they have a natural disdain for fire (and other dangerous situations) and are known to lead children, in particular, to safety and even to 'paw out' a fire or a lit cigarette."

We humans seem to have a massive blind spot where we refuse to look in the right places for truth or to understand what we are seeing. We seem to be intent on raping the creation for our own private desires and passions when we should be nurturing, listening, and understanding.

We humans seem to have a massive blind spot where we refuse to look in the right places for truth or to understand what we are seeing.

Scientists are currently trekking through the Amazon jungles looking for the evasive "cancer cure". Whatever they find, however, they must extract and synthesize in order to obtain a *patent,* and therein lies the problem. Their "cure" will result in another high-priced drug that is also highly toxic.

Patiently, our Creator is nudging us to get these truths through our thick skulls and into the quiet place of *heart receptivity*. But first we must be willing to sacrifice our pride, our fear and many of our doctrinal and other "traditional" positions on the altar of humility and brokenness. This is our best hope for a truly healthy future!

Can We Communicate with Animals?

Does this mean we start exchanging ideas with animals? I am not sure what it means, but consider this: The story is told, purportedly true, of how St. Francis of Assisi resolved a local crisis involving a man-eating wolf. The wolf had killed numerous small children in a local village. The townsmen and protectors had been unable to trap or kill the wolf. Francis was in the area at the time, so the townsmen explained their predicament. One day St. Francis walked to the edge of the woods and called out to the wolf. The wolf came before him, only a few feet away, head to the ground. Francis explained the problem and commanded the wolf to stop. From that day on no more children were harmed.

Whether true or not, the story does raise the intriguing possibility that our mental link to animals may be much stronger than most of us imagine. Allen

Boone, author of *Kinship with all Life*, writes in a chapter entitled, "Mental Bridges," "It is not easy to make clear in words the exact technique for exchanging ideas with a dog by means of silent communication. One obstacle to an understanding is the general attitude which resists the unfamiliar, especially if it has to do with animals."[14]

Later on, commenting on his experiences with the brilliant canine movie star "Strongheart," a regal German Shepherd, "Another difficulty arises from the fact that attempting to expand one's rational relations with a dog in this manner must of necessity be a pioneering adventure. One is forced to do his own mental navigating, to arrive at his own conclusions and prove them in first hand experience. *One finds himself moving contrary to almost all conventional notions of human-animal relationships.*"[15]

In the Genesis story of Adam and Eve we have a hint of this human ability to communicate with animals. Adam had the responsibility of naming the animals at the beginning of creation. God created them but Adam named them. We can only guess at what that connection was. But some experts have postulated that by intuitive observation Adam was gifted to recognize the real *nature* of each species, giving each the correct descriptive *name*. Or even more dramatically, Adam was co-laboring with the Almighty and actually imparted to the animals their different particular natures by creative revelation, because the *name is the nature*! Either way, Adam's task required very specific skills!

Nor did it appear out of the ordinary for Eve to carry on a conversation with a serpent! What else happened in that pristine situation of inter-relating and communicating with the creation is difficult if not impossible to guess. However, young children, before we educate it out of them, seem to have some of that innate ability! They run into the house and say something like, "Mommy, Frisky isn't feeling well today, her tummy hurts!"

How does the child know that? And furthermore, how else do we explain the three Scriptures quoted above from the book of Job? Maybe we have a lot of doctrine to shed, a lot of preconceived notions to release, and human junk to discard, before we can enter into this realm. And if we are in tune with the God who created everything, as His sons, should we not be able to be in tune with everything God made? That is a question that begs to be answered!

If we are in tune with the God who created everything, as His sons, should we not be able to be in tune with everything God made? That is a question that begs to be answered!

There is also something called "non-verbal communication." Some trainers seem to have this ability intuitively. Have you noticed some trainers are *a natural* in their work—the animals respond to them almost effortlessly?

One trainer explained to me: "A good trainer always pictures in his mind what he wants the animal to do. If the dog is on the couch, and the trainer wants him off the couch, he *pictures him on the floor*! The average person commands the dog to "get off the couch!" but pictures the reality of where Fido is presently *on the couch*. The dog is entirely confused, because the mental pictures he picks up are contrary to the emotional tones and words the person is commanding *at* him. There is a power struggle, talking "at" rather than "with". The dog doesn't *know* what to do, and certainly doesn't get a clear message."

I have also learned that animals in the wild communicate by non-verbal pictures. For instance, when a pack of wolves are stalking their prey, the lead wolf flashes mental pictures giving direction to his companions, so that they can move in unison. Although dogs and wolves have about 15 different bark sounds, and all of them mean something in canine language, that method is not effective in the chase. There is too much noise, dust and confusion. But somehow they can "read" each other, and the process has been understood by wildlife specialists as a primitive form of non-verbal communication: mental word pictures being communicated from one wolf to another.

There is a primitive tribe in Africa that speaks very few words. When the men go on a hunt and are successful in the catch, the women back in the camp have the water boiling. When there is no catch, no preparation goes on back at the camp. How do the women know? Anthropologists explain they communicate by a sort of internal knowing, the primitive ability of word-picture communication. "Knowing" of this variety has been reported frequently among identical twins. They can be thousands of miles apart and yet know immediately when something unusual happens to one or the other. This is hard to explain in modern scientific terms.

When I am in my clinic and ready to take a blood sample, I mentally picture the dog relaxing his paw into my hand. I wait for him to relax and follow my mental picture of his paw in my hand. Using this technique, and "asking" for permission, I find things flow well. I am able to easily withdraw the blood test without a struggle. I don't remember ever being bitten!

Because we are attempting to establish both kind words and non-threatening non-verbal communication, I am not forcefully dominating something the dog must consciously resist! I am, as it were, getting into his field of recognition as a friend. Sound weird? Probably. But the above explanations make sense to me, and I do find precedence for this in the three Scriptures I quoted above!

Proverbs 12:10 says, "*A righteous man regards the life of his animal, But the tender mercies of the wicked are cruel,*" and Proverbs 27:23, "*Be diligent to know the state of your flocks, and attend to your herds.*" These Scriptures, like all the rest of the Bible, were written at a time in history when the vast majority of the world's population was agrarian. They were much closer to the land and to their animals than we are today, and we are the poorer for it. We have lost sight of a vital connection that was second nature to them. Somehow, we must get it back!

Contrary to the counsel in those Proverbs, most of the people who come to my office bring their animals to me weeks, months, and sometimes even years after subtle symptoms of a problem first appear. Why do they wait so long? Usually it is unawareness and lack of knowledge. They don't know anything is wrong because they lack intuitive and instinctual observation. Today only 2- 3% of our population lives on farms. Probably only 1 in 1,000 have the heart of a true husbandman, the nurturing of a mother, or the shepherding ability of a King David!

Resolution of this problem of blind-spot negligence begins with *you* and *me*. According to the prophet Hosea, God's covenant agreement with His people includes the following: "...the beasts of the field, the birds of the air...the creeping things of the ground...." (Hos. 2:18). Then he prophesies: "'*It shall come to pass in that day that I will hear,'" says the Lord; "'I will answer the heavens, And they shall answer the earth. The earth shall answer with grain, With new wine, And with oil; They shall answer Jezreel*" (Hos. 2:21-22) ("Jezreel" is Hebrew for "God sows".)

Probably only 1 in 1,000 have the heart of a true husbandman, the nurturing of a mother, or the shepherding ability of a King David! Resolution of this problem of blind-spot negligence begins with you and me.

This prophetic utterance has a definite meaning. There may be a profound spiritual truth, but let's not discount the obvious literal implications. The entire creation is in relationship, in vital communication—and a message is out there crying to be heard. Who is that true husbandman of the vineyard and the shepherd of the sheepfold who will hear and understand? A "groaning" is going forth. *Will we get the message?*

Some of you may ask, "Does God's covenant really include the *animals*?" If that is a new concept for you, let me remind you of the Flood and the rainbow.

After Noah, his family and all the animals came out of the ark, God declared a new covenant with all His creatures:

> [8]*Then God spoke to Noah and to his sons with him, saying:* [9]*"And as for Me, behold,* ***I establish My covenant with you and with your descendants after you,*** [10]***and with every living creature that is with you****: the birds, the cattle, and every beast of the earth with you, of all that go out of the ark, every beast of the earth.* [11]*Thus I establish My covenant with you: Never again shall all flesh be cut off by the waters of the flood; never again shall there be a flood to destroy the earth."*
>
> [12]*And God said: "This is the sign of* ***the covenant which I make between Me and you, and every living creature that is with you****, for perpetual generations:* [13]*I set My rainbow in the cloud, and it shall be for the sign of the covenant between Me and the earth.* [14]*It shall be, when I bring a cloud over the earth, that the rainbow shall be seen in the cloud;* [15]*and I will remember* ***My covenant which is between Me and you and every living creature of all flesh****; the waters shall never again become a flood to destroy all flesh.* [16]*The rainbow shall be in the cloud, and I will look on it to remember* ***the everlasting covenant between God and every living creature of all flesh that is on the earth****."* [17]*And God said to Noah, "This is the sign of* ***the covenant which I have established between Me and all flesh that is on the earth****"* (Genesis 9:8-17, emphasis mine).

Notice that in those ten verses God mentions His covenant with man and "every living creature" *five times*! Doesn't it look like God thinks this is important?

In Matthew 10:29 Jesus asks, "Are not two sparrows sold for a copper coin? And not one of them falls to the ground apart from your Father's will." Revelation 5:13 says, "And *every creature* which is in heaven and on the earth and under the earth and such as are in the sea, and *all* that are in them, I heard saying: 'Blessing and honor and glory and power Be to Him who sits on the throne, and to the Lamb, forever and ever'" (emphasis mine). The note next to that verse in my reference Bible reads: "Universal Worship." May I rest my case?

Summary

1. Animal and plant husbandry are part of our creation mandate.
2. By astutely considering "the beasts" we would undoubtedly learn many major principles about nutrition and other key truths relating to ourselves as well.
3. We need to lay aside our pride, humble ourselves and once more allow the animals to teach us.
4. Our mental link to animals may be much stronger than most of us imagine.
5. If we are in tune with the God who created everything, as His sons, should we not be able to be in tune with everything God made?
6. The entire creation is in relationship, in vital communication—and a message is out there crying to be heard.

Chapter Seven

MEGA-SHIFT

"The most thought provoking thing about our thought provoking age is that we still are not thinking."

—Martin Heidegger, German philosopher following WW II

"The Third-rate mind is happy when it's thinking with the majority. The second-rate mind is happy when it's thinking with the minority. The first-rate mind is happy when it's thinking."

—Walter Gannon

Today we live in a world that is constantly changing. For much of human history progress was slow, change infrequent. The more knowledge we have gained, however, the faster change has come until today the sum total of human knowledge doubles every few years. Our intellectual and technological advances have outstripped our moral sensibilities to the point where we face a continual array of ethical and moral challenges—situations we have never dealt with before—and we do not know how to handle them. Does simply possessing the ability to do something give us a mandate or even the right to do it? Does the mere *potential* of advances in disease prevention and cure through embryonic stem cell research justify killing human embryos to harvest those stem cells?

Human culture worldwide is undergoing a massive mega-shift in perspective. The diabolical attacks of 9/11 forever destroyed the complacency of the west. Add to the mix a Europe that has become completely secularized, even to the point of officially denying its Christian heritage, one million parishioners a year leaving the church in America, unprecedented dissatisfaction with politicians, failing ecological stewardship, genocidal wars and corporate greed, and the result is a world in such chaos that a new urgency of spirit is being born within a disenchanted generation of questioning youth!

Failing ecological stewardship, genocidal wars and corporate greed...result [in] a world in such chaos that a new urgency of spirit is being born within a disenchanted generation of questioning youth!

Our world is not the same today as two generations ago. There is a rising sense of urgency among many, particularly the young; a shift in perception of earthquake proportions. Pessimism grows along with optimism, depending on who you talk to. Some question whether answers are to be found and fear that it is already too late. NO! ABSOLUTELY NOT! Answers *are* available. And they can be found right here on earth in the here and now!

Are you and I ready to be part of the solution? Or are you and I still part of the problem? That is the question!

Are you ready for homework!

It's time for some interaction. Below are listed thirty statements that I believe reflect characteristics of this great mega-shift we are seeing in the world today. Let me encourage you to read each of these statements carefully and thoughtfully, then underline the (+) or (-) to indicate whether you agree or disagree with the statement. Use the blank lines after each statement to indicate your core reason for agreeing or disagreeing. The purpose of this exercise is to get you pondering deeply rather than simply feeding you facts. *You are free to disagree!* The more you are challenged to think deeply, the more you will understand and the more you understand the more likely you will be to become personally engaged. So here we go!

Thirty Characteristics that Typify an Expanding Group of the Stressed World Population

1. People are looking for *answers* that satisfy the deeper longing of their heart and spirit. Success and worldly goods have not satisfied. Although many continue to relish the "good life" (if it is available), there is an ongoing recognition of an internal dark hole

or void that has reached the crisis point of ache, anxiety and bewilderment. (+)/(-) ________________________________
____
____.

2. This mega-shift is occurring among both Christians and non-Christians. (+)/(-) ________________________________
____
____.

3. It is not limited to "conservatives" or "liberal" but is occurring across the political spectrum. (+)/(-) ________________
____
____.

4. There is a growing sense among many that the Creation is not to be exploited without regard to responsible *stewardship*. (+)/(-)
____
____.

5. War, drug reactions and poverty are pricking the universal conscience. The problem is that all current answers are undefined, vague and confusing. (+)/(-) ________________________
____
____.

6. It is time to sound a trumpet blast: all must return to core Scriptural foundations which alone have the true answers! (+)/(-)
____
____.

7. The burning question of the hour is: How can we make the scriptural message relevant to the 21st century? (+)/(-) __________
____
____.

8. Pulling down religious and cultural strongholds will require a message that is non-sectarian, non-threatening, positive in nature, and which resonates at the level of heart and spirit. (+)/(-)
____
____.

9. On the other hand, strong language is required, language that will reach, tug and potentially convince both the heart and the spirit. (+)/(-)____
____.

10. People are asking, "Why are we here?" Our challenge is to respond with a clear and compelling answer! (+)/(-) ________________
____.

11. We have messed up. Now *we* are called to un-mess the mess! (+)/(-) ____
____.

12. We must demonstrate a *vision* and appropriate the clout and power to activate the heavenly vision: "Thy will be done *on earth* as it is in heaven." (+)/(-) ________________________
____.

13. We must become living Scriptural examples of "speaking" to the Creation. We must nurture the creation with "creative word." This means words of *blessing*. Only blessing will reverse the negative word that cries out from all the major networks and from the hopeless heart of betrayal that exudes from mankind in general. The clear command of the Scriptures is to "Bless, and curse not!" (+)/(-) ________________________________
____.

14. Are we bordering on "New Age" philosophy, or are we authentically Scriptural? New Age has in many ways stolen our truth but typically has clothed it either in Gnostic mysticism or Greek Western intellectualism. *No matter who has truth, truth is still truth!* And leaven is leaven. And it may be that the traditional church has been so smug in itself (like the lukewarm Laodicean church that Christ threatened to spew from his mouth, see Rev. 3:16) that as a result New Age philosophy has become a reservoir of answers that must be re-examined as gems of truth that have been overlooked, despised or ceremoniously buried alive by the church. Is that a heretical statement? Or does it merely recognize that such a great hunger exists for true answers that answers, whether genuine or counterfeit, will spring up anywhere they find water? (+)/(-) ________________________
____.

15. Gnosticism is a spiritual stronghold that leads to emptiness. Documented as one of the oldest heresies of the Church, gnosticism denies the goodness of the physical creation and, consequently, denies that Jesus came in the flesh (that Jesus was fully human). The fact that Jesus *did* take on our flesh and blood and

did care for the physical needs of people shows that God is not schizophrenic, pitting the spiritual against the physical. Gnosticism tends to revolve around the spiritual, the symbolic, the subconscious mind, mystical experiences and elite mystical "knowledge" that often have little relevance to the challenges of daily life. (+)/(-) ______________________________________

______________________________________.

16. Westernized Greek philosophy is another stronghold that leads to emptiness. The Greek paradigm tends to glorify the body. It tends to literalize the symbolic and humanize the spiritual. The Greeks had gods with human tendencies, conceived after the image of man. It is also philosophical chatter without genuine action, hearing without doing, philosophy without feet, and breath without spirit. The emphasis is head knowledge and the five senses. The apostle Paul encountered Greek philosophers on Mars Hill. These Greeks gathered every day to hear new ideas, which means they tended to be broadminded! But they were also great at shooting down and scoffing at anything new if it didn't fit their preconceived paradigm. (+)/(-) ______________________________________

______________________________________.

17. What I see happening today are people speaking bits of "truth" without understanding *the truth*: creation without the Creator, Christianity without Christ, vision without seeing, hearing without perceiving and touching without feeling. This yields a worldview with no eternal perspective, resulting in dead-end alleys. What is lacking is the creative instinct of the Father—the DNA of God operating in His children in its restored capacity!(+)/(-)

____

______________________________________.

18. I sense a sincere friendliness and esteem for many of the New Age people. Most have rejected traditional Christianity. Could it be, however, that many New-Agers are closer to God than some professing Christians? Could they be embracing key spiritual truths that "religious" inflexible Christians reject, to the detriment of Christians and to the benefit of mankind? On this point Bruce, a friend of mine, commented: "You'll probably get some flak for saying that, but I whole-heartedly agree with you. We have friends who have a deliverance ministry and have much experience dealing with people involved in the occult. They see these people (some, not all, obviously) as being *so close* to the truth that *all it*

takes is for them to see the Gospel in its pure simplicity and power, and they will embrace it whole-heartedly and become some of the most on-fire, powerful witnesses for Christ the modern Church has ever seen! Many people that the Church tends to write off as being so lost it's not worth our time even to pray for them (take the terrorist suicide bombers, for example), are putting us to shame simply by their willingness to lay down their lives for what they believe. Saul of Tarsus is a good biblical example of a "wild-eyed fanatic" who only needed a revelation of who Yeshua was to turn his life around. If the New-Agers and others keep searching they undoubtedly will run into the One who *is* the Truth. Romans 2:14-16 opens the door for all true searchers after truth! Hebrews 11:6 proves the way to God is very uncomplicated! (+)/(-) ____
____.

19. Many seekers do not recognize God in Westernized Christianity yet nevertheless from their hearts many still do the "works of God." This group may be among those who enter in, having "given a cup of cold water" in His name without ever having heard or understood his human name. Which is more important, understanding and walking in God's nature, or intellectually knowing how to pronounce his name? That is a colossal question! And probably if questioned, 10 people would give 10 different answers! Many outwardly "religious" people are filled with pharisaical pride and may therefore be among those to whom Jesus will speak the words, "I never knew you; depart from Me" (Mt. 7:23). This group may have intimate knowledge of the correct technical name as well as other important facts about God, but they definitely do not understand how to walk in the *nature* of God, which includes charitable giving, stewardship and guardianship, and the power and nature of unconditional love. Understanding the true nature of God broadens our scope where we must understand that *God judges the heart rather than legalistic protocol!* (+)/(-) _______
____
____.

20. It's time to release creativity! We must take creativity out of theory by sharing and practicing graphic living examples, both from the past and the present. There is nothing new under the sun! We must discover and re-discover. The captives must be set free! Many of our greatest scientists moved in this principle. For

instance, Einstein writes that one day he was lying on a hillside looking at the blue sky, meditating, when an inspiration suddenly flashed into his mind and heart. Out of that inspired moment was birthed the mathematical truth of relativity. Because of that hillside experience, the world will never be the same again! Sadly most people function on no more than 7-10% of their total brain capacity. God has created us with the potential for so much more! Don't you want to reach for it? (+)/(-) ____________________

____.

21. God gave Adam (mankind) *legal authority* over the earth. Some teach that Satan rules over the earth as the *prince* of the power of the air. That is one interpretation of the Scriptures. Another interpretation is that, "All authority has been given to Me (Christ) in heaven and on earth" (Mt. 28:18). Ephesians 1:17-23 says that *we* have been given the "spirit of wisdom and revelation," that the "eyes of [our] understanding" have been opened, that his power works mightily in those who believe, that Christ's resurrection placed Him far above every demonic power and might, and that in that position everything is now under His feet. In addition, Ephesians teaches that all *this authority has been invested in the church, which is His body,* His flesh and blood representative on this earth. So if Satan is a "prince," we must remember that we are kings under the direction and authority of the King of Kings! This message must be restored. (+)/(-) ____________________

____.

22. Welcome to the frontier! Limber up your thinking and open up your heart! It's time to free ourselves from our man-made boxes of traditional thinking. We have entered new territory. We must move beyond stagnant orthodoxy, closer to that boundary which many perceive as *dangerous*! Life-as-usual is not even close to dangerous. Jesus lived life "on the edge!" He brought a revolution to mankind, an awareness that released chains of and mental stagnation. (+)/(-) ____________________

____.

23. Therefore we must ponder the imponderable. We must give voice to fragments of *truth* that have been hidden in the crevices of history. (+)/(-) ____________________

____.

24. We must ask, "Why do we think the way we think? Why do we take on a 'herd mentality?' What *fear* has kept us back from being the man or women who we were meant to be in Christ?" (+)/(-) ____.

25. Many have a morbid fear of Eastern thinking. Jesus was born in the East! We have westernized Christianity! It is not a question, actually, of Eastern or Western, but of biblical! (+)/(-) ____.

26. We must use the "eyes of our heart" and not just our limited intellectual approaches to everything. The spirit of revelation and creativity must be restored. We have been robbed! It is time to take captivity captive! We have been made free, free men and women in Christ. There is a quest for this higher level of freedom worldwide. (+)/(-) ____.

27. We must overcome our fear of imagery and imagination. In the 16th century, Protestants threw out images and symbols. Perhaps the Protestant *protest* went too far! We become what we "see" through the windows of our imagination. We must fix our eyes on Jesus. Every scientist and inventor creates what he has first seen in his imagination! (+)/(-) ____.

28. We have a bad case of cultural blindness and blind spots. We have naively bought into the lie that *the answer* to every problem lies in better training or more money. Usually it is neither! (+)/(-) ____.

29. We live in a day of great opportunity, a day of rapid acceleration. Meanwhile, so many continue to live in pessimism and fear. The world is full of evil. Many people fear or suspect that the end is near! Although there is much truth to that, our perspective and focus should be just the opposite. We should instead ask: what can we do to facilitate freedom? How can we serve? How should we *occupy* ourselves until Jesus returns? The Word of God proclaims that we can do all things through Christ who strengthens us (Phil. 4:13). It is time to advance and proclaim the true Kingdom message. (+)/(-) ____.

30. We live at a time in history when Law is again being challenged by Grace. The world, including man-made religion, operates on law. The Kingdom of God operates on grace. Grace is rarely understood. Romans 6:14-15 teaches that we are not under the law, but under grace. What is Grace? Yes, it is true that grace is unmerited favor. But Grace is more than that. Grace is the *power to overcome* human limitations. GRACE IS THE *POWER* TO FULFILL THE LAW! The people of the world need to be taught the difference and introduced to the God of grace and the gospel of grace (see Acts 20:24, Galatians 1:6)—to this gift and calling which imparts extraordinary divine power to bring mercy, peace, purpose and answers into every situation. (+)/(-) ____________
____
____.

Summary

1. Today the sum total of human knowledge doubles every few years.
2. Human culture worldwide is undergoing a massive mega-shift in perspective.
3. Are we going to be part of the solution? Or are we part of the problem?
4. Consider 30 questions and respond by underlining the positive or negative, then also write the reason for your response.
5. Both Greek and Gnostic philosophy fall short of the truth.
6. Many have a morbid fear of Eastern thinking. Jesus was born in the East!
7. Sadly most people function on no more than 7-10% of their total brain capacity. God has created us with the potential for so much more!
8. If Satan is a "prince," we must remember that we are kings under the direction and authority of the King of Kings!
9. Grace is the *power to overcome* human limitations. GRACE IS THE *POWER* TO FULFILL THE LAW!

Chapter Eight

TEN STEPS TO HEALING YOUR INDIVIDUAL CREATION

A great mega-shift is underway in the world today. God is up to something. A new generation is waking up. A seed is growing. More and more of us are recognizing that something is seriously *wrong*! The scientists and the "white coat crowd" have misled us. Billions of dollars are spent every year on health care and disease research and yet we are getting sicker instead of healthier. So is our planet. All creation is groaning for the sons of God—the husbandmen/caretakers of the earth—to be revealed. Who will answer the call?

Malachi chapter 4 speaks of the restoration of the fathers, the family and the faith. In this sense "fathers" means all parents and parenting. There is no sexism here! The husband and wife co-labor! The need is great and the situation grave, so much so that many would say, "The job is too big! I'm only one person! What could I possibly do that would make any difference at all?"

All of us must begin where we are: with ourselves, our homes and our families. It's always best to begin with little steps because little steps successfully completed build confidence and lead to bigger steps. Here are ten (plus one bonus) "little" steps any of us can take to start doing our part to heal the creation right where we are.

1. Hear

Faith comes by hearing! Actions grow from thoughts that enter our minds and implant themselves in our hearts. Thoughts are vibrations, energy frequencies that implant action and response in our being. In a sense, a prophetic word is sought and manifests.

Before going to sleep at night, ask God to speak to you in the night seasons and open your mind to His response. Begin to hear and to "see" in your mind's eye the very thing you are aspiring to attain. "See" healthy herds, healthy plants, healthy soil and healthy people. "See" them responding to the word going forth from your heart, the word which you *heard.* We must give ourselves over to faith, hearing and inspiration. Inspiration means taking in instruction from the Creator. This includes allowing for correction! For example, if a farmer aspires to have a healthy herd, does he simply lie in bed and dream about it? No! He learns everything he can about how to grow and maintain a healthy herd, and then he does it! He provides the proper environment and the proper nutrition. He gets his hands dirty and becomes personally involved. He co-labors with the Creator. Like the farmer, we too must set into action the very things we *hear* and believe for. This is the essence of stewardship.

Inspiration means taking in instruction from the Creator. This includes allowing for correction!

2. See

Allow your imagination to work where it is motivated by inspiration. We all have an imagination and it works overtime 24/7. The only problem is that many of us ignore it or discount it, especially as we get older. Some of us have even been taught that our imagination is evil. No, not evil, just often misused and misunderstood! Imagination itself is not the problem; it's *what* we imagine that often gets us into trouble. Too many times we imagine the wrong things. We get into "vain imaginations" by feeding on the wrong kinds of thoughts and stimuli. We must switch our images from mental left-brain thinking to intuitive heart pondering and meditation! That is the key!

Imagination is a gift from our Creator and He wants us to use it, but use it properly. Some of the best counsel of all for using our imagination is found in Philippians 4:8: "*Finally, brethren, whatever things are true, whatever things are noble, whatever things are just, whatever things are pure, whatever things are lovely, whatever things are of good report, if there is any virtue and if there is anything praiseworthy—**meditate** on these things*" (emphasis mine). We need to learn to control our thoughts and focus on things that are right, good, edifying and lovely.

In Genesis chapter 11, when God saw the people building the Tower of Babel, He said, "Behold, the people is one, and they have all one language; and this they begin to do: and now nothing will be restrained from them, which they have *imagined* to do" (Genesis 11:6, emphasis mine). Then He stopped their progress on the tower by confusing their speech so they could not understand one another. Make no mistake, the human imagination is powerful! What we can imagine we can attain *if we can see it*! *If we can believe it*!

Imagination (the thoughts we *see* and allow into the image of our mind) is the *seed*, the open door to greater things. Hitler, Stalin and Napoleon were all experts at this! So were Einstein, Newton, Edison and the apostle Paul! Imagination is the eye of understanding. We are called to have godly dreams! One third of the Bible revolves around visions and dreams, but 100% of it revolves around inspiration! Imagination and inspiration: use them rightly!

3. Touch

The human touch is a key instrument to health and healing. Dr. Bernard Grad of McGill University, Montreal, discovered that barley seeds in a sealed container sprouted better and more often when a healer laid hands on the container of water used for germination. Dr. Grad let depressed psychiatric patients do the same thing, which reversed the results. Dr. Paul Brand, in his book, *In His Image*, talks about the power of human touch by relating how lepers respond positively when touched.[16] Traditionally, lepers have been regarded as unclean in many cultures, and that perception lingers in some parts of the world today. In ancient Israel, lepers were forced to live in separation and were required by law (under pain of death) to cry out, "Unclean, unclean!" whenever anyone approached. As a class they became known as the "Untouchables." Dr. Brand discovered that it was the *power of touch* that began their healing, both emotionally and physically.

In the same way, we must learn to feel, to touch, to participate directly in the lives of others in close proximity to us. The power of the human touch is truly awesome! Babies will grow and develop poorly and even die if they are denied the touch of loving hands. Our highly industrialized machine age with all its advanced technology has provided us with many helpful benefits, but as wonderful as all those things are, we must as a culture rediscover the value of touch! Machines are only an extension of man; they can never replace or even substitute for the human factor.

We need to learn to touch, feel, experience and heal! Like hearing and seeing, touching is one of the five physical senses. It represents outer feeling that connects and leads to inner feeling. The apostle John said that he "touched" Jesus. This statement was the first evidence he gave as proof that his message was first-hand and valid: "That which was from the beginning, which we have heard, which we have seen with our eyes, which we have looked upon, and *our hands have handled,* concerning the Word of life—the life was manifested, and we have seen, and bear witness, and declare to you that eternal life which was with the Father and was manifested to us—" (1 Jn. 1:1-2 emphasis mine). Touch means close enough for first hand revelation. Get close, feel, experience and know!

4. Believe

Belief requires an active faith. Passive faith is useless. James 2:26 says that faith without works is dead. Genuine faith must be built on truth and true knowledge. For example, I let my teeth go too long without proper care as I wavered in the valley of indecision, resulting in serious infection in the bones of my upper jaw. I "believed" for restoration and healing of the problem, but not according to sufficient knowledge. The end result was negative; the healing did not take place. Now I have re-positioned myself into active healing based on accurate knowledge arising from careful research. Can old bone infections regenerate without dental surgery? It has happened for others, so why not me? I have instituted a careful program combining several pieces of information, all based on research that has worked for others. Will it work for me? I am my own experiment! Good things are beginning to manifest, but the jury is still out. Perhaps the final result will appear in my next book!

Here is another example of the importance of active faith—faith combined with knowledge. In Colombia in the 1970s a colleague of mine kept a group of chickens in a tropical pen, feeding them only water and corn. "I am believing for eggs!" he exclaimed to me one day.

"Fine," I replied, "but I can still tell you your eggs won't happen. You are defying the laws of nutrition and the formation of eggs." In my mind his was an obvious case of belief without knowledge. Call it idealism, ignorance of poultry nutrition, or whatever. Sometimes our beliefs are based on false expectations. In the end, my colleague was disappointed; his undernourished hens produced no eggs.

There is an open heaven for those who believe *and* at the same time put their belief into action. But there are also boundaries. Faith must be built on the correct foundation. We must believe for the right things. Paul says, "Faith comes by hearing," (Rom. 10:17). Did my friend "hear," or was his "faith" vain imagination? We must be honest with ourselves: unless there is visible fruit, we have built on a wrong foundation.

Hearing also requires action. In fact, belief actually presupposes action. Belief translates into action with inspired knowledge. James says, "Show me your faith without your works, and I will show you my faith by my works" (Jas. 2:18b). When I was in my early 20s I heard (perceived) that I should become a veterinarian. It happened under a strange set of circumstances. Growing up on a goat dairy farm, I had occasion once to write to two veterinarians who specialized in goats, requesting their advice. Unknown to each other, both of them wrote back that I should become a veterinarian! Nobody had ever suggested that to me before. At that time the idea was not even on my radar screen! But when I received those letters, bells rang inside me. Somehow that revelation resonated deep within my spirit. From that simple idea began a journey that included a long and difficult phase of diligent study, training, qualification and application. Take it from me, true faith does not mean sitting on your rear in a lazy dream state! The Bible is a manual for *action*, not just study. If the only thing we gain from reading and studying Scripture is knowledge, then we have missed the point. Faith requires that we act out the Word we hear, the vision we see and the passion God has placed in our heart.

Are you read for some revolutionary thinking? Once while listening to a tape about faith, I heard these two statements:

1. "You do not have enough faith to get healed if you don't eat right."
2. "You do not have enough faith to have a good marriage if you don't love."

Interpreted in our context, this means, first of all, that genuine, effective faith—faith that gets results—combines belief with the wisdom of God. If we desire healing, we need to combine our belief for healing with the wisdom that facilitates healing. For example, stop eating the very junk that is making you sick! Go and sin no more!

If we desire healing, we need to combine our belief for healing with the wisdom that facilitates healing. For example, stop eating the very junk that is making you sick! Go and sin no more!

Secondly a successful marriage is built on love. When Jinnie and I got married, the preacher told us, "The Bible doesn't say to marry the one you love; it says love the one you marry!" Whether in marriage or any other arena of life, we often expect miracles without changing our habits. But unless we change our habits it is unlikely we will receive our miracle. Belief presupposes inspired action. Inspiration comes from hearing. Change comes when we "touch" a situation with compassion. You see, everything fits! When we see + hear + touch + believe, then miracles increase from the paltry 5%, the statistical average for those who go forward in healing meetings, to over 50% for those who in their daily life "walk it out" by combining all levels with equal fervor.

5. Empower Others

Teach others and receive from others. Legacy is built on community. Others have a part to play in bringing each of us to our full creative potential. Be open-minded, therefore, and teachable. Give and share. Grow together with others of like heart and mind. There is power in being *part of a team*. A team accomplishes what an individual could never do alone.

Every time I teach or share what I have discovered or learned, my conscious goal is to impart something of significance to those listening. My son, Dr. Reuben De Haan, has the same vision: "Empower those you teach, so they can go out Monday morning and do what you just taught!" By practicing that process, by sowing into the lives of others, inevitably I receive from them the very keys and encouragement that I need for my own greater success! Every good teacher learns by teaching just as every good farmer learns by sowing and harvesting. A nutritionist learns by how his clients respond to various treatments. As we share and give graciously, the windows open for more. As we give, we receive more in return, pressed down and running over. Give out more, reach out more, and the byproduct is receiving more!

Give out more, reach out more, and the byproduct is receiving more!

Even as I write this chapter I am at the same time involved in a unique health care project involving spices. I am part of a team putting together a product that we believe could impact the health of millions of people. The key person on the team discovered the healing power of spices quite by accident, as a last resort when everything else had failed. The family Cocker Spaniel, upon being administered a spice regimen, revived from near death from several unresponsive diseases. Tumors disappeared, Cushing's disease was resolved, appetite was restored, the hair grew back—all due to a divine incident. So now I am part of a team of doctors doing clinical tests, while others are using their skills in marketing, advertising, manufacturing and financing. I will not know the final results before this book goes to press. However, because it is a team effort, our chances of success just went from 10% to over 50%! (Nationally, 90% of new companies go belly up within 5 years.) Our likelihood of success is great because each member of the team, all of whom have prior experience and a good track record, have been released (empowered) to move in their individual giftings and creative skills.

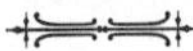

The family Cocker Spaniel, upon being administered a spice regimen, revived from near death from several unresponsive diseases.

6. Seek Counsel

We are part of a family of human beings. Every culture and every ethnic group has something to give. Build relationships. We are in the internet age. The answers are out there. Pay heed to Jesus' counsel: "Ask, and it will be given to you; seek, and you will find; knock, and it will be opened to you. For everyone who asks receives, and he who seeks finds, and to him who knocks it will be opened" (Mt. 7:7-8). Proverbs 24:6 says that there is safety in a group of wise counselors. No one is an island alone. In any area of growth, that growth is best facilitated in groups of trust, groups of two or three, preferably three! In the Bible, the number three is often used to represent completeness. Ecclesiastes 4:12b says, "A threefold cord is not quickly broken."

7. Be Patient

Often we receive one piece at a time. Grow with your vision. Wait on God. Take advantage of the small things. Generally, our character has to grow before we can handle real answers. Some fruit trees bear the first year while others have to grow for five years before they produce their first batch of fruit. There are even some fruit trees that require twenty years of growth and preparation before they bear! Quite often it is the fruit that takes the longest that is the most highly prized.

Many of the great heroes of the Bible were in preparation and training for many years before they were ready to fulfill their destiny: Joseph—13 years as a slave in Egypt; Moses—80 years (40 years in Pharaoh's court, 40 years in the wilderness of Midian); David—12 years or more from the time he was anointed king to the time he ascended the throne; Paul—at least 14 years after his conversion before his first missionary journey. Usually years of learning, growth, sweat and painful steps are required before each growth spurt occurs. Many become discouraged and quit along the way—often just before rounding the final bend that will carry them to success. Don't let that happen to you! Be patient. Keep your dream alive!

8. Experiment

Be proactive. Conduct research. Get your hands dirty. This is a dig-in, hands-on opportunity we are talking about. We have hands and feet for what purpose? To do the work of God; to be a servant and a *king in disguise* at the same time. Are we willing to experiment and fail? All great successful people failed frequently before their talent came into its prime. It is often quoted that Thomas Edison failed 999 times before finding the right filament material to produce a successful light bulb. That's persistence! He "saw" the light bulb in his mind, believed in it, and finally succeeded. And how the world was changed because of his vision! Experience really is our best teacher. The more of our five senses we can engage, the faster and more thoroughly we learn. There is no better school than the University of Trial and Error, the University of the Wilderness! But where defeat abounds, grace abounds even more. That's when we are surprised by joy!

It is often quoted that Thomas Edison failed 999 times before finding the right filament material to produce a successful light bulb. That's persistence! He "saw" the light bulb in his mind, believed in it, and finally succeeded. And how the world was changed because of his vision!

9. Follow the Plan

As I said before, the answers are out there waiting to be revealed. God's divine plan is for His Kingdom to be revealed "*on earth* as it is in heaven." He created us to be co-laborers with Him in the execution of His plan. We are His representatives on earth, charged with the mandate to be the vessels through whom the Kingdom of Heaven is realized on the earth. This is a high calling and a great task, and it is vital that we discover where we fit into the great scheme of things. As Rick Warren put it so succinctly in the title of his best-selling book, we all have the opportunity to enter a "Purpose-Driven Life!"

Connect with your purpose! Which cell, which joint or organ or gland are you a part of, for the greater good of humanity? God's plan calls for the ultimate "restoration of all things" (Acts 3:21). Have you tapped into God's overall plan? Do you know your special place in it? If not, it is time to diligently search it out. There is priceless treasure buried deep inside each one of us—deep within our spirit! As Psalm 42:7 says, "Deep calls unto deep." First Corinthians 2:10 says that the Holy Spirit searches out "the deep things of God," and that same Holy Spirit resides in the heart of every believer. Everything is subsequently confirmed in the Book of Books as well as in the Book of Nature. That which God buried as treasure in *each person*, and further revealed in His *Word* and in *nature* (see Rom. 1:20), comprises a trinity of completeness. The three are *one*! All three, our heart, the

Word, and the message we receive from God's marvelous creation, should all wind up confirming the same conclusion. God has ways of confirming His plan for you. All that is left is to obey and follow that plan!

10. Never Never Give Up

Problems are for overcoming. Press in *always*. Change your methods if necessary. Be adaptable. If you are convinced you have heard rightly and are pursuing the right thing, keep looking. Remain diligent and eventually the way will be revealed to you. But if you allow discouragement to achieve the upper hand, you will go down in defeat.

During some of Great Britain's darkest days early in World War II, the great British statesman and prime minister Winston Churchill rallied the people with the call to, "Never, never, never give up!" And they didn't! When it looked like defeat was inevitable, the tide of battle turned for some mysterious reason. The enemy made a strategic misjudgment. History is now clear: God intervened due to prevailing prayer. Perhaps we should ask, Was God simply answering prayer, or was it something even more convincing, the people practicing their divine privilege of intercession, expressing their God given nature of dominion, which was restored in Christ, and that sudden shift in the war was the fruit of that intercession? I suspect it was the latter!

11. (Bonus) Be a Well-Grounded Dreamer

Some have their head on another planet of impracticality. I know people like that and I'm sure you probably do too: people who always have their head in the clouds, seemingly out of touch with practical living. It is important to dream. Be a dreamer, but make sure you remain a realist with both feet on the ground. By all means, talk of high ideals, but don't forget to wash the dishes, sweep the floor, and keep your nose clean! Idealism only works if put into practice! The best lessons of life are learned at the bottom! Learn from your setbacks and your failures. Someone said that a successful person is simply a failure who got up one more time. Don't fear failure. Those who never fail never become innovators!

By all means, talk of high ideals, but don't forget to wash the dishes, sweep the floor, and keep your nose clean! Idealism only works if put into practice!

Summary

1. Begin with little steps because little steps successfully completed build confidence and lead to bigger steps.
2. Begin to *hear* and to "*see*" in your mind's eye the very thing you are aspiring to attain.
3. Allow your imagination to work where it is motivated by *inspiration.*
4. The human *touch* is a key instrument to health and healing. We need to learn to touch, feel, experience and heal!
5. There is an open heaven for those who believe *and* at the same time put their belief into action.
6. Teach others and receive from others. Legacy is built on community. Others have a part to play in bringing each of us to our full creative potential.
7. Every culture and every ethnic group has something to give. Build valuable life-time relationships.
8. Generally, our character has to grow before we can handle real answers.
9. Experiment. Be proactive. Conduct research. Get your hands dirty.
10. Connect with your purpose! Aspire to have a "Purpose-Driven Life!"
11. Never, never, never give up!
12. Be a dreamer. Don't fear failure. Get up one more time!

Chapter Nine

TAKE CARE OF YOUR TEMPLE

By all appearances the universe seems to be going through an agonizing transition. One source I read spoke of the earth shifting a little on its axis from the violence of the December 2004 undersea earthquake that caused the devastating tsunami in Asia. Another report revealed that a couple of years ago the electrical polarity of the sun switched. One expert said that the basic earth shuman resonance, which remained steady for centuries at around 7.2 hertz, recently rose to around 13 hertz over a period of only a few months. Weather patterns are becoming increasingly sporadic and changeable. At the same time, changes of similar magnitude are occurring within the hearts and minds of mankind. Even as social violence continues on the upswing in many places, cries and aspirations for justice and peace are increasing accordingly. It seems we are on a collision course with destiny!

Even as social violence continues on the upswing in many places, cries and aspirations for justice and peace are increasing accordingly. It seems we are on a collision course with destiny!

During this time of transition, it is more important than ever that we prove faithful to live and practice what we intuitively know and learn—the wisdom and common sense we have all been given by our Creator. This will not be easy, living as we do in a humanistic age where the trend is in the opposite direction. In order to weather the storms of life, we must arm ourselves with facts, truth, faith and love. The biggest question is where to start. With so much information available and so many directions we could go, how do we decide where to turn first?

When it comes to health care and disease prevention, perhaps the best thing to do is to go back to the basics: nutrition, exercise, rest and sleep. Simple, yes, but sometimes we tend to overlook or lose sight of these basics because they *are* simple and get lost amidst the clutter of on overly complicated world.

As we consider these basics in this chapter, let's be careful to keep a few things in mind. First, we need to remember that some people are genetically tough and "disgustingly" healthy (disgusting to us, but a blessing to them!). These are the people who seem to be able to violate all the rules and still remain healthy. They are also the ones who tend to drop dead of heart attacks in their 40's and 50's!

Second, keep in mind that other people have constitutions that have been weakened by circumstances and/or injured genes. Some of those weaknesses may be beyond their control, while others are the result of ignorant living.

Third, in every case or difficult circumstance, liberal grace is in order. We need to give grace freely to others, just as we hope it will be given to us. Paul put it this way: "Receive one who is weak in the faith, but not to disputes over doubtful things. For one believes he may eat all things, but he who is weak eats only vegetables. Let not him who eats despise him who does not eat, and let not him who does not eat judge him who eats; for God has received him. Who are you to judge another's servant?" (Rom. 14:2-4a)

So with these three factors in mind, let's begin.

Basic Nutrition

The nutritional landscape has become so cluttered with information, misinformation and supposedly "scientific" studies that often contradict one another that getting to the truth of basic principles of nutrition is no longer an easy task—unless you know where to look. In this, as in every other area of life, we need to look to the Book for guidelines. The Bible is God's Word and our basic standard for every dimension of life. When it comes to nutrition, our first principle is that we need to return to "Creation Law." Creation Law consists of those principles God put into the very fabric of creation for each system of that creation. Since the laws of nature are the laws of God, it is plain common sense that we should give those laws careful study. Every type of creature was *designed* to operate best on certain types of fuel, so would it not be wise to select those specific types of fuel?

Termites eat wood. Alligators eat live flesh. Chickens eat grass, grain and insects. What should humans eat? How about dogs and cats? Horses and cows? Any answers we come up must provide *solutions* for the stressful world we live in. We have inherited compacted and lifeless soils, poisons in our atmosphere and contaminated food and water. Processed and manufactured foods are now a part of our everyday life. But is this the way it *should* be? Can we lay aside our assumptions, alter our thinking and climb out of tradition's box?

Creation Law requires us to go back to the basics, such as *whole foods, in season*, plus concentrated yet "live" natural food supplements to make up for the severe soil and mineral deficiencies. In addition, Creation Law calls for variety and rotation as very basic needs for proper organ and gland functions. This is best achieved through balance among the various food groups.

There is also the *principle of individuality*. As we have already seen, every species is unique from every other and every individual within a species is unique from every other individual of that species. This is called, "biochemical individuality." For example, male and female puppies from the same litter may have very different heredity and chemical makeup. Husbands and wives frequently have totally different metabolisms from each other. Within the basic principles of Creation Law, "balanced" nutrition for one may not be balanced for the other. Each must learn his or her own proper balance.

Husbands and wives frequently have totally different metabolisms from each other.

Violation of this principle can have serious effects on one's health. I know personally of one case where a father forced his daughter to eat eggs, even sitting her at the table for hours at a time until she ate those eggs. He thought he was being a good father, teaching her life principles about healthy eating and nutrition. His daughter, however, had a constant draining cyst on her tailbone that simply would not heal. Eventually, an astute health practitioner discovered that she was totally allergic to eggs. He told her father that eggs were like rattlesnake poison to her! Once eggs were removed from her diet, the cyst immediately dried up and disappeared. *Principles are good. Knowing when to shift gears is also good!*

The four basic principles for nutrition, then, are whole foods, variety and rotation, balance, and individuality. Let's look at each one a little more closely.

1. Whole Foods. Use the entire edible part of the plant. That includes the peelings, if they are edible, the germ, even the seeds! If edible, eat the leaves and roots as well. Why? Because each plant is an entire living system, with synergistic qualities. Potatoes are a good example. The essential mineral potassium is just under the peeling. We need potassium for our heart. We need the fiber in the peelings for healthy bowels and for blood sugar regulation. "Eat you all of it" is a good principle demonstrated both in the Old Testament Passover meal and New Testament communion. To pick and choose misses the principle.

2. Variety and Rotation. In nature this principle is enforced by the rotation of the seasons. Different plants, nuts and berries mature at different times. The cleansing varieties of certain vegetables and fruits are the first to mature in the spring. Their job is to help facilitate a "spring cleaning" due to winter stagnation. Grains, however, mature in the fall, to help us get through the long winter. When prehistoric human remains were thawed from the deep freeze of the ice age by archeologists, they found over *one hundred* different herbs, vegetables and fruits mixed together in the same stomachs! *Those folks knew something we don't.* Not only did they live longer but the also displayed no signs of tooth decay or any other degenerative disease!

3. Balance. God hates a false balance, says Proverbs 11:1, and so does our body! Too much or too little of any nutrient throws us way out of balance. In veterinary school I had an entire course in farm animal nutrition. One of the course requirements involved "nutritional balancing." Using scientific charts we had to ensure the animals' food ration was balanced with the right amounts of protein, carbohydrates, fats, vitamins, minerals and fiber. *Why don't we teach those principles as a part of every health course in junior high, and make it a requirement for graduation from high school?*

4. Individuality. We are each as unique as snowflakes. One practitioner has theorized that women tend to live longer than men because they instinctively cook meals for their own body type, which may be different than that of their husbands. No matter how wonderful those meals might taste, that diet could shorten the life of the husband—because of his unique biochemical individuality. Even if this observation sounds off the wall, note that there are published guidelines that are relevant to individual blood and body types. In addition, however, we each are also created with the instinctive ability to choose correctly. That instinct has been educated out of us by astute advertising, personal addictions, social training and cultural habits. It is time to renew our connections with what we were gifted with from the beginning. Its time to get off the cookie-cutter processed food mentality and think for ourselves!

We each are created with the instinctive ability to choose correctly. That instinct has been educated out of us by astute advertising, personal addictions, social training and cultural habits.

The animals are better at this than we are—yet we are a higher order of being! We must learn once again to listen to our body, the resonating output messages from our cells, organs and glands to our brain and their transference back to our heart and subconscious instincts.

Now I have three questions for you. First, using this God created mechanism, have you personally *learned or relearned* how to choose a balanced variety of foods in order to meet your particular and specialized individual needs? Secondly, have you learned the correct amount of each type of food to put on your plate for that day? And finally (and especially), have you learned when to leave food on your plate and/or push your chair away from the table? Don't worry when you make mistakes. Simply learn from your mistakes and go on.

Retrain Your Eating Habits

Here is another secret: eat breakfast like a king, lunch like a prince, and the evening meal like a pauper. Why? Because food is fuel. Fuel is energy for work. This is precisely the opposite of how most of us have been trained to eat (unless you were brought up on an old-fashioned farm!)

For many of us today, breakfast tends to be a modern rush of coffee and donuts. Then a rush of soda and pastry for the midmorning sugar dip at the 15-minute break. This is subsisting on poor quality fuel, a divisive habit that ultimately paves the way for both hypoglycemia and diabetes as well as arthritis and many other degenerative illnesses. Next comes a hefty supper of meat and potatoes—a time of the day when our system is theoretically programmed for a light meal in order to cleanse and repair. This combination of food also helps clog the arteries and leaves brain cells undernourished. Where are the 2-3 fruits and 4-7 vegetables that holistic nutritionists tell us we need in our daily diet? We have the whole thing backwards and up side down; no wonder we're sick!

We must retrain ourselves to eat in order to have the energy to work rather than work in order to eat! Our appetites must not control us! Admittedly, it is not a simple task to retrain ingrained and habits, but nothing worthwhile comes without concentrated effort. The rewards, however, are exceptional: you will be healthier, stronger, live longer and have a better mental attitude. But only if you bring your appetites under control!

We must retrain ourselves to eat in order to have the energy to work rather than work in order to eat! Our appetites must not control us!

The February 2005 issue of the *AVMA Journal* published the results of a large study on the advantages of controlling appetite. In this study, canine litter-mates were separated into two groups. One group could eat all the food they desired, any time they desired; —free choice. Their food intake was carefully measured. The other group was fed just twice a day and given exactly 25% *less* food than the first group. In a result that has now been repeated and verified with many litters of dogs, the dogs in the second group lived, on average, *two years longer* than the dogs in the first group. Between the two groups, only the amount and timing of the food intake differed; every other parameter remained exactly the same. Two years in a dog's life calculates to over *ten extra years* in our life span. This means that we can eat ourselves into an early grave or, conversely, live a longer and better life—our choice!

Similar double blind studies have calculated the difference in osteoarthritis. Merely by decreasing the amount of food by 25%, osteoarthritis in large breed dogs has been cut by 75%. This means that the dogs given less food manifested only ¼ the level of arthritis as did the control groups. When longevity was factored in, these same dogs also lived, on average, two years longer. Further studies like these have brought consistent findings. *Just think what good things would happen if the diet had been improved from a commercial brand to a truly nutritious diet that fit the standards of Creation Law!*

Merely by decreasing the amount of food by 25%, osteoarthritis in large breed dogs has been cut by 75%.

As I have already said, many illnesses today are a direct result of nutrient deficiencies. Some are brain deficiencies. All of these deficiencies developed because we abandoned the basic principles of nutrition. Non-whole foods are the main staples of our diet. We lack sufficient variety in the foods we eat. The balance scale has been completely overturned and we have made no allowances for individual metabolic differences. How did this happen? *Where did we get off track?*

Much of the blame lies at the feet of the current worldwide influence of powerful agri/business corporations and chemical farming enterprises. We bought into the easy way of living and assumed science knew best. We thought the nutritionists in the corporate kitchens had our best interests at heart. Besides, their products tasted so good. The truth is, we fell into the horrifying trap of food addictions. Habit and nutritional laziness ruled our lives. It was so much easier simply to trust the food giants than to *think for ourselves.*

What can we do about it? Get off the generic, processed, sterile, chemically preserved and mass-manufactured brands of food. For help in understanding this issue, let me recommend the book *Beating the Food Giants,* by Paul Stitt.[17] The information provided by this author, who once worked as a food scientist for these giant corporations, will change your eating habits!

As an example, rats can live a normal life on whole wheat or whole corn, water and a good mineral supplement. Stitt describes what happened when rats were fed breakfast cereals like puffed wheat, puffed rice, or corn flakes, water and the same mineral supplement. The rats lived longer eating the cardboard box! And the companies knew it!

Retrain your eating habits. A good place to start is by supplementing your diet with whole and *live foods,* pure water and balanced food supplements. In addition, I recommend that you learn to grow 20 to 50% your own organic fresh food. Resources for doing this are readily available and the benefits are outstanding. Use your backyard to full advantage! Learn the techniques and subtleties of raising and preparing an abundance of great tasting food. Teach your children to cook, how to grow vegetables and how to care for a flock of chickens or ducks! If you fail, keep experimenting and keep believing! Turn off the TV! Develop your touch, your faith and your health. Go for the gold!

Exercise, Rest and Sleep

Life is downright hazardous in our modern society. Stress is at an all-time high, while more and more jobs are sedentary in nature, requiring little or no vigorous exercise of the body, hands or feet. Make no mistake about it, mental stress is physically toxic! Add to this a desk job, driving to work, and sitting on the couch in front of the TV—this vicious cycle allows many different types of toxins to accumulate in the body without being expelled.

Following digestion, nutrients enter the blood stream to nourish the cells while the toxic waste products are excreted back into the intracellular spaces to be collected by the lymph system. The lymph system has no pump. It depends entirely on physical activity and exercise to move those toxic by-products into the blood stream and out through the kidneys!

The lymph system has no pump. It depends entirely on physical activity and exercise to move those toxic by-products into the blood stream and out through the kidneys!

Speaking of the kidneys, make sure you drink 6-8 glasses of water every day to avoid chronic dehydration. Water is only part of the answer, however, as healthy lungs, and a healthy stomach and spleen are also part of the equation. But you need 6-8 glasses of pure water so the kidneys properly filter the wastes from the blood stream. Water, the right minerals, healthy lungs, stomach and the spleen all work together! I say "pure" water, because for every cup of coffee or soda, you need *two extra* cups of water to undo the damage of caffeine on your kidneys!

Brisk walking, aerobic exercise, movement (such as the use of a mini-trampoline) and stretching are awesome ways to satisfy the exercise needs of the physical body. And best of all, plant a garden, raise some animals and prepare a compost pile to tend! There is nothing so physically and mentally invigorating as watching good soil producing good food. It is awesome to watch billions of earthworms at work once they set up house in the compost pile. When we first came to our present clay soil we could not find a single earthworm. Now I have billions of wiggly workers. But first it took some sweat and work on my part to establish their housing. Now I have billions of happy campers on my property, the kind that pay their own way!

In addition to planting and enjoying beautiful flowers, the side benefit is superior food for the benefit of your family and friends! Walk your land every day, observing, meditating and planning. Meditation means allowing the thoughts of Yahweh Elohim (LORD God) to enter your heart and mind, giving you insight, answers and guidance. Write those insights down! (I carry a pen and pocket notebook with me to catch those pithy phrases and words of guidance while they are hot!) As a bonus, this daily exercise will stimulate your feet, hands and lymphatic system for great physical exercise.

Exercise needs to be balanced by regular periods of rest. By "rest" I am speaking of special times of relaxing the body, the mind and the spirit during the *daytime*. Learn some relaxing exercises, deep breathing exercises, and the art of meditation. Take a 3-5 minute catnap at least once daily. Learn to quiet the mind to allow God to speak into your heart. Drop to your knees in a spirit of quietness and prayer various times during the day. That is easy for me, because I have a home office! In my experience even a 1-2 minute session brings my mind back into focus. Do I have to wait till God "shows up"? No, He is always present! I am amazed that when my heart is inspired, my mind knows exactly the next thing I need to focus on, just because of that moment of "waiting on the Lord."

Take small breaks to say something nice to a friend. Write a note of appreciation. Don't forget to smell the roses. Appreciate small things and swing your arms when you are walking! These are some of the things I mean by "daytime rest". Just do it!

Just as important to optimal health as exercise and rest is to get adequate sleep every night. Sleep is the time when the body revitalizes. Both the body and the mind need time to recycle, rejuvenate and cleanse. The Bible says "Day unto day utters speech, and night unto night reveals knowledge" (Ps. 19: 2). We often wrongly assume that knowledge comes only in the daytime from applied study and research. According to the Bible, however, true knowledge is *heart* knowledge, with God as its source. And He often imparts that knowledge to us at night as we sleep. The heart (the subconscious mind of secular psychology) is where we process knowledge and information and reach internal subconscious conclusions. That important activity is best empowered during times of rest and sleep. This is a process that initiates and forms internal conclusions beyond our personal belief system. Our personal belief system can limit us. The "knowledge that comes from above" is what actually empowers and changes us! *It is from heart knowledge that we communicate with God!*

*According to the Bible, true knowledge is **heart** knowledge, with God as its source. And He often imparts that knowledge to us at night as we sleep.*

Without empowering daytime rest periods, and without restful nighttime sleep, in what is called the "alpha" zone of sleep, our inner guidance system is left in confusion and toxicity. This is why those who reach the truly restful alpha zone of sleep at night will often wake up in the morning having solved a complicated problem. Pay attention to those first thoughts in the morning! If you have prepared your heart and mind correctly, meditating on God's Word, you will wake up more frequently with God-directed thinking.

All of these are things I had to learn. And I am still learning! None of this came naturally to me. I am a workaholic by nature, a project-driven type of guy. It is hard for me to rest, harder still to slow my mind down and get into that meditative state of quietness. Not doing "something" *seems* totally counterproductive to me.

Please do not misunderstand me. I definitely am *not* advising going into neutral, or into that blank zone of mental nothingness. That is both dangerous and counterproductive because it neutralizes our will out of the equation. Never relinquish your will into neutral!

But as we come into rest, God can get our attention. His thoughts begin to regulate, infiltrate, and fill our lives with productive insights! Yes, our bodies are temples of the Holy Spirit. We are called to present our bodies a living sacrifice, clean, rested, and undefiled from the accumulation of gross amounts of mental and dietary toxins. Both cleansing and growth take place during times of sleep and rest. Did you know a child's primary physical growth takes place at night while asleep? Heart knowledge also grows during the same time. So work hard, eat well, get plenty of exercise, take regular rest breaks and enjoy some well-earned sleep at night. Your body will thank you!

Summary

1. During this time of *cosmic* transition, it is more important than ever that we prove faithful to live and practice what we intuitively know and learn—the wisdom and common sense we have all been given by our Creator.
2. When it comes to nutrition, our first principle is that we need to return to "Creation Law." Creation Law consists of those principles God put into the very fabric of creation for each system of that creation.
3. The four basic principles for nutrition are whole foods, variety and rotation, balance, and individuality.
4. Eat breakfast like a king, lunch like a prince, and the evening meal like a pauper.
5. Eat to work; don't work to eat.
6. Get off the generic, processed, sterile, chemically preserved and mass-manufactured brands of food.
7. Supplement your diet with whole and *live foods*, pure water and balanced food supplements.

8. Learn to grow 20 to 50% of your own organic fresh food.
9. Brisk walking, aerobic exercise, movement (such as the use of a mini-trampoline) and stretching are awesome ways to satisfy the exercise needs of the physical body.
10. Exercise needs to be balanced by regular periods of rest. Take a 3-5 minute catnap at least once daily. Learn to quiet the mind to allow God to speak into your heart.
11. Just as important to optimal health as exercise and rest is to get adequate sleep every night. Sleep is the time when the body revitalizes.
12. If you have prepared your heart and mind correctly, meditating on God's Word, you will wake up more frequently with God-directed thinking.

Chapter Ten

CLEAN OR UNCLEAN—DOES IT MATTER?

In the last chapter we reviewed briefly four basic principles of good nutrition, but because of the high level of confusion about this subject, particularly among Christians, I believe it is important to devote another chapter to the subject and related issues. Christians across the board hold many different ideas and attitudes toward health and nutrition and the extent of the church's responsibility to take the lead in these areas; and every "camp" of opinion points to the Scriptures to support their view. Admittedly, we must allow much grace toward one another with regard to these matters, but can we draw from the Bible general principles that apply to us today? YES, I believe we can.

From the very beginning the Bible lays down the foundation for nutritional wisdom. No sooner had God created man—male and female—than He announced to them their mandate to be fruitful, multiply and exercise dominion on the earth. On the heels of that mandate He gave them instructions regarding their diet: "See, I have given you every *herb* that yields seed...and every tree whose *fruit* yields seed; to you it shall be for food" (Gen. 1:29 emphasis mine). Interestingly, in the very next verse God establishes a similar vegetarian diet for *all* the beasts of the earth. Even after the fall of man in the Garden of Eden the same dietary principle held forth: "Cursed is the ground for your sake...And you shall eat the *herb* of the field" (Gen. 3:17-18 emphasis mine). It was not until after the cataclysmic flood in the days of Noah that meat was introduced into man's diet. God said to Noah, "Every moving thing that lives shall be food for you. I have given you all things, even as the green herbs" (Gen. 9:3).

Although this verse does not mention it, Noah and his family undoubtedly understood that their "meat allowance" was restricted to the meat of *clean animals*. Genesis 7:2-4 makes it clear that even before the flood Noah already knew the difference between clean and unclean animals. When God said to gather seven of each clean animal and two of each unclean animal for preservation on the ark, Noah needed no explanation. He already understood the distinction. Sometimes we forget that the principle of clean and unclean animals preceded the Levitical law by a thousand years or more. It did not arise in the days of Moses—but had been known and understood for centuries.

Sometimes we forget that the principle of clean and unclean animals preceded the Levitical law by a thousand years or more.

Unfortunately, within the church there has been great misunderstanding and misinterpretation concerning this newly established diet. By mixing, misinterpreting, and misjudging the differences between eternal Creation Law (natural law) and the temporary Leviticus ceremonial temple laws spoken by revelation to Moses, we have turned our health upside down. Because of our penchant for eating anything and everything our heart desires, with no restrictions or distinctions—"clean" and "unclean" meats, animal fats, high-carbohydrate foods, especially sugars and starches, and natural as well as toxic artificial sweeteners—we have created for ourselves a virtual monster of sickness and disease.

Have you ever wondered what skill or ability Noah possessed that allowed him—in only seven days—to gather and pull together all those animals into the ark? Did he "call" to them somehow so that they came to him? Was this a reflection of man's innate dominion authority over all the animals? Did Noah and his sons have to trap, catch, drag and herd each species to the giant ark, hold them in corrals, then somehow get them to march up the gang plank into the ark into separate holding pens? How exactly did Noah accomplish this task?

Some have suggested that God Himself drew the animals to gather at the ark, and while this is certainly possible, God says quite plainly to Noah, "*You* shall take with you seven each of every clean animal..." (Gen. 7:2), so Noah definitely had a part to play in the process. However it was accomplished, the Scriptural account indicates that loading the ark occurred in a very orderly manner. Then for a whole year they lived together: eight humans on a boat the size of the *Queen Mary*, filled with animals and birds of every kind, both domesticated and feral, carnivore and herbivore. *And everybody got along!*

Have you ever wondered what skill or ability Noah possessed that allowed him—in only seven days—to collect and draw all those animals into the ark?

What did Noah have that we have lost? What spiritual or natural ability did this family possess that we obviously need to relearn today? Can you imagine the difference it would make in our world today in our efforts to solve the chronic and seemingly irresolvable health problems of our time if we could recover that ability? Is the astonishing talent that Noah and his family possessed with those animals still available for us today? Or has it disappeared forever?

As you ponder your answer, consider these tantalizing clues:

- the "animal whisperer" who talks to and trains unmanageable dogs with voice and hand motions.
- the wild horse tamer who uses "horse language" to train wild horses and within 30 minutes saddles and rides them in total control using only his voice and body motions.
- the poisonous snake trainer who handles and trains frustrated and fearful pet snakes so that they relax and cuddle within 30 minutes.

Are the Dietary and Hygienic Laws of Moses Still Applicable Today?

As concern rises among more and more Christians regarding the deteriorating state of our health and our planet, the question of the current applicability of the Old Testament dietary and hygienic laws for us today is being raised more frequently. Certainly there is no "law" under the new covenant in Christ that *requires* us to abide by those ancient guidelines for nutrition and cleanliness. We appear to be completely free in Christ in regard to these matters. The requirements of the law were apparently fulfilled through His death and subsequent resurrection.

Does this mean, however, that there is no wisdom we can derive from those guidelines, no counsel that can help us chart a course to a brighter and healthier future? Did the foundational principles behind the Old Testament dietary and hygienic laws change or cease to exist when Christ initiated the new covenant through His blood? The answer to both of these questions, I believe, is NO. Let me explain!

Many of the dietary and hygienic laws of Moses accurately represent the *original* revealed Creation Laws, the revealed "master plan." This master plan includes fundamental dietary principles for the health of man and the entire creation. These human laws and principles were revealed to a fallen creation as precepts and principles to maintain health in body, mind and spirit. Noah knew these laws. So did Moses and David, as well as the early Christians. Wild animals know them instinctively. For mankind they were passed down from father to son, and later transcribed by Moses in the Torah. It is we, modern man, who have trashed that knowledge. Over the last century or so we have discarded the wisdom of the ages regarding nutrition, believing in our arrogance that we could "improve" on nature through highly refined and processed, chemically-preserved and enhanced, mass-produced food.

Many of the dietary and hygienic laws of Moses accurately represent the original revealed Creation Laws, the revealed "master plan." This master plan includes fundamental dietary principles for the health of man and the entire creation.

Part of our problem in the church is that some of us have misunderstood and misinterpreted Peter's symbolic vision in which he was told to "rise and eat" unclean beasts (see Acts 10:10-20). The obvious *purpose* of the vision, however, was to break Peter's anti-Gentile prejudice and his stubborn Jewish resistance to God's universal plan of human redemption. This is made clear by Peter's own understanding of the vision. As he entered the home of Cornelius, a Roman centurion, Peter said, "You know how unlawful it is for a Jewish man to keep company with or go to one of another nation. But *God has shown me that I should not call any man common or unclean*" (Acts 10:28 emphasis mine).

Peter's vision had to do with evangelism, not nutrition and diet. It dealt with Peter's need to understand that not the Jews alone but the Gentiles also were part of God's master plan of salvation in Christ. Peter clearly understood this, therefore there is *zero evidence* that he started eating ceremonially unclean food after receiving this vision. His eating habits were neither the point nor the problem.

I make the case for the wisdom of observing many of the Old Testament dietary laws strongly and in detail in my first book in this series, *We Don't Die... We Kill Ourselves.* One woman who enjoyed the book gave it to her pastor, expecting that he would be blessed by it. To her surprise, however, he wrote her a letter explaining in detail why he thought I was completely wrong and unbiblical. Among other things, this pastor claimed that the church has no mandate or responsibility to teach health and nutrition. Furthermore, he charged that my position on the Old Testament dietary laws was unbiblical because those laws were fulfilled and made obsolete in Christ—and used the example of Peter's vision in Acts chapter 10 to prove his point. (For my full response to this pastor's letter, see Appendix One.)

Rather than proving his point, I believe he *missed* the point. Peter's vision had nothing to do with diet. And as for the church's responsibility to teach health and nutrition, does not the New Testament say that our bodies are temples of the Holy Spirit? And are we not to honor the Spirit by showing proper care and respect for our bodies, which are His temples? And does not proper care and respect for our bodies include issues of nutrition and hygiene? If all these things are true, then it would seem self-evident that instruction in principles of healthy nutrition, diet and hygiene should be an integral part of the overall teaching ministry of the church. Yet the church essentially has relegated responsibility for those areas to the secular culture—and we are reaping the bitter consequences!

Please do not misunderstand me. The Scriptures are *clear* that the food we consume with our mouths does not affect our *eternal status* one iota. It is not what we eat that defiles us, but what comes from the inside—meaning the evil, lust and corruption of our sinful hearts. Jesus said, "Do you not perceive that whatever enters a man from outside cannot defile him, because it does not enter his heart but his stomach, and is eliminated, thus purifying all foods?" (Mk. 7:18b-19). Some translations end Jesus' words after "eliminated," making the final phrase a parenthetical comment by Mark: "'Don't you see that nothing that enters a man from the outside can make him "unclean"? For it doesn't go into his heart but into his stomach, and then out of his body.' (In saying this, Jesus declared all foods 'clean')" (Mk. 7:18b-19 NIV). Either way, the point is the same. All foods are "clean" in the sense that nothing we eat will cause us to violate a spiritual "law" that could affect our eternal destiny.

Let's illustrate this truth one step further. Matthew clarifies this interpretation within the same context in chapter 15. In the context this illustration is in the form of a parable. Parables always require interpretation. "Peter said, "Explain this parable to us," "'Are you still do dull?' Jesus asked them." Whereupon Jesus carefully explained that it is not what goes into the mouth that defiles a man, but what goes out of the mouth. He applied the same principle to washing the hands (Matthew 15:16-20, NIV.) Defilement is clearly a spiritual word. Therefore, from the *spiritual standpoint* foods and dirt don't defile us—it is the junk that comes out of the inner being that defiles us! What do we conclude? We conclude that eating "unclean" food is *permissible*, but that doesn't mean it is *wise*! We must interpret this illustration in the context of the entire Word of God, both Old and New Testaments.

Eating arsenic is also permissible, but that would not be wise either. I know some children and animals that eat dirt; it is a disease we call "pica." That definitely is not wise! Eating unclean foods like lobster, horsemeat and pork may not be wise either.

Neither would it offend me for you to eat pork! Occasionally on the road, where choices were limited, I have ordered a bacon and eggs dish, with no twinge of conscience. It is, however, a nutritional compromise. To eat unclean meats knowingly or unknowingly, and regularly, when we have other choices, clearly *could* be a "sin" against the metabolism of our own body! *If* the Creator of our body has revealed clearly in His "Manufacturer's manual" that unclean meats are not safe fuels for the human body, would it not be smart for us to pay attention to the guidelines in that manual?

Why "Clean" and "Unclean"?

The laws regarding clean and unclean animals are laid out in the 11th chapter of Leviticus. They are detailed and specific. After defining the parameters for determining between clean and unclean, and after listing specifically the animals and sea creatures in each category, the chapter ends with these words: "This is the law of the animals and the birds and every living creature that moves in the waters, and of every creature that creeps on the earth, to distinguish between the unclean and the clean, *and between the animal that may be eaten and the animal that may not be eaten*" (Lev. 11: 46-47, emphasis mine). As a "law" these stipulations were mandatory for the Jews under the covenant of the Law. They are not mandatory for us who are under the Covenant of Grace—yet they remain wise and prudent principles and guidelines for a number of reasons. If followed generally, they will definitely promote better health and longer life. Read on!

Defining Clean and Unclean Animals

"Clean" animals, those that were healthy and permissible to eat, included those species that have both a cloven hoof and that chew the cud: cattle, sheep, goats, deer, antelope, elk, buffalo. The fish include all lake, river, sea and ocean fish that have fins and scales. Permissible birds include chickens, turkeys, quail, partridge, duck and many others.

The list of "unclean" animals included those that did not have a cloven hoof or that did not chew the cud or both. Camels, rabbits and swine are some of the first on the list. The horse and donkey were also included. "Unclean" water creatures included all fish and sea creatures without fins and scales, such as the shark, the catfish, lobsters, shrimp and clams. "Unclean" birds included the eagle, the vulture, the raven, the owl, the hawk, the bat and any fowl that "creeps," such as the penguin. Beasts with four paws were also unclean: the weasel, the ferret, the cat, the dog, the lion, etc.

The validity of separating animals between clean and unclean from the standpoint of health considerations is now backed up by solid scientific evidence that has been confirmed by cancer specialists, professors of parasitology, and numerous (though still a minority) medical nutritionists. Studies have revealed the underlying principles between these two very different types of creatures to be as follows:

1. The unclean animals, birds and fish are generally "scavengers" of live or dead meat. These meats are more heavily parasitized with infections that easily pass to man. Most of the clean animals eat vegetation and have a 4-stomach system which allows them to more effectively eliminate the bacteria, toxins and parasites that might end up in their flesh and negatively affect the human body. Clean fish have scales which help them repel toxins in the water. They also tend to be picky eaters, rejecting dead foods, polluted or otherwise contaminated areas to feed in.

2. Scavenger flesh takes approximately 18 hours to digest in the human digestive system. This delay creates another toxic load on the system, an extra workload for the stomach, intestines and kidneys and liver. "Clean" meats, on the other hand, digest in only 3-6 hours. Imagine what happens to a food like pork, rotting in our body at 98 degrees body temperature, during the 18 hours it takes to break down the scavenger proteins! That creates an additional toxic overload of incompletely digested flesh! Yuk!

3. During the 1950s, a Johns Hopkins cancer specialist scientifically tested both categories of meats. This medical doctor imported frozen meats from all over the world. Testing them in a laboratory setting he discovered that 100% of the *unclean* meats had a significant toxic effect on human blood, similar to the toxic blood of cancer and schizophrenia patients. Their blood was acidic, poisonous and filled with parasites and disease! This same finding can also be confirmed using a modern dark field microscope.

*In a laboratory setting he discovered that 100% of the **unclean** meats had a significant toxic effect on human blood, similar to the toxic blood of cancer and schizophrenia patients.*

Conversely, this cancer specialist discovered, the "clean" meats consistently had a neutral to positive effect on the blood. Again, science is finally catching up with Creation Law—as it is consistently revealed in the Scriptures! Unfortunately, few paid attention to his results and his research got buried on the dusty back shelves with the rest of the medical literature that does not pass the test of pharmaceutical orthodoxy.

What, Then, Should We Eat?

As humans we are called to have dominion over the creation. That includes our own creation, our body! If we are to fulfill our destiny as a creative, imaginative, focused generation with answers, we will require a healthy body, a healthy heart and a healthy brain.

Herbs, vegetables and fruits should *always* be the primary foods for modern man, with the clean meats consumed in moderation. Instead, a gluttonous and carnivorous meat-eating diet has become a universal standard. That, combined with excessive amounts of refined hybrid grains, pastries and soft drinks, with an occasional side dish of nutrition-less iceberg lettuce, has brought about the sad, sickly state of affairs we are in today. It is time that we become known as the healthiest people on the planet!

*Herbs, vegetables and fruits should **always** be the primary foods for modern man, with the clean meats consumed in moderation.*

The California Cancer Society recommendations and a short-lived USDA "food pyramid" have both been attacked as irrelevant and quickly re-revised under financial and political pressures from the meat, dairy and fast food industries. Nevertheless, true science is catching up with the Bible! Beginning at the bottom, the basic foundation of a wise food pyramid, the following recommendations fit the currently understood human nutritional guidelines that also fit the biblical model. Watch out, some of these may surprise you!

Seven guidelines toward a truly healthy diet.

1. *Vegetables, herbs and spices.* Humans should eat 4-7 helpings of a variety of veggies daily. Some should be raw, with the remainder steamed, stir-fried, cooked or baked. A pleasant variety of nutritional herbs and spices will add to the flavor as well as contribute health benefits of their own. For centuries, wars were fought to control the herb and spice trade. Vegetables, herbs and spices are still foundational keys as foods and as medicines! You may really have to work at this one, especially if you are locked into the meat-bread-potatoes mode. If you have young children at home, make it a game; get them involved early. Build healthy habits in them now and they will thank you later on. Choose a variety of vegetables of every color and shape. One of the diabetic foundations recommends dividing a plate into four sections. Two sections, meaning one half of the daily portion, should be low glycemic vegetables!

For centuries, wars were fought to control the herb and spice trade. Vegetables, herbs and spices are still foundational keys as foods and as medicines!

2. *Whole grains, nuts, beans and peas.* These truly are the staff of life. For most people, however, 3-6 helpings a day probably should be the maximum. This is significantly less than the typical food pyramid recommendation, especially for the grains. The key is to not overdo the carbohydrates. And make sure they are whole foods, not refined, pasteurized, defatted or de-germed. Minimize or eliminate the hybrid high-gluten grains such as wheat, corn and soy, which are *highly pro-inflammatory*. Emphasize instead buckwheat, millet, rice, oats, amaranth and the like. Also, everyone should enjoy nuts and beans such as almonds, walnuts, peas, lentils, and garbanzos. This includes those wonderful 7- or 9-bean and pea mixes in dishes, salads and soups. Don't forget grain, seed and bean *sprouts*. Sprouts are live foods!
3. *Fruit.* A daily portion of 3-4 helpings of a wide variety of fruit is highly recommended. Include in-season fruits, berries, and fresh juices of every color. The dark- and bright- colored fruits have the

highest levels of anti-oxidants, so don't skimp on the grapes and grape juice! Concord grapes are one of the best choices. Fruits should be your dessert and the answer to your sweet tooth. Substitute 100% fruit juice for soft drinks—but dilute half-and-half with water to lower the glycemic index.

4. *Meat and fish.* In moderation, these may be enjoyed fully 3-5 days per week. For most people that amount is not only acceptable and healthy, but most of us require at least some lean meat for optimum health. But toughen yourself up to avoid the typical American habit (a learned habit) of eating meats and high protein meals three times a day. That will overload your liver and kidneys. It could also be a form of gluttony! Add occasionally some eggs, quality yogurt and natural, unprocessed cheeses. Goat cheese is superior! Let's agree to beat this gluttony of *over-indulgence* on meat products!

5. *Good fats.*[18] Real butter and the essential fatty acids are required in moderation. The healthy brain requires lots of good fats, as do the glands. Avoid hydrogenated oils, saturated fats (coconut oil seems to be an exception), and all margarines—even the ones which claim to be "natural." "Natural" does not mean to them what it means to us!

6. *Natural sweets.* Jams, honey, molasses, maple syrup, snacks, real chocolate and healthy candies, cookies and an occasional pastry may be enjoyed in moderation. These are at the tiny tip top of the food pyramid! A century ago the average consumption of white sugar was 1-3 teaspoons per person daily. Today it is half a pound daily, mostly from "hidden" sugars in soft drinks, cereals, processed food, pastries, etc, etc, etc (practically everything)! However, eliminate *all* the artificial sweeteners such as Aspartame and Sucralose. Sorry, but these are synthetic drugs and are toxic![19]

7. *Water and liquids.* Probably this should just read water! However, in all of the healthiest cultures other beverages have been used with benefit. Biblically, grape juice and wine are acceptable in moderation. Teas, and especially mixed herb teas, are great substitutes as well as being healthy. Remember, if you drink fruit juices, dilute them half and half with water. Minimize or eliminate white sugar and artificial sugar substitutes, which *always* compromise health! A cup or two of *quality* coffee, especially if organic and home ground, or dark unprocessed chocolate drink, are acceptable for most people—with

the exception of those with specific allergies. Recent research actually proves that for most people wine, coffee and chocolate are healthy and beneficial *in moderation!!!!* Remember, however, that caffeine and sugar imitate drugs. Both tend to deplete minerals, tie up vitamins, compromise the immune system, and are addictive. WATER IS THE SAFEST OF ALL *IF* YOU DRINK NATURAL SPRING WATER, FILTERED OR FROM REVERSE OSMOSIS SOURCES.[20] Rapid flowing mineralized and oxygenated mountain stream water and clean rainwater are other sources.

Summary

1. The principle of clean and unclean animals preceded the Levitical law by a thousand years or more. It did not arise in the days of Moses but had been known, assumed and understood from prior centuries.
2. Many of the dietary and hygienic laws of Moses accurately represent the original revealed Creation Laws—the revealed "master plan."
3. Principles of healthy nutrition, diet and hygiene should be an integral part of the overall teaching ministry of the church.
4. Eating "unclean" food is *permissible*, but that doesn't mean it is *wise*!
5. Herbs, vegetables and fruits should always be the primary foods for modern man, with the "clean" meats consumed in moderation.
6. Many scripture passages as well as science confirm the Torah dietary health laws. Besides the scriptures quoted within this chapter, note other interesting scriptures set apart in a box that relate to this challenging chapter.
7. Follow the seven guidelines toward a healthy diet. You will be glad you did!

Scriptures Relating to Creation Law Dietary Guidelines

Psalm 104:14: *"He causes the grass to grow for the cattle, And vegetation for the service of man, That he may bring forth food from the earth."*

Proverbs 18:9: *"He who does not use his endeavors to heal himself is brother to him who commits suicide." (Amplified)*

Proverbs 17:22: *"A merry heart does good, like medicine." (Medicines in those days were herbs, oils, fruits and ointments.)*

Proverbs 25:16: *"Have you found honey? Eat only as much as you need, Lest you be filled with it and vomit."*

2 Kings 20:7: *"Then Isaiah said, 'Take a lump of figs.' So they took and laid it on the boil, and he recovered." Medical science has recently proven that a fig poultice is specific for healing boils.*

Hebrews 6:7: *"For the earth....bears herbs useful for those by whom it is cultivated."*

Ezekiel 47:12: *"Along the bank of the river......will grow all kinds of trees used for food.....Their fruit will be for food, and their leaves for medicine." (margin: medicine="healing")*

Revelation 22:2: *".....On either side of the river, was the tree of life....each tree yielding its fruit every month. The leaves of the tree were for the healing of the nations."*

Science is currently revealing the medicinal healing power of tree leaves, for instance the Mediterranean Olive leaf and the Australian Tea Tree leaf. Both are more effective than most antibiotics. In addition, the powerful "super-bug" microbes do not develop resistant strains to these natural remedies, like they do with all the synthetic antibiotics.

Genesis 43:11: *"Israel said to them.....Take some of the best fruits of the land in your vessels and carry down a present for the man—a little balm and a little honey, spices and myrrh, pistachio nuts and almonds." A gift of food today would more likely be a store-bought pie, a tray of refined commercial pastries or a box of sugar filled chocolate candies. Which gift passes the "health test"? Are you searching for a gift to bless someone with? Go with the biblical guidelines!*

Chapter Eleven

NUTRITION AND GENETICS MYSTERY SOLVED

If you have read this far it should come as no surprise when I say that nutrition affects our genetic health. Nutrition affects *everything* related to our health! The link between nutrition and genetic disorders has been suspected for decades but only in the last couple of generations has the question been put to rest. A continually growing mountain of scientific evidence make it clear that virtually all genetic disorders have their root cause in some kind of nutritional deficiency. This is true for both humans and the animals we live with. Once we understand—*and correct*—the nutritional problem, in most cases the disease or disorder goes away. In the case of genetic disorders, the cure is progressive, requiring at least three generations of offspring before normalcy returns because repair must take place at the genetic level—the DNA must be repaired. Let me give you an example from the world of veterinary health.

I recall treating an entire litter of German Shepherd puppies that suffered from severe hip dysplasia. As the caretakers of these animals became aware of the nutritional laws involved, they took steps to correct the deficiencies. A few years later, that same pair of Shepherds sired a new litter—and not a single puppy developed hip dysplasia! What changed from one litter to the next? The nutritional element. This was an awesome lesson. The owners, following the advice of their veterinary nutritionist, were finally applying the nutritional law principles that were relevant to preventing hip dysplasia. The results were that the disease of hip dysplasia was totally lifted!

Hip dysplasia is primarily a disease of the larger breed dogs that grow rapidly. It results in ligament degeneration, a sloppy hip joint and, finally, severe arthritis. The final result, of course, is a swollen joint with pain that hinders the dog's quality of life. Most hip dysplasia, unless it is caused by trauma, such as a car accident, is due to chronic *nutrient deficiencies* in the sperm and egg of *both* parents, in the *diet of the mother* during gestation and, finally, with *faulty nutrition in the puppies*. These deficiencies and imbalances ultimately result in faulty links in the DNA of both the sperm and the egg of the *next generation*. Some call this "junk DNA."

Matt Ridley, in ***Nature VIA Nurture***, and in his bestseller, *Genome,*[21] reveals some of the latest research into genes that updates our understanding of how traits are passed on to succeeding generations. In the early 1960s I was taught that genes were predictable and followed exact genetic rules. We calculated how these genes would express themselves with mathematical formulas in future generations. I got an A in that course, proving, with some certainty, that I understood genetics.

But today, thanks to Matt Ridley and other pioneering scientists, we know that the DNA of genes operates on far different principles than we were previously taught. Ridley says that genes "absorb formative experiences, react to social cues, and even run memory."[22] Amazingly, one can turn genes off and prevent them from expressing themselves. Or one can pollute and pervert the gene, especially under conditions of poor nutrition, chemical exposure, vaccinations, drugs and stress, resulting in a *perverted expression*!

DNA of genes operates on far different principles than we were previously taught.

Five Scary Lessons in Genetic Manipulation that are Preventable!

1. When there is an ongoing chronic condition in the body at the cellular level, a gene can become permanently blocked or modified. In a human, this permanent change takes place after approximately 16 years of wrong nurturing. For the shorter-lived domestic animals it takes approximately 2.5 years. The blocked or modified gene is then passed on to future generations. Thus we have a great window of opportunity to make positive corrections—if we understand that we can actually modify an outcome in a positive direction resulting in future personal benefit. I say, "Go for it!"

2. Laboratory tests have revealed that when one group of bacteria is exposed to certain external influences such as sound, light, chemicals, electromagnetic frequency or even strong thought, another group of related bacteria, although separated by a thick glass wall and with a different ventilation system, will vicariously take on the changes in the first group! That change is then passed on to their progeny. Admittedly, not every condition has the power to impact the genetic code. But once it reaches that level of influence, that weakness or strength is semi-permanently transmitted to future generations.

3. Then there is the modern problem of "super-bugs." When any bacteria are exposed to environmental threats, such as antibiotics, chemicals, strong energy fields, or psychological threats to their well-being, *the survivors incorporate that survival ability into their genetic code and pass it along to their progeny!*

4. I once held a phone consultation with Dr. Bob Smith, an international expert in mineral analysis and toxicity. He reminded me of an experiment where scientists purposely induced zinc deficiency by limiting that mineral in the diet of a group of dogs. They discovered that this deficiency created an abnormality in the dogs' DNA, so that in time they lost the ability to metabolize zinc at normal levels. That factor was passed on for three generations before it could be genetically corrected at the DNA level. For three entire generations, all of the offspring required higher zinc supplementation than normal in order to maintain health, just in order to survive. This has far-reaching implications!

5. Recent discoveries prove that *food additives can permanently affect our DNA.* Unfortunately, this genetic damage is also passed on to future generations. My naturopathic-trained sister shared with me about a research release from the medical school from the University of Michigan, revealing that scientists had recently discovered that *approved* food colorings are collecting on our DNA. Medical doctors are concerned, as they should be. After all, food coloring is harmless and non-toxic; everybody knows that, right? Wrong! This is just one more shocking revelation that the effects of diet, drugs and chemicals, of thinking and belief, and of society and customs—can actually influence and modify the DNA codes of our chromosomes.

Recent discoveries prove that food additives can permanently affect our DNA.

I have on my clinic bulletin board a list of the health effects of food colorings. Red #2 causes thyroid tumors, chromosomal damage, and hyperactivity. Red #40 causes lymphatic tumors and hyperactivity. Blue #1 causes chromosomal damage. Blue #2 causes brain tumors. Green #3 causes bladder tumors. Yellow #5 causes thyroid and lymphatic tumors. Yellow #6 causes kidney tumors and chromosomal damage. Three of the seven are *known* to cause chromosomal DNA damage! And these are FDA approved "non-toxic" artificial colors!

It is now understood that this modified DNA passes to the third and forth generation. This is a shocking yet important discovery. Armed with this knowledge, we now have the opportunity to employ strategic steps to protect ourselves and future generations. What many of us suspected for several decades has now been proven in the laboratory. I don't know about you, but I have no interest in receiving or passing on "junk DNA! Let the wise take heed and move preventatively!

We Have a Creative Opportunity to be Guardians of the Future!

Fortunately, there is a positive flip side to this dilemma. By employing Scriptural and scientific answers, we can reverse the damage to our genes. If we apply the right principles and teach them effectively to our children by daily living example, Scripture promises that "mercy" will pass to a thousand generations (see Deut. 7:9). Who is included in this promise? It includes all those who "love and keep the commandments." Personally, I believe that keeping the commandments includes keeping the nutritional commandments! This should encourage us to go for the positive promises!

This is also why we must solve our deficiencies, change our wrong thinking and throw out our brainless dietary habits. You will recall from chapter four that Dr. Pottenger discovered this same principle in his landmark cat study. When the cats were fed a totally cooked diet it took three generations to reach the edge of final and total disaster—and another three generations to reverse the genetic damage. Only then was the "junk DNA" purged and health restored to normal.

What we do today *does* affect our children and our grandchildren! What we feed and how we treat our animals will, by the same token, also affect *their* future generations. How we treat the soil will also have long lasting effects. Let us influence them for good! Let's get serious about understanding the statutes of Creation Law. Let's get back to sound Scriptural principles, and back to a way of life that will nurture and multiply the life that God intended us to have. *Multiplication, not division, must be the norm!*

*What we do today **does** affect our children and our grandchildren! What we feed and how we treat our animals will, by the same token, also affect **their** future generations.*

Picture this: junk DNA is like dust collecting on an item in the barn. The dust gets thicker with each passing year. Eventually rot, tarnish and oxidation take place. Finally, the condition becomes irreversible. Repair becomes impossible. The point is that this same unfortunate process of oxidation happens inside the cell! In a healthy body there is a constant process going on of repair and cleansing. When that process is interfered with by poor nutrition, lack of antioxidant nutrients, chronic obesity, chemicals, drugs and poisons—including emotional toxins—the cellular DNA becomes clogged, deranged, and tarnished. *As in the barn, so in the cell!* When the cleaning mechanisms go on strike the end result is dysfunction!

Perhaps comparing the cell to a barn is a rather unusual way of comparing gene dysfunction. But it does accurately describe how genes can be affected by the process of stagnation and oxidation. Thus the title of Matt Ridley's, *Nature VIA Nurture*. That title refers to the fact that genes must be nurtured and cared for, or the potential in the gene will not correctly manifest. The so-called "genetic diseases" will inevitably result. But the problem isn't really the gene, which has a perfect holographic memory, but the junk that has collected on the gene, preventing its perfect expression. Many people do not understand that distinction.

Do I now have you curious and wondering how much junk we humans have collected on our DNA over many generations? Would it not be wonderful to have a mechanism to clear out the cells, to restore the DNA, and to even clean up our brain cells? Wow!

According to God's Word, and according to the principles of science, there *is* a way to clean up this mess! That day is now, and in another sense that day will more fully manifest in the future age. But if we understand the principles now, would it not be prudent to begin the first steps *now*? It begins by co-laboring in what the Scriptures call the "restoration (recovery) of all things" (see Acts 3:21). Does co-laboring with the Creator by preventing and solving these pesky earthly genetic coding problems fit your job description as a son of Yahweh Elohim? It fits mine!

Canine Hip Dysplasia is NOT Genetic

Let's get back to our German Shepherd story. Did the puppies in that first litter actually inherit a bad gene for hip dysplasia? The probable answer is no. Scientists have never discovered a gene for hip dysplasia! What the puppies really inherited was junk DNA, which paved the way for imperfection and weakness of the ligaments and joints of their hips. Tobacco, marijuana, soda pop, food coloring and a junk diet have similar effects with human babies. This is well-established fact—even in the popular journals at the grocery store.

How's this for a shocking statistic? Only 25% of our physical and emotional makeup is genetic; the other 75% is due to the ability or inability of our body to express those genes—because of how those genes are nurtured via the environment. The environment includes what happens in the womb, which has a powerful influence in shaping the ultimate health and future status of that fetus. In other words, the mechanisms and causative factors for the general health of a child are in place long before the day of birth. This is cutting-edge science.

Only 25% of our physical and emotional makeup is genetic; the other 75% is due to the ability or inability of our body to express those genes.

Certain puppies, therefore, are actually *born* with weakened joints and the predisposition toward this devastating disease. The preexisting problem is then multiplied by deficient and out-of-balance nutrition fed to these rapidly growing puppies. *Nurture affects nature* both before and after the puppy is born. Here is what happens after the puppy is born:

1. When high protein commercial "puppy diets" are fed during the rapid growth phase, this breed of dog (and other similar large and giant breeds prone to arthritis and hip dysplasia) grow too big and too fast. Their rapidly developing joints become increasingly unstable. I am convinced that the maximum protein should be no more than 23% for the large and giant breeds when feeding them

processed commercial food. This protein problem is exacerbated when feeding *poor quality proteins* like meat byproducts and cooked soybean meals. I *never* recommend soy products for carnivores!

2. The next problem is due to the addition of inexpensive and inferior refined mineral salts or mined soil minerals laced with cheap synthetic vitamins. The canine was originally created to metabolize live chelated plant minerals and live natural vitamins. These are found only in healthy foods that the puppy would normally obtain in a pristine or more natural environment.

   There is also evidence of a deficiency of vitamins C, E, and the mineral selenium (look for selenomethionine, not sodium selenite) in the typical commercial diets. Standard science texts teach that dogs have the ability to manufacture their own vitamin C. This is probably true in the pristine wild state. But under our 21st century conditions of chemicals, cooked food and super stress, everything has changed dramatically! Today, the ability of a dog's system to manufacture its own vitamin C is seriously overestimated. And vitamin C is a key player in the manufacture and repair of—you guessed it—collagen, ligaments and bone!

3. Hip dysplasia (and osteo-arthritis as well) is further complicated by the modern method of "self-feeding," where food is available to the animal 24 hours a day so that it can eat whenever it wants and as much as it wants. Many animal caretakers believe this to be not only convenient (for them) but also healthy and beneficial for the animal. It's the old principle, "Let your stomach be your guide." After all, we humans do it, so why not our pets?

   There are several fallacies to this line of thinking. You will recall from chapter nine the test that demonstrated that dogs who self-fed from food available 24 hours a day lived on average two years less than dogs fed twice daily with 25% less food. The self-fed dogs ate more, got fatter, grew faster—and manifested 3 to 4 times more arthritis and hip dysplasia than did the dogs whose feeding was controlled.

   These and other studies confirm that "slim and trim," along with slower or average growth, results in tighter and stronger joints. They prove the fallacy of the common concept that "bigger is better!" Picking the biggest and fattest puppy in the litter may not be the best decision in the long run.

4. There are significant *deficiencies* of biologically active collagens, live enzymes, soluble fibers, and natural vitamins in the typical commercial puppy diets. This is a fact. Most of these cooked, extruded, synthetic, preserved and beautifully-bagged foods are filled with inferior, second-rate junk—and this junk just does not meet the standards of long-term health.[23] Fortunately there are a few exceptions; there are several dependable brands of pet food on the market.

   Neither does home cooking always solve the problem (just in case you were wondering) unless it is formulated and prepared with understanding! But sometimes we can utilize a combination of both. I have presented this material at several veterinary conferences. Animals (and people) need live food!

5. Finally it has been discovered recently that high amounts of grains in the canine diet are pro-inflammatory, pro-arthritic, and pro-disease. Think with me. In nature a wild dog eats fresh meat, live organs and raw bones. They also relish the vegetable stomach contents of their prey. They browse in nature, nibbling occasionally on grasses, herbs, fruits and berries. As the generations passed, in companionship with we humans, dogs admittedly were fed a limited amount of cooked grains from the masters table, especially whole grains. These were minor additions to the diet, however, not major *byproduct* ingredients such as are present in today's typical commercial concoction.

It has been discovered recently that high amounts of grains in the canine diet are pro-inflammatory, pro-arthritic, and pro-disease.

Here is my point. Over the last 50 years everything has changed, some of it in the wrong direction. Because grains and byproducts are *cheap* compared to real meat and high quality food, it was only a matter of time before grains like corn, wheat and soy would become the *primary* ingredients in commercial pet foods.

If you don't believe me, check it out. Most of the mass-produced dog foods use corn as their first ingredient. Next come cheap meat *byproducts* and then even cheaper grain byproducts. After that come saturated animal fats and sweeteners such as corn syrup, sucrose and fructose sugars, preservatives and flavor enhancers. Finally, synthetic vitamins and mined or processed mineral salts are added. Every one of these ingredients is pro-inflammatory, unnatural, acidic, and pro-illness! Hip dysplasia, arthritis, allergies, asthma, cancer, obesity, heart disease, diabetes, prostate disease and auto immune diseases are all diseases characterized by *excessive inflammation* and an *acid environment.* Get the picture?

It is Time to Jump Off the Merry-Go-Round and into the Answer Apparatus!

In my office I diagnose and treat the painful diseases of arthritis and hip dysplasia every week. At 8 to 12 weeks of age some puppies already exhibit inflammatory pain when their little hip joints are carefully rotated and stretched. "Ouch! That hurts!" they wince!

Please remember this time-tested truth: *"Prevention is always the best medicine."* In a related vein, here are two truisms you should mount on your refrigerator door and inscribe on your heart and mind:

1. "*Let food be your medicine.*"
2. "*Leave your drugs in the chemist's pot if you can heal the patient with food.*"

Whose words are these? They were spoken—and taught—by Hippocrates, the father of modern medicine.

The model I just explained is very simple. However, most real answers *are* relatively simple. Yet many educated people might reject the answers I just presented because they do not fit the standard and accepted scientific model. The defenders of that substandard model are many, and they will fight tooth and nail to preserve it—even if it is wrong. They cloud the issue and delay action by demanding more tests and more scientific proof when tests and proofs abound. They seek a quick fix rather than a real fix. In the meantime more drugs will be sold. Big money is involved in influencing these critical health decisions, but truth takes the power out of the hands of the corporate business conglomerates and puts the answer back into the hands of the caretaker! This is a fight worth fighting and a fight worth winning!

The defenders of that substandard model are many, and they will fight tooth and nail to preserve it—even if it is wrong.

Remember, every problem has answers and answers are based on clearly understanding the roots of the problem. There are very few quick fixes. We must get to the root causes. Only then will we benefit from the true fix.

The principles of nutrition and genetics explained through the hip dysplasia story has applications for humans too. Here are five ways you can apply these truths to yourself and your family:

1. To birth truly healthy children and grandchildren, get your own health fixed first!
2. It all begins with the health of the sperm and egg.
3. Our environment influences our genes!
4. What we eat in our formative years paves the way for our health as adults.
5. What we eat as adults paves the way for how we live out our golden years.

Buy and eat real food according to knowledge. Then practice the right principles *together*. Together means your family, your animal companions, the barnyard, the orchard and the soil!

Summary

1. Virtually all genetic disorders have their root cause in some kind of nutritional deficiency.
2. One can turn genes off and prevent them from expressing themselves.
3. Food additives can permanently affect our DNA.
4. By employing Scriptural and scientific answers, we can reverse the damage to our genes.
5. What we do today *does* affect our children and our grandchildren!
6. The mechanisms and causative factors for the general health of a child are in place long before the day of birth.
7. Prevention is always the best medicine.
8. Let food be your medicine.
9. Leave your drugs in the chemist's pot if you can heal the patient with food.

Stewardship Regained in Guatemala!

"I will provide for them a land renowned for its crops, and they will no longer be victims of famine..." Ezekiel 34:29, NIV

"Take Almolonga, a small town of 20,000 in the highlands of Guatemala. In the early 1970's, the alcoholism rate in this dark and impoverished community had reached a staggering 99%. The entire town seemed locked in a downward spiral of superstition, corruption, and poverty. When I visited Almolonga in early November (1998) I discovered God had been at work. Upwards of 92 percent of the town's population is now born again! The evidence, which may be seen at every turn, includes a forest of churches and workplaces dedicated to the Lord. The results of this transformation have been nothing short of amazing. Previously impoverished farmers displayed 5 lb. beets and carrots as big as a man's arm. Before the spiritual turnaround these growers were exporting 4 truckloads of produce a month. Now they leave town forty times a week!

Alcohol addiction has abated dramatically and the town's jails have been closed for lack of use. Idolatry and superstition have also fled, leaving behind a people dedicated to fervent prayer and honest labor. One farmer told me their growing time has dropped from 65 days to 25 days—with yields so robust that agricultural experts from the United States have been flocking to Almolonga to examine their farming techniques. Asked to explain this phenomenon, the farmers point to stickers affixed to the windshields and mud flaps of their shiny, new Mercedes trucks. The messages are simple and straightforward: "The gift of God." "Go forward in Faith" and "God is My Stronghold."

—(page 32, Can You Feel The Mountains Tremble?
by Dr. Suuqiina as reported by George Otis in
The Sentinel Group Newsletter of Nov 25, 1998)

Chapter Twelve

HEALING YOURSELF AND YOUR ENVIRONMENT: ADDITIONAL TIPS

As I have stressed throughout this book, our current model of health-care and disease treatment/prevention with its emphasis on chemically-, drug- and surgically-based therapies is broken, perhaps beyond repair. The season is ripe for a return to older, time-honored and more natural approaches. In this chapter I will discuss several additional practical tips for healing yourself and your environment through natural means. The next chapter will present some more spiritually- and scripturally-based tips for achieving the same end. Remember, our spirit, our body and the earth are all connected. Insights from each arena can work together to bring effective change.

Vaccinations

Let's start by looking at the whole vaccination picture. This may well be my most controversial subject! But current honest research clearly demonstrates that shotgun multiple vaccinations are doing more harm than good for our animals. And as we have already seen, things that affect the health of our animals also affect our health, and vice-versa. The results are in: vaccinations have a definite detrimental effect on immune systems by reprogramming them at the DNA level. This is now solid science.

An increasing number of disease experts are predicting that deadly plagues will devastate the world population in the near future. *This doesn't have to happen!*

Nor is the answer more vaccinations, in my opinion. Several safer, wiser and more natural alternatives to vaccinations are already available. These include, but are not limited to, powerful herbal, dietary, homeopathic remedies—combined with major lifestyle changes.[24] Get educated or get boxed in. Isn't it time to break out of our box?

Several safer, wiser and more natural alternatives to vaccinations are already available.

During the 1918 swine flu epidemic, approximately 50,000,000 people died worldwide. The mortality rate for flu victims being treated by doctors and hospitals was 60 to 80%. In contrast, the mortality rate for patients under the care of homeopathic and naturopathic physicians was under 3% to 15%! One good homeopathic doctor, records show, treated 275 cases with no deaths! What we need today is a stronger immune system kept strong with better nutrition—not one reprogrammed by questionable shotgun vaccination practices.

I realize this advice contradicts modern practice and orthodox wisdom. Resources to check this out are available on such sites as: www.mercola.com, (type in "vaccinations" under the Mercola Google "search" engine for over 100 educational articles concerning vaccinations), www.vaccine-education.com, the National Vaccine Information Center at www.909shot.com and many others.

Many other educational resources are currently available. One is "*Vaccinations Deception & Tragedy, The Truth About Vaccines and the Dangers They Pose*," by Michael Dye, Hallelujah Acres Publishing, 704-481-1700. Here is a quote from the back cover of that highly documented book: "The truth is that vaccinations are not only unsafe, but they actually work against our God-given immune system. This book explains how this God-given natural immunity works, and how vaccinations can destroy this self-healing system."

Another resource is: "*Vaccine-Free Prevention & Treatment with Homeopathy*," by Jeffrey Starre, M.D.[25] Dr. Starr provides the reader with information regarding the common diseases for which vaccines are available and the corresponding homeopathic alternatives. It is a practical guide for anyone interested in knowing what homeopathy has to offer as an alternative to vaccinations.

Recent science, plus my own experience, substantiate that many of the current immune problems are due to *over-vaccination*. I have seen multiple problems following vaccinations, including life-threatening autoimmune hemolytic anemia and cancers appearing at the vaccinations sites. One cat I treated had up to 50 epileptic seizures daily beginning hours after a required rabies vaccination. Not long ago I examined a young dog that had digressed sharply in mental clarity and focus after being vaccinated, even to the point of forgetting to go outdoors to defecate. These are not isolated cases. Many dog breeders have told me of expensive litters of puppies that have suddenly died following shotgun vaccinations. But once they stopped or sharply curtailed those vaccinations, the puppies stopped dying.

A study in England involving 2,700 dogs showed a much greater incidence of illness using cocktail vaccinations. The report also revealed that dogs boosted annually were more likely to become ill than those that were not boosted annually. In the first three months following vaccination, illnesses were reported at an average of 55% higher than expected. These ailments included diarrhea, epilepsy, loss of appetite, skin problems, vomiting, weight loss, behavioral problems, tumor growth at the vaccination site, encephalitis, short attention span, autoimmune diseases, dry eye, and others.

Obviously, there are other interrelated factors that affect the immune system, such as too much stress and too much drug and chemical exposure. Another major contributor is serious malnutrition in the midst of plenty—empty foods that are devoid of live nutrients, live enzymes and "live foods."

Can we do something about these problems? Yes, of course we can. There are many things we can do, but first we have to get off the industrial and pharmaceutical bandwagon. Answers and alternatives are readily available to those who are willing to take the leap. *But you'd better not leap until you have your own personal convictions, because when you do, the pressure to conform will hit you from all sides!* Among my clients are a number of medical doctors and nurses. Many of them have shared with me the pressure they face every day to conform and to enforce conformity. Regarding vaccinations, however, the law is actually on your side—if you decide to reject most of them. Remember, I am not saying to break any laws. What I am saying is to *know your rights, and know your risks.*

Remember, I am not saying to break any laws.
What I am saying is to know your rights, and know your risks.

Dr. Jonathan Wright, MD, in an article in the October 2004 issue of "Nutrition & Healing,"[26] writes that the human measles vaccine disrupts the protective "viral-human cycle". He says there is a "serious risk to unborn children and infants from measles that's actually been *created* by measles vaccination—a hazard that never existed before." Dr. Wright believes there is a "well documented link between measles vaccination, intestinal inflammation, and autism." He also believes there is another major problem—that vaccinations actually weaken the immune system by altering the natural cycle, and this is "not for the better."

Dr. Wright also states that research done in the 1920s and repeated in the 1990s proves that measles is entirely preventable and that a single good-sized dose of vitamin A "cut the death rate from measles to zero in treated children." He concludes: "While you still have that right (to reject mandatory vaccinations), I urge you to exercise it by staying informed on all aspects of pediatric health care, including—and especially—vaccination. Your child's life depends on it."

Let me add that we must make our decisions based on solid information from both sides of the controversy—not in FEAR. Views on health are in transition and major flux. But please realize that we all have more "rights" than we have been led to believe. The key is research and becoming informed.

Research done in the 1920s and repeated in the 1990s proves that measles is entirely preventable and that a single good-sized dose of vitamin A "cut the death rate from measles to zero in treated children."

Foliar Sprays

For those who are growing your own food (as well as those who are considering it), if you currently are not knowledgeable on the cutting edge science of foliar spraying, let me encourage you to learn! Foliar spraying is the science of mist-spraying small (micro) amounts of nutrients over and under plant leaves. The optimum time for spraying is in the early morning or late afternoon when the stomata, or respiration pores, of the plant are open. I have been astounded by the results of my own experiments with foliar spraying over the past twenty years. Application of these vital nutrients on your plants and crops may be done by hand with mist bottles as well as by using small or large commercial pressure sprayers to treat lawns, gardens, orchards, field crops, ponds and, yes, even animals and herds.

Foliar spraying can include natural nutrient remedies, flower essences, homeopathics, fish, kelp or sea water emulsions, molasses, minerals, "compost tea" or dozens of other possibilities. Compost tea is an active culture of *oxygen loving good bacteria* and *good* fungus and microbes. The technology of this tea goes back at least 3000 years in several cultures. It has recently been advanced and proven to be effective at several agricultural universities, and is now being promulgated by Dr. Elaine Ingham and many others who are on the cutting edge of plant and soil health. In fact I now own and have used one of the first "compost home tea brewers" that have ever been manufactured commercially.

My brewer cost around $900, but sketch plans are available for making your own for a fraction of that cost. There are also internet websites that will instruct you on how to brew your own active tea culture loaded with trillions of these highly beneficial organisms. Just type in "compost tea" on a web search engine. You will be surprised at how much useful information you will find. This tea acts both as a fertilizer and as a welcome alternative to the overuse of pesticides and fungicides. Spray it on the plants to *head off* bacterial or viral wilt diseases. The "good" organisms will grab the leaf sites that the disease organisms are looking for. The idea is: "Sorry, we were here first!"

This technology has been practiced successfully on farms nationally and internationally. Foliar sprays have resulted in economical forms of nutritional and health balancing. Some have even theorized that this technology, when properly balanced, may even be useful in regulating and enhancing the internal DNA of the chromosome.

The cost of foliar spraying can be as low as $10.00 per acre. I have found it to be a joy to experiment using these homemade sprays. Personally, I have rescued several garden crops from near disaster, bringing them instead into good and even great production. Do you remember the melon miracle I shared in chapter two? A significant part of that success was accomplished with foliar sprays.

For instance, when we lived in Massachusetts many years ago, I planted a new garden on what I thought was virgin rocky New England soil. Our finances were tight, and I wanted to grow fresh food for our family. So we got permission from the landlord to tear up a plot of soil to grow our garden. Imagine my dismay as the plants barely hung on in survival mode. I thought to myself, "Well, now is the time to try some of these new (to me) concepts of foliar sprays." To my amazement the plants responded. Tomatoes, beans, eggplant, peppers, okra and radishes all took off and produced in abundance. Friends told me it was the most productive garden they had ever seen!

Anyone can learn this technology and be successful. The principles involved are simple. It does require some training, however, along with the proverbial "green thumb" of a caretaker, an open mind, and some personal creativity.

The Treasure of Good Soil

Someone said, "As goes the soil, so goes the nation." Perhaps those bred in the city will not understand that statement. It is a historical truism, however.

Commerce and business will only survive when a nation nurtures its God-given land. When the husbandman of the soil is despised, when agriculture is misguided, when the laws of nature are not followed, that nation will not long survive. Healthy soil is like money in the bank. When the wisdom of the intellectual fails at this level of understanding, it has failed in everything.

Today few understand the breakneck speed at which our lands are being raped. This cannot go on indefinitely. The land needs a Sabbath rest to regenerate. You and I should be on the forefront of conservation. We should be thinking of efficiency and long-term goals in every aspect of our planning. It requires a people of great wisdom to actually practice the principles of wise soil management. If we do not, then nature and nature's God will enforce those laws. Proverbs 26:2 (KJV) states, "The curse causeless shall not come." This is just another way to speak of the law of sowing and reaping. Man-made disasters of pestilence, wars and famine will strike down rich and poor alike. We will merely inherit the results of our own stupid decisions!

It requires a people of great wisdom to actually practice the principles of wise soil management. If we do not, then nature and nature's God will enforce those laws.

But it is not too late for people to get the message, get back to caring for the land and provide an example for families of understanding to follow. Will you and your family be among those people? Start in your own backyard! Do you have a compost pile? Are you nurturing the billions of "good" microorganisms in every square inch of your soil? Are the earthworms happy and rejoicing? These are just a few questions to ask if you aspire to be a good steward in your sphere of local influence.

The following is a column written several decades ago by the late Dr. Robert Rodale, the founder of the organic movement in the United States and for many years publisher of *Organic Gardening and Farming*. I believe his thesis could prove to be prophetic.

SOIL IS BETTER THAN GOLD[27]

by Dr. Robert Rodale

I read a story not long ago that made me think about which is a better investment—gold or soil. It was told by an American economist, and happened in Italy about 20 or 30 years ago. I can't remember the name of the economist, or his exact words, but here is roughly how the story went.

> "I was working in Italy after the war, and had a very intelligent young Italian man on my staff. He told me that every month he would take part of his pay and buy a small gold coin, which he gave to his wife to keep in a safe place. I told him that was a foolish investment."
>
> "Don't you Americans tell us about gold," the young man snapped back at the American. "If things get bad again, I tell my wife that she can take one of those gold coins to a farmer and get enough food to eat for a month."

That story tells clearly the true appeal of gold. It is the investment of the disaster-minded. Gold does not pay dividends or yield interest, but it increases in value as confidence in paper money declines. And there is always the thought in the back of the gold-hoarder's mind that—especially if the yellow metal is owned in the form of small coins—it can be used as currency in times of economic collapse or war.

Is gold really the best disaster investment, though? What about the farmer who grew the food that the young Italian couple was relying on to supply to them when catastrophe struck? When you stop to think about it, the farmer was in a pretty good position, too. His investment, the soil, paid dividends during times of stability and peace, yet he was also there to supply the "good-as-gold" food when regular money couldn't buy anything in the store.

Is gold really the best disaster investment, though?

COMPARING THE ADVANTAGES OF GOLD VERSUS SOIL

The disruption of normal social and economic activities caused by a worldwide food shortage would probably increase the attractiveness of both gold and soil as investments. But I feel that if you compare the relative merits of each, *soil is clearly the winner.* And because of the shortage of food that is likely to occur within this decade, soil will soon replace gold as the most-talked-about and symbolic thing of enduring value.

That is going to happen because people have always put a higher value on things that are rare. Gold has always been rare, and will remain so, even though more is being mined all the time. But soil has never before been in short supply on a worldwide basis. Erosion and encroachment of deserts have ruined the soil of large regions, and there have been famines caused by bad weather. But never have people had to contend with the thought that on a global basis, there isn't enough soil to go around. Within a few years, that will change. *Soil will, for the first time, become rare.* And worldwide television and news reports quoting crop production statistics and high food prices will carry that news everywhere.

Erosion and encroachment of deserts have ruined the soil of large regions, and there have been famines caused by bad weather.

A new symbolism of soil will develop. Until now, soil has symbolized dirt in the minds of many, especially city people who have little or no feel for the tremendous productivity capacity of good soil. I think we are going to see that attitude change rapidly. Access to good earth will become the greatest of all forms of protection against inflation, and a much stronger security blanket than it is now.

Don't minimize the importance of the idea that the symbolic value of soil can and will increase. The value of gold is mainly symbolic. People think it's money; therefore it actually is money. They wear it around their necks to show other people their wealth, or keep pieces of it in a safety deposit box and dream of its growing value. *For thousands of years gold has worked that mental magic. Soon, soil will begin to have the same appeal.*

When you spend gold, it is gone. Soil, properly cared for, is permanent. You can even take land that is poor and build it into rich earth of great productivity capacity by planting green manure crops and by adding to it manure, compost, mulch and natural mineral fertilizers. Especially on a garden scale, *you can take land that is not productive now and turn it into black gold by building its fertility.* Soon, that regeneration of earth will become one of the most rewarding of all challenges.

Land close to cities could become the most valuable of all, because of the people who live nearby. They are both customers for surplus food and productive workers. The working partnership between people and the land will become a much more important ingredient in the productive capacity of soil in the future. People are needed to make land produce. Farmers substitute for people by using large, energy-guzzling tractors and other machines. Even with that mechanical help, they produce much less food per unit of land than do gardeners working the earth in a more personal way. Land for gardening is already more high priced than is farmland. The difference in value could become even greater.

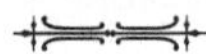

You can take land that is not productive now and turn it into black gold by building its fertility.

I want to make one final point. Suppose you do have a hoard of small gold coins at home, and a food shortage develops here in the U.S. Hopefully, the cause will not be war; and it may not even be an absence of food in central storehouses. The shortage could be caused by transportation breakdowns, most likely a lack of fuel to carry food from farms to processing plants to supermarkets.

Where would you take your gold coin to buy food? In post-war Italy, as in this country several decades ago, small, diversified farms could be found near all towns and cities. There were even truck farms within the city limits of New York. All are gone now. Many Americans would have to walk or ride their bicycles for hours to get to a farm, and then likely would find an agribusiness operation with bins of one or two commodities on hand. Spending your coin would present a real challenge.

So the best fall-back position is not gold, but a large garden and a pantry full of home-produced food.

I couldn't agree more with Dr. Rodale's conclusion!

My Dream: A Worldwide Network of Training Facilities

It should be our active and ongoing ambition that God will raise up training opportunities all across this nation and around the globe. Some of the knowledge and break-through technology is already available. But discipleship and training must be our long-term goal. My own mission is to paint the living picture that I see both up close and from a distance. *A picture and a dream always come before the living reality.*

My own mission is to paint the living picture that I see both up close and from a distance. A picture and a dream always come before the living reality.

Before I left Colombia, we had a training facility on the drawing board. Our plan was to design a "discipleship training" curriculum in the areas of agriculture, health, carpentry and mechanics. This curriculum was geared toward the life and needs we experienced on the community farms. I prepared a sketch of the proposed building and we were looking for ways to finance the project. Before long, however, the failing health of my dear wife necessitated our return to the U. S.

Meanwhile, in the dense jungles behind us, other training camps were being financed and built for guerilla warfare. More than a year before we left Colombia, a guerilla undercover agent from M-19 lived in our home for ten days. He had disguised himself as a Jesuit priest in training and even showed us convincing photos. At his request, he flowed with the work in the community and was quite cordial.

The morning he disappeared from our lives, however, he shared in confidence his real mission. He explained that we had already been "investigated" by all ten of the other existing guerilla fronts. Then he showed us his "black bag" filled with guns, ammunition and explosives. Finally, he told us he was pleased by what he saw and asked forgiveness for deceiving us.

Not long after we left Colombia, M-19 and other guerilla front groups were on the front pages of the national and international newspapers. As things degenerated, they began to rob our camps, made plans to kidnap some of our children, and they burned some of our buildings.

Sadly, they won that round, and we were forced to disband. However, the vision still lives on in hearts and homes. In fact, when I visited Colombia in 2003 I taught the same nutritional principles I have discussed in this book in three separate cities. Amazingly, I received more interest, more excitement and far better reception than I do here in the States! Intuitively they knew the truth. Many in third world countries are closer to the land and closer to nature, even those who live in the cities. On almost every block there is a small store with fresh fruits, vegetables, eggs, meat and daily supplies. If we don't "get it," guess who may be the next ones to carry the torch!

But the mega-challenge and team-effort required to get this message flying will require dedicated leadership. There is a supreme requirement for strong leadership with enough respect and anointing to bust through the massive walls of ignorance, mental roadblocks and the dullness of spiritual blindness.

It is precisely here and that I am beginning to see *hope*. Major leaders finally are beginning to give mental assent. They are taking beginning steps with their own health and families. But active and progressive breakthrough leadership has definitely not yet manifested. Maybe the time is not ripe yet. Both leadership and society in general are cautious in approaching this critical mass of interest. It is time to stoke the fire! Let's join and flow with teamwork! The need is there and if it is combined with a grassroots cry for team leadership, I am confident that leadership will manifest somehow somewhere. The question is: will the current leadership be ready to meet the need? Or will God have to raise it up from some other direction?

In my own experience, this training need could be met by circulating anointed teaching videos, seminars, printed or internet books, as well as by correspondence textbooks. Have people gather in study groups! Provide the advertisement and energy needed to assure success. This could rapidly develop into a loud and clear trumpet call. There must be a clarion call and challenge that activates and brings together both the wisdom of maturity and the energy of youth. Can you see the writing on the wall?

There must be a clarion call and challenge that activates and brings together both the wisdom of maturity and the energy of youth. Can you see the writing on the wall?

Here is what I "see." I picture sufficient resources at every level of need. I see principled and quality teaching material on shelves and bookcases that are widely distributed and locally owned. These materials are available for home study via printed materials and the internet for small home-based or locally based schools. Weekly or bi monthly discipleship training is taking place at every local level. This includes local tutoring and frequent study trips. The purpose is to develop a *stewardship mentality*. Take tours, visit farms, orchards, forests, parks and training institutes. Summarize and critique every trip to stimulate critical observation and the learning process. Do research reports. Ask students to look deep into their own hearts to draw out ideas and revelation beyond external observation. Stimulate the creative process. We must burst out of the doldrums of traditional education. The future of our children depends on breaking through to the next level. Do you see what I see?

We must burst out of the doldrums of traditional education. The future of our children depends on breaking through to the next level. Do you see what I see?

Each student would apply for general studies as well as electives and individual research projects. Groups in target areas would come together to disseminate the results of their projects. These groups would also invite experts in the subject to share their own experiences and discoveries. These progressive training groups would also sponsor a yearly gathering, a "Practicum" of applied sharing, lectures and demonstrations. We also envision a monthly or quarterly newsletter to serve as a means of sharing these discoveries, to disseminate knowledge and to share answers in print. None of these are new ideas. They are as old as human history. But they need to be applied in an innovative way.

Sound impossibly big and ambitious? Perhaps. But no great achievements or paradigm-shifting movements ever grew from *small* dreams! Dream big! The bigger we dream the greater the chance that we just might see it come true!

Summary

1. Vaccinations have a definite detrimental on immune systems by reprogramming them at the cellular and DNA level.
2. Several safer, wiser and more natural alternatives to vaccinations are already available, including powerful herbal, dietary and homeopathic remedies.
3. Foliar sprays have resulted in economical forms of nutritional and health balancing.
4. As goes the soil, so goes the nation.
5. The best fall-back position is not gold, but a large garden and a pantry full of home-produced food.
6. It should be our active and ongoing ambition that God will raise up training opportunities all across this nation and around the globe.
7. We must burst out of the doldrums of traditional education. The future of our children depends on breaking through to the next level.

Chapter Thirteen

INTUITIVE AND SPIRITUAL TIPS FOR HEALING THE CREATION

Throughout this book I have stressed that the physical and the spiritual go hand in hand. In creation the natural and the supernatural are like two sides of the same coin or two facets of the same diamond. Neither is complete without the other. (Of course, I exempt God Himself from this statement. Being eternal and uncreated, God is always complete within Himself. When I talk about the physical and the spiritual being incomplete without each other, I am referring to the *created order*: the *created* natural realm as well as the *created* spiritual realm.)

With the natural and the supernatural linked as they are, it stands to reason that not all the answers to the ills of our natural world are to be found in nature alone. The spiritual realm has tremendous power to effect change in the natural order, either for good or bad. We need to learn how to connect with and appropriate the power of God's kingdom to improve the earthly kingdom as well as learn to use the intuitive gifts that God has given us. We can illustrate this in several ways.

The Anointing

The healing of ourselves, our crops, our animals and our land to achieve extraordinary 100-fold success and fruitfulness will require a great deal of prevailing prayer, inspired leadership and a unique anointing. Anointing comes from a relationship with God. I recall the success of our own organic farm in the 1950s. How vivid are my memories of watching my father walking the fields on Sunday afternoons and on his knees in prayer early in the morning before beginning chores. Success came through a *combination* of hard work, daily diligence, seeking answers, heart guidance, inspiration, meditation and connected prayer. Dad used to say we could raise more on five acres, using intensive organic farming methods, crop rotation, knowledge and hard work, than the average chemical farmer could raise on fifty acres. The product we produced was also far superior in quality, quantity and, especially, taste!

Dad used to say we could raise more on five acres, using intensive organic farming methods, crop rotation, knowledge and hard work, than the average chemical farmer could raise on fifty acres.

We can still expect miracles tomorrow by sowing the right seeds today. Use of Kingdom methods and Kingdom principles will bring about Kingdom breakthroughs. One such principle is the "anointing."

The anointing is the ability to accomplish tasks under the inspiration and personal direction of the Holy Spirit. It is a divine impartation of power that enables us to do more than we could ever accomplish on our own. Through the anointing the Holy Spirit leads us into the knowledge of the truth. The anointing helps us to grasp the full picture, to find the true balance, and to keep our focus on the right things.

As each member of the team adds his part to the whole, the sum of the whole adds up to greater than the sum of the individual parts. This is divine arithmetic, a whole new dimension in math, where 1 + 1 equals not 2 but instead, 3 or more! The number 3 is the number of divine intervention, which is just the edge we are looking for and that the anointing gives us.

You will recall that in chapter one I shared the story of amazingly productive black-eyed pea plants in Colombia, planted by a mentor of mine from the States. "Brother Sam," as we knew him, was a man who preached often on the Anointing. He said, "The anointing breaks the yoke". A man who had consecrated and dedicated his life to doing the will of the Father, Brother Sam believed and walked in the anointing. He preached about "incorruptible corn" and "incorruptible tomatoes". Some of it was over our heads, because he was a man ahead of his time.

Months after the black-eyed pea "miracle," Brother Sam and his airplane went down over the mountains of Ecuador. I never did get the chance to ask him his secret. Someday I will, and expect his secret will have something to do with the anointing, with the blessing, with impartation, having touched in faith the workings of the Holy Spirit to do miracles.

Common Sense

Some days, despite our best efforts and searching, we lack obvious answers. How then do we proceed? Let's say, for example, that we have a major ongoing responsibility of some kind. Big changes are not yet indicated or imminent but there is still the desire for progress. What do we do? In this case, the only recourse is to continue doing what we intuitively know to do. Then we also experiment, using common sense.

How "common" is common sense?

I have discovered personally that God often plants a seed thought or impression into my mind and heart. When I need answers, thoughts begin to flow. Frequently, this happens as I wake up in the morning. It also happens sometimes when I am considering and meditating on a situation. *Intuitive thoughts and authentic answers should be common for everyone who is knocking and seeking and expecting.*

If the thought is unusual or cutting-edge, I typically will ask questions and inter-relate with others I trust—parents, peers, businessmen—who are experts in that particular area of need. You see, other mature people often can be our safeguard because they also have been given common sense as part of their maturing process.

Other mature people often can be our safeguard because they also have been given common sense as part of their maturing process.

Rarely do we humans get full answers in one overnight lesson. How I wish it was that easy! Usually the lessons are separated into "chapters" and continue to expand and grow over many years. God allows most answers to come line on line, here a little, there a little. Frequently, a key element in that "little by little" will come from another inspired human source or resource. Sometimes the answer will come from some other part of the natural creation, often unexpectedly.

An expert in shrimp farming once told me that while in Ecuador he observed that following heavy tropical rains, shrimp still grew well in the rain-swollen ponds. Until that discovery he had raised shrimp in ocean saltwater ponds like everyone else. The goal was always to keep the water at the perfect salinity as genuine ocean water. Following this observation he began to experiment raising shrimp in fresh water ponds. By trial and error he discovered that if he acclimated the shrimp gradually over a two-week period, they would survive and grow normally. No one had ever done this before. This inspiration was based on observing something that occurred in nature. And he was tuned in! Then he used common sense as he perfected his experiment. Today he successfully manages large fresh water shrimp ponds in Arizona. As we increase our observational and intuitive capabilities, common sense answers begin to come more readily and more often. We develop more confidence. *Common sense becomes more common!*

Often, common sense will be inspired through the reading of books or articles. Something "leaps" off the page at us and we "know" intuitively that it is part of our answer. Taking what we perceive, we then test that conclusion on an experimental basis, watching for good fruit. Wisdom and knowledge can also be supernatural gifts, as it was with Solomon. But moving effectively in our gifts usually also requires experimentation, learning and expanding that which already produces promising results. Rather than a lack of faith, this is precisely the mechanism used to "test the spirits" in order to honestly judge the source. Testing means to give it a trial run. Does it bear good fruit or not? If not, shuck it. If so, add it to the list of successes! We are all called to "prove all things" (1 Jn. 1:4), and then to "hold fast to that which is good" (1 Thess. 5:21).

A lesson I learned from my father, although he did not use these precise words, was, "Nothing ventured, nothing gained." Remember Thomas Edison, who failed hundreds of times before finding the right filament material to make a successful light bulb. *We must be willing to experiment, innovate and press on beyond past failures if we are to "win the prize!"*

Be A Lighthouse

As you and I diligently practice what we firmly believe, others will observe, ponder and occasionally ask questions. It consistently amazes me, however, how unobservant and dogmatic human nature is. Most people want to be part of a tight matrix system. They are not ready to be unplugged from the umbilical cord of the system and go out under their own power. This probably describes many, perhaps most, of our personal friends, relatives, fellow workers and neighbors. Traditional religion, educators and professionals are at the top of this unfortunate list. Nearly everyone is fearful of being a "maverick". They will fight to protect a failed system because they are hopelessly dependent upon that system. They have an innate fear of disrupting the system because it might adversely affect their security, their paycheck and their retirement.

Nearly everyone is fearful of being a "maverick". They will fight to protect a failed system because they are hopelessly dependent upon that system.

Many are tied to the system by tight financial and commercial interests. Their minds cannot conceive of something different or better. They have built something and become dependent on its continued success. Going back to natural law is inconceivable to them because their present status depends on merchandizing goods, personal power or political correctness as the backbone of their success. Sometimes the desire to be free stirs in their hearts but more often than not, *fear wins out over faith*! And so they fight to keep their flimsy failing system alive.

Let me share a gem of practical counsel. It is a truism that for any commodity to be effectively exported, its benefit must first be proven at the local level. When the home environment benefits from practical "home spun" but revolutionary answers, that same creative discovery becomes a powerful catalyst for change. So my advice is that we must carefully prove our solutions first in our own backyard, our neighbors field, and in our local environment *before* excitedly exporting it as our awesome "solution"! First, refine it, test it, prove it and then market it!

For instance, my own solutions or methods must consistently serve first in my veterinary clinic before I teach it at a veterinary conference. Any solution you develop must be proven to work in your home or job or field before you shout it from the housetop. Otherwise, we will both be chasing wind.

It is not easy to unplug from a system that has become a "comfort zone". But there is always a "better" mousetrap, an improved answer to an old problem! And as children of God, we are the ones called to be that answer.

Remember my melon story from chapter two? I was able to grow and demonstrate to others 300 melons growing on 3 hills of melon plants. This is virtually impossible. I was more shocked than anybody! In fact I was stunned! What I didn't tell you earlier was that at the same time nearby I also had hills of corn that produced 2 and sometimes *3 full ears per stalk*. I showed a few folks, and of course received positive remarks. They thought this was interesting and unique—but to my disappointment not a single person asked me for my secret! Mere observation of the phenomena seemed to be the limit of their interest. None of them displayed any interest in learning how to grow melons or corn like that for themselves.

But for me that experience was a stunning turning point. It was another confirmation that I was on the right track. And there will be more opportunities to be a lighthouse in the future, when some other individual or group of individuals is ready to be "turned on" by the possibilities of 100-fold supernatural production!

Use Professional Guidance

Professional guidance is often useful and even wise, but don't become dazzled or addicted to the experts! I am impressed by how many sincere professionals are out there, who often help to reveal a part of the solution. But if I follow any professional blindly, I also accept his or her limitations. "Here a little, there a little," seems to be a clear divine principle.

For instance, a few years ago I attended a seminar with the man who is listed in the Guinness Book of World Records for the growing world's tallest tomato plants. He had to build wooden frames with ladders around his plants, with various landings, just to pick the tomatoes—tomatoes harvested by the bushels full! I was glad to be challenged by his extensive experience. If I were a tomato grower I would accept this man as my mentor!

So brothers and sisters, glean in every field where you are invited and accepted. More importantly, ask for divine guidance; accepting it by any means that God chooses to reveal it. For the Lord God Himself is the professional of professionals!

Here is another key: do not go beyond your own internal peace, wisdom, and heart witness. How often I have heard this lament, "I knew it was wrong, but didn't know what else to do!" Or, "My pet died unexpectedly because of the wrong treatment!" Did you know that upon autopsy approximately 50% of both animals and humans were found to have been treated for the *wrong disease*? These are the hard lessons of life. We alone must bear the personal responsibility for the health decisions of both our animals and of ourselves. Therefore, never relinquish that responsibility to another "professional," no matter how impressive his or her credentials. *Above all, never violate your own inner sense of conscience or witness!* The Word says to "Wait on the Lord." That means to "wait" until you receive specific direction, peace of heart, or an inner knowing of how to proceed.

Prayer

We have both a mandate and an opportunity to bathe our work and our labors in prayer. We have the ability within us to minister with both our hands and our hearts. We are only limited by the box we live in. We can stretch and anoint everything we do with prayer, with oils and nutrients, and with life-enhancing sprays.

Specific prayer for the land, for the soil and for the animals must be counted as both a work of love as well as a privilege. Could there be a better way to join and harmonize with nature and nature's God? If prayer can move that proverbial mountain, then what effect might prayer have on living creatures? If prayer could shrivel a fig tree overnight, and it did, what might it accomplish in bringing a fig tree back into productivity? If prayer can direct the fish in the sea, so many fish that Peter's net was tested to the limit, what effect might it have on grasshoppers, viruses and bacteria in the opposite direction? What power and authority have we left untapped because of *unbelief*?

If prayer can move that proverbial mountain, then what effect might prayer have on living creatures?

Remember that we are ambassadors of Christ, commissioned by God to minister the "word of reconciliation." Too often, however, we have our hands out for blessings before we deal with the mess in our own lives and hearts. Solving those heart issues is the first step in ministering to the creation, ministering the word of reconciliation! We cannot minister out of lack. We must minister out of overflow!

Scripture counsels us to "seek first the Kingdom of God and His righteousness," and all the other things we need will automatically follow (see Mt. 6:33). The answers to the world's problems are very simple. Man was created to rule over the earth, but to do so by being in fellowship with God. Without God our own strength automatically gets us into a peck of trouble. *By the end of this age all mankind will have learned this important lesson: that we cannot make it without God!*

Therefore we must each reach out and pour God's redemptive love into everything under our roof, in our fields and on the job. Literally and actively we must touch and redemptively love and empower everything under our jurisdiction. Paul said to "bless and curse not." Blessing is the highest way to effect change! We can only empower creative change by staying in tune and in flow with the promises given in God's Word! Bless the land. Bless the animals. Bless our co-workers. Bless the bugs and bless the beetles! As we reach upward and outward, we must also remain humble. *We have a destiny to travel into places of discovery and creativity that few have ever even dreamed of!*

It will take great strength to reach outward in our resistant society. Often we will be sharply misunderstood. It will take proactive steps to correct those age-old curses over our homes and over our fields. We are called to break those curses! We are called to break them by dealing with our own root problems. In many cases this will require forgiveness and repentance—dealing with and releasing the roots of our own bitter judgments and experiences. The roots of these negative judgments are usually found to have their source in our own internal spiritual darkness. Bitterness, anger and fear only multiply in the dark.

We must right now let the light shine inside ourselves before it can reflect outward. Only then do we have the hope of bringing genuine healing and light into society. Only then will our light shine brilliantly before men. Then and only then will others respond to a power and authority greater than themselves—and greatly desire it for themselves! All this is empowered through the energy and authority of prayer. Prayer changes things!

Summary

1. The spiritual realm has tremendous power to effect change in the natural order, either for good or bad.
2. Use of Kingdom methods and Kingdom principles will bring about Kingdom breakthroughs.
3. The anointing is the ability to accomplish tasks under the inspiration and personal direction of the Holy Spirit.
4. Intuitive thoughts and authentic answers should be common for everyone who is knocking and seeking and expecting.
5. Moving effectively in our gifts usually also requires experimentation, learning and expanding that which already produces promising results.
6. For any commodity to be effectively exported, its benefit must first be proven at the local level.
7. Professional guidance is often useful and even wise, but don't become dazzled or addicted to the experts—because experts also have limitations.
8. Above all, never violate your own inner sense of conscience or witness!
9. We have both a mandate and an opportunity to bathe our work and our labors in prayer.
10. It will take proactive steps to correct those age-old curses over our homes and over our fields. We are called to break those curses!

Chapter Fourteen

LEARNING TO LISTEN TO GOD

"Lord download into us! Download Your likeness, restore Your image, empower us with creativity! I want my internal program to be compatible with Yours! My heart, mind and spirit are ready to be changed into Your likeness! I want You to program me because You know me better than I know myself. You know what I need to fulfill Your call on my life."

This might be an appropriate prayer for many believers in this high-tech, thoroughly computerized age in which we live today. In many ways, the human body could be likened to a complex machine. The human brain certainly is a highly sophisticated computer almost infinitely more complex than any devised by man.

Unfortunately, there is a disturbing trend in today's scientific and philosophical communities to attempt to reduce man to nothing more than a biological machine, an evolutionary accident, highly complex, to be sure, but an accident nonetheless. And this reductionist viewpoint is making its way into the larger culture.

Let me be clear: when I speak of the human mind and body in terms of computer programs, I am speaking symbolically. The human spirit is the most awesome computer ever invented, masterminded by the Creator of the universe. God is Himself Spirit, and He placed His image in each of us, somewhat like a divine computer program or operating system, so that we would think and act like Him.

The human spirit is the most awesome computer ever invented, masterminded by the Creator of the universe.

However, currently we are infected with a rogue virus; our monitor display is distorted and our files corrupted. We need a strong anti-viral program installed and a thorough system purge. The distortions and corruptions must be removed so we can interpret our divine programming accurately and display it properly. The old system is too corrupted to be salvaged. It must be completely replaced by a whole new system. The Bible calls this process *receiving a new heart and a new spirit, becoming new creatures in Christ.*

Whenever we write and add new materials to the "hard drive" (our heart) of our new system, we must depend on the divine "spell check" to help us avoid misunderstandings and misinformation. Up to now we have limited the Almighty. The smallest in the Kingdom of Heaven has the potential to be greater than John the Baptist! (Mt 11:11-12) John was the last faithful model of a passing age. He said that he was not worthy to untie the sandals of the Messiah, Jesus Christ, who was the new model for the coming age. Jesus Himself promised that *corporately* our works would be greater than His were during the time when He was limited to a human body on this earth. This miracle would be possible because He could now in this present age work through millions of people as each was faithful to bring heaven down into the earthly realm. He would be the "head" directing restoration of the realm called earth. Believers would be his "body" with heart, hands and feet to demonstrate His ongoing works on earth. This would include "making disciples" by teaching Kingdom principles to benefit every nation on the earth. Is this exciting or what? Are we finally ready to enter fully into that calling?

When we were birthed into this world as babies we were totally dependent on our parents. As adults we have become independent and selfish. We must again become as little children. Nicodemus did not understand this mystery. When Jesus told him, "Unless one is born again, he cannot see the kingdom of God," he asked, "Can a man be born when he is old? Can he enter a second time into his mother's womb and be born?" (Jn. 3:3-4)

Nope, that was not God's plan. Nicodemus was right: no one can be reborn physically. Jesus was talking about a *rebirth of spirit,* where believers are given a new heart and a new spirit and enter into spiritual life, life that has no end! We were created to be sons and daughters of God—chosen by divine invitation and personal decision to be recreated spiritually so that a *new script* could be written.

This means that we have been adopted into a great spiritual family made up of spiritual brothers and sisters from every nationality, ethnic group, language group and tribal affiliation. Collectively, we are *a new Man for a new age*!

In this newness of life we are to nurture child-like faith, a faith totally dependent on a trust relationship with our heavenly Father, whose desire is to nurture, discipline and train us into our highest destiny and calling. We are called to be raised on our Father's knee and to be fed suitable daily food that nourishes our heart and spirit. We are called to depend on the Father just as Jesus did. Scripture reveals that Jesus did not speak until the Father spoke and did not move until the Father moved. That is *total dependence on the Father,* and we must learn it if we are to grow into His full image and nature, move like He moves, and create like He creates. It is then that he will "give us the Kingdom." Giving us the Kingdom has been God's plan and purpose from the beginning of the creation. But first we must prove ourselves faithful in the "little things." This invitation is open to anybody. How exciting it is to live in a day of such great opportunity!

Giving us the Kingdom has been God's plan and purpose from the beginning of the creation..... How exciting it is to live in a day of such great opportunity!

A True Story

Opportunity profits us nothing, however, if we ignore it. This is true whether we are talking about healing the land, healing ourselves or listening to God. To illustrate, let me share with you a sad, tragic story.

I know a brilliant doctor who cured himself of terminal cancer. Unfortunately, the same was not true for his wife. For long years she faithfully studied and worked at his side. Together they built a successful healing practice based on the principles and processes he had developed in dealing with his own disease. Through their compassionate and commonsense ministry, thousands of people found hope and healing from the ravages of cancer and other serious illnesses. This wonderful couple saw their work blossom as a true and valuable service to mankind.

Eventually, however, the wife was diagnosed with malignant breast cancer of an extremely aggressive nature. The cancer spread rapidly, invading many of her internal organs. Her husband pleaded with her to begin an aggressive cancer program, the same one that had worked so well for himself as well as for hundreds of their clients and friends. For some unidentified reason, she adamantly refused to do for herself what both he and she had counseled many others. He was devastated.

Apparently, she did not want to be bothered with the radical change of diet and supplements that would be necessary, not to mention aggressively facing and conquering the emotional fears associated with malignant cancer. *Why was it too much for her to do for herself the very same programs that she had successfully taught to others?*

One day their son said to his father, "Dad, let me take Mom to our mountain cabin, and I will have a talk with her. She will not listen to you. I believe I can convince her." The next morning, however, his mother angrily threw all of her nutrients across the room into the wall and split the jar. She absolutely refused to cooperate. What she often had advised others to do, with positive results, she refused to do for herself. Sadly, the son informed his father later that morning that he too had failed. She died a few months later. The husband, this brilliant, successful, compassionate and caring health care professional, sadly lamented that he had lost "the love of his life." Why?

All of us are born with a personal destiny planned by God. But we also have freedom of choice. Each day of our lives is filled with opportunities to make choices, either good or bad. For some unknown reason this cherished women, who had many accolades to her honor, gave into the spirit of personal hopelessness. When faced with a life-threatening disease some part of her wanted to quit—to die rather than live.

This is not easy to explain. She had everything a person could desire: success, reputation, a huge bank account, a loving husband and family. But something inside her still remained empty, undecided and hurting. Offered both hope and help, she closed herself off. That empty space inside refused to respond to the answer of hope that was available. In her mind, death was the easier road and she took it. I had met this woman often and knew her quite well. Her decision to give up fit neither her temperament nor her nature. What is it that robs the will to live from the heart and soul of a person who, by all appearances, had everything to live for?

In her mind, death was the easier road and she took it.... What is it that robs the will to live from the heart and soul of a person who, by all appearances, had everything to live for?

Dr. Christopher taught in one of his courses: "Every disease known to mankind has been cured. However not every person with any particular disease can be cured. The problem is many refuse to follow the path to cure!" Stated another way: "*Every disease has a cure, but not everyone will avail themselves of that cure.*"

Preparing Our Hearts to Hear

Everyone on earth faces this same predicament of hope versus hopelessness. Our quality of life and health depends as much and even more on the choices we make as it does on external circumstances and other related factors. Things are getting tougher out there on the world stage. Disease is on the march, much of the land, water and air is poisoned—and every day millions of people make unwise and unhealthy choices at every level of life. Currently, the prognosis does not look too good!

Asking the question, "*Doctor, can you help me*?" is one way to approach the present dilemma. A better question is: "*Doctor, will you join me as one part of my team—a team that will work together on the road to finding my solution*?"

Millions are in the valley of decision. However, very few are looking in the right place for the right answers, even though answers abound. For Christian believers (as well as *all* who genuinely seek the truth), one of the right places to look for answers is in the wisdom and Word of God. If we will only learn to listen and heed the counsel of our Creator, we will save ourselves bushels of trouble!

Millions are in the valley of decision. However, very few are looking in the right place for the right answers, even though answers abound.

Like anything worthwhile, learning to listen to God takes practice and planning. God is always speaking but we do not always hear Him because we have not trained ourselves to listen. We have not positioned our hearts spiritually through obedience and right living to be sensitive to His voice. There are some positive steps we can take to increase our sensitivity and better prepare ourselves to hear the voice of the Lord when He speaks.

For the material that follows, on the art of hearing from God, I am indebted to Dr. Mark Virkler of Christian Leadership University.[28]

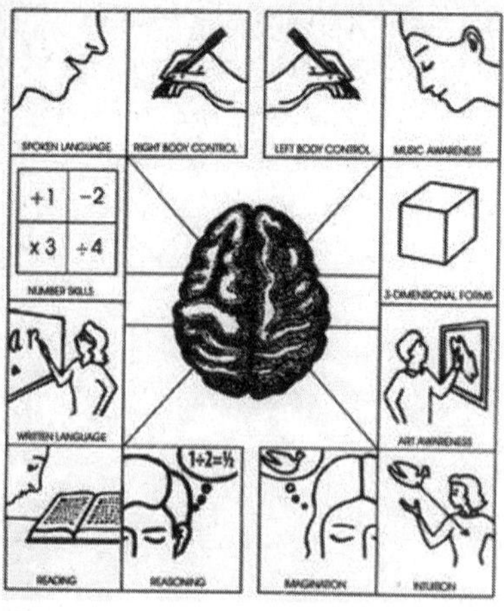

You Can Hear God's Voice!

By Dr. Mark Virkler

Reprinted by Permission

The age in which we live is so married to rationalism and cognitive, analytical thought that we almost mock when we hear of one actually claiming to be able to hear the voice of God. However, we do not scoff, for several reasons. First, men and women throughout the Bible heard God's voice. Also, there are some highly effective and reputable men and women of God alive today who demonstrate that they hear God's voice. Finally, there is a deep hunger within us all to commune with God, and hear Him speak within our hearts.

As a born-again, Bible-believing Christian, I struggled unsuccessfully for years to hear God's voice. I prayed, fasted, studied my Bible and listened for a voice within, all to no avail. **There was no inner voice that I could hear!** Then God set me aside for a year to study, read, and experiment in the area of learning to hear His voice. During that time, the Lord taught me **four keys that opened the door to two-way prayer.** I have discovered that not only do they work for me, but they have worked for many thousands of believers who have been taught to use them, bringing tremendous intimacy to their Christian experience and transforming their very way of living. This will happen to you also as you seek God, utilizing the following four keys. They are all found in Habakkuk 2:1-2. I encourage you to read this passage before going on.

I prayed, fasted, studied my Bible and listened for a voice within, all to no avail. There was no inner voice that I could hear

Key #1 – God's voice in our hearts sounds like a flow of spontaneous thoughts. Therefore, when I tune to God, I tune to spontaneity.

The Bible says that the Lord answered me and said...(Hab. 2:2). Habakkuk knew the sound of God's voice. Elijah described it as a still, small voice (I Kings 19:12). I had always listened for an inner **audible** voice, and surely God can and does speak that way at times. However, I have found that for most of us, most of the time, **God's inner voice comes to us as spontaneous thoughts, visions, feelings, or impressions.** For example, haven't each of us had the experience of driving down the road and having **a thought come to us** to pray for a certain person? We generally acknowledge this to be the voice of God calling us to pray for that individual. My question to you is, "What did God's voice sound like as you drove in your car? Was it an inner, audible voice, or was it a spontaneous thought that lit upon your mind?" Most of you would say that God's voice came to you as a spontaneous thought.

I have found that for most of us, most of the time, God's inner voice comes to us as spontaneous thoughts, visions, feelings, or impressions.

So I thought to myself, "Maybe when I listen for God's voice, I should be listening for a flow of spontaneous thoughts. Maybe spirit-level communication is received as spontaneous thoughts, impressions, feelings, and visions." Through experimentation and feedback from thousands of others, I am now convinced that this is so.

The Bible confirms this in many ways. The definition of *paga*, the Hebrew word for intercession, is "a chance encounter or an accidental intersecting." When God lays people on our hearts for intercession, He does it through *paga*, a chance-encounter thought, accidentally intersecting our thought processes. Therefore, when I tune to God, I tune to chance-encounter thoughts or spontaneous thoughts. When I am poised quietly before God in prayer, I have found that the flow of spontaneous thoughts that comes is quite definitely from God.

Key #2 – I must learn to still my own thoughts and emotions, so that I can sense God's flow of thoughts and emotions within me.

Habakkuk said, "I will stand on my guard post and station myself on the rampart..." (Hab. 2:1). Habakkuk knew that in order to hear God's quiet, inner, spontaneous thoughts, he had to first go to a quiet place and still his own thoughts and emotions. Psalm 46:10 encourages us to be still, and know that He is God. There is a deep inner knowing (spontaneous flow) in our spirits that each of us can experience when we quiet our flesh and our minds.

There is a deep inner knowing (spontaneous flow) in our spirits that each of us can experience when we quiet our flesh and our minds.

I have found several simple ways to quiet myself so that I can more readily pick up God's spontaneous flow. Loving God through a quiet worship song is a most effective means for me (note II Kings 3:15). It is as I become still (thoughts, will, and emotions) and am poised before God that the divine flow is realized. Therefore, after I worship quietly and then become still, I open myself for that spontaneous flow. If thoughts come to me of things I have forgotten to do, I write them down and then dismiss them. If thoughts of guilt or unworthiness come to my mind, I repent thoroughly, receive the washing of the blood of the Lamb, and put on His robe of righteousness, seeing myself spotless before the presence of God (Is. 61:10; Col. 1:22).

As I fix my gaze upon Jesus (Heb. 12:2), becoming quiet in His presence, and sharing with Him what is on my heart, I find that two-way dialogue begins to flow. Spontaneous thoughts flow from the throne of God to me, and I find that I am actually conversing with the King of Kings.

It is very important that you become still and properly focused if you are going to receive the pure word of God. If you are not still, you will simply be receiving your own thoughts. If you are not properly focused on Jesus, you will receive an impure flow, because the intuitive flow comes out of that upon which you have fixed your eyes. Therefore, if you fix your eyes upon Jesus, the intuitive flow comes from Jesus. If you fix your gaze upon some desire of your heart, the intuitive flow comes out of that desire of your heart. To have a pure flow you must first of all become still, and secondly, you must carefully fix your eyes upon Jesus. Again I will say, quietly worshiping the King, and then receiving out of the stillness that follows quite easily accomplishes this.

Key #3 – As I pray, I fix the eyes of my heart upon Jesus, seeing in the Spirit the dreams and visions of Almighty God.

We have already alluded to this principle in the previous paragraphs; however, we need to develop it a bit further. Habakkuk said, "I will keep watch to see," and God said, "Record the vision" (Hab. 2:1-2). It is very interesting that Habakkuk was going to actually start looking for vision as he prayed. He was going to open the eyes of his heart, and look into the spirit world to see what God wanted to show him. This is an intriguing idea.

I had never thought of opening the eyes of my heart and looking for vision. However, the more I thought of it, the more I realized this was exactly what God intends for me to do. He gave me eyes in my heart. They are to be used to see in the spirit world the vision and movement of Almighty God. I believe there is an active spirit world functioning all around me. This world is full of angels, demons, the Holy Spirit, the omnipresent God, and His omnipresent Son, Jesus. There is no reason for me not to see it, other than my rational culture, which tells me not to believe it is even there and provides no instruction on how to become open to seeing this spirit world.

The most obvious prerequisite to seeing is that we need to look. Daniel was seeing a vision in his mind and he said, "I was looking...I kept looking...I kept looking" (Dan. 7:2,9,13). Now as I pray, I look for Jesus present with me, and I watch Him as He speaks to me, doing and saying the things that are on His heart. Many Christians will find that if they will only look, they will see. Jesus is Emmanuel, God *with* us (Matt. 1:23). It is as simple as that. You will see a spontaneous inner vision in a manner similar to receiving spontaneous inner thoughts. You can see Christ present with you in a comfortable setting, because **Christ *is present with you in a comfortable setting.*** Actually, you will probably discover that inner vision comes so easily you will have a tendency to reject it, thinking that it is just you. (Doubt is Satan's most effective weapon against the Church.) However, if you will persist in recording these visions, your doubt will soon be overcome by faith as you recognize that the content of them could only be birthed in Almighty God.

The most obvious prerequisite to seeing is that we need to look.

God continually revealed Himself to His covenant people using dream and vision. He did so from Genesis to Revelation and said that, since the Holy Spirit was poured out in Acts 2, we should expect to receive a continuing flow of dreams and visions (Acts 2:1-4,17). Jesus, our perfect Example, demonstrated this ability of living out of ongoing contact with Almighty God. He said that He did nothing on His own initiative, but only that which He ***SAW the Father doing, and HEARD the Father saying*** (Jn. 5:19,20,30). ***What an incredible way to live!***

Is it actually possible for us to live out of the divine initiative as Jesus did? A major purpose of Jesus' death and resurrection was that the veil be torn from top to bottom, giving us access into the immediate presence of God, and we are commanded to draw near (Lk. 23:45; Heb. l0: 19-22). Therefore, even though what

I am describing seems a bit unusual to a rational twentieth-century culture, it is demonstrated and described as being a central biblical teaching and experience. *It is time to restore to the Church all that belongs to the Church.*

Because of their intensely rational nature and existence in an overly-rational culture, some will need more assistance and understanding of these truths before they can move into them. They will find this help in the book *Communion With God* by the same authors.

Key #4 – Journaling, the writing out of our prayers and God's answers, provides a great new freedom in hearing God's voice.

God told Habakkuk to record the vision and inscribe it on tablets...(Hab. 2:2). It had never crossed my mind to write out my prayers and God's answers as Habakkuk did at God's command. If you begin to search Scripture for this idea, you will find hundreds of chapters demonstrating it (Psalms, many of the prophets, Revelation). Why then hadn't I ever thought of it?

I called the process "journaling," and I began experimenting with it. I discovered it to be a fabulous facilitator to clearly discerning God's inner, spontaneous flow, because as I journaled **I was able to write in faith for long periods of time,** simply believing it was God. I did not have to test it as I was receiving it (which jams one's receiver), because I knew that when the flow was over **I could go back and test and examine it carefully,** making sure that it lined up with Scripture.

I did not have to test it as I was receiving it (which jams one's receiver), because I knew that when the flow was over I could go back and test and examine it carefully, making sure that it lined up with Scripture.

You will be amazed when you attempt journaling. Doubt may hinder you at first, but throw it off, reminding yourself that it is a biblical concept, and that God is present, speaking to His children. Don't take yourself too seriously. When you do, you become tense and get in the way of the Holy Spirit's movement. It is when we cease **our labors** and enter His rest that God is free to flow (Heb. 4:10). Therefore, put a smile on your face, sit back comfortably, get out your pen and paper, and turn your attention toward God in praise and worship, seeking His face. As you write out your question to God and become still, fixing your gaze on Jesus, Who is present with you, you will suddenly have a very good thought in response to your question. Don't doubt it, simply write it down. Later, as you read your journaling, you, too, will be blessed to discover that you are indeed dialoguing with God.

Some final notes: No one should attempt this without having first read through at least the New Testament (preferably, the entire Bible), nor should one attempt this unless he is submitted to solid, spiritual leadership. All major directional moves that come through journaling should be submitted before being acted upon.

Summary

1. The human spirit is the most awesome computer ever invented, masterminded by the Creator of the universe.
2. Jesus Himself promised that *corporately* our works would be greater than His were during the time when He was limited to a human body on this earth.
3. In this newness of life we are to nurture child-like faith, a faith totally dependent on a trust relationship with our heavenly Father, whose desire is to nurture, discipline and train us into our highest destiny and calling.
4. All of us are born with a personal destiny planned by God. But we also have freedom of choice.
5. Our quality of life and health depends as much and even more on the choices we make as on external circumstances and other factors.
6. Four keys to hearing God's voice:
   - Key #1 – God's voice in our hearts sounds like a flow of spontaneous thoughts. Therefore, when I tune to God, I tune to spontaneity.
   - Key #2 – I must learn to still my own thoughts and emotions, so that I can sense God's flow of thoughts and emotions within me.
   - Key #3 – As I pray, I fix the eyes of my heart upon Jesus, seeing in the Spirit the dreams and visions of Almighty God.
   - Key #4 – Journaling, the writing out of our prayers and God's answers, provides a great new freedom in hearing God's voice.

Chapter Fifteen

TAMING THE TIGER!

"Welcome to our dimension. May you find it as exciting as we do!"
—Bea Lydecker, Animal trainer

"For every kind of beast and bird, of reptile and creature of the sea, is tamed and has been tamed by mankind."
James 3:7

At a conference recently a health professional asked me for advice. She had been feeding a feral cat for about a year. During that time she observed that her family cat and this semi-wild cat were "in love," as she put it. But somehow she as a human was not included in that bond. Although she fed the feral cat, it would never let her get any closer than three feet. Although feral, it was an attractive animal, sleek and beautiful. This lady's question to me was whether there was anything she could do to facilitate a better relationship? She wanted to gain the trust and affection of this suspicious cat.

Throughout history there have been many touching stories of innovative people who had the ability to develop close relationships with wild or abused animals. St. Francis of Assisi is probably the most familiar, although there are dozens of other historical figures who had a similar gift.

Animals have a natural fear of mankind. This is probably for their own good, given mankind's history of abusing the creation. Currently, according to researchers, as many as 1000 species die off every year because of man's abuse of the planet. *We who were intended to be stewards of the creation have gone mad!* Morally we have broken trust with the created order we were supposed to manage. Man once hunted out of necessity, to provide food and clothing for survival. Now he hunts for pleasure, and not always in the forests and woodlands.

Some people, especially those who live in the concrete jungle, have been known to kill for a measly dollar or for a pair of designer sneakers. Certainly everyone remembers the appalling tragedy the Spring of 2007 when a deranged student at Virginia Tech University intentionally murdered 32 people before taking his own life. Humans have been known to torture, rape and mutilate for the pleasure of it. No wonder animals prefer to keep their distance! Smart dudes, these animals!

And no wonder God put the "fear and dread" of mankind in animals' hearts after the flood (Genesis 9:2.) Without this inborn wariness of man "the destroyer," many beautiful creatures would have been long extinct, erased from the planet by the cruelty of violent men as they trap and kill, sometimes in ignorance but many times out of rage and violence.

Nature in its raw state is not nearly as violent as man! Have you ever visited a place deep in the forest or jungle and noted the quietness and peace that prevails there? Hunters and explorers who come to an area of the wild untouched by man often experience a peculiar awe in such a place. Many have remarked of an incredible sense of peace and quietness so tangible that they naturally found themselves speaking in whispers. *To many people, wilderness untouched by man feels like one is suddenly on holy ground, in a quiet sanctuary or an ancient cathedral filled with the presence of God.*

Hunters and explorers who come to an area of the wild untouched by man often experience a peculiar awe in such a place.

The lady who approached me at the conference was searching for a way to dispel the innate fear of her in this feral cat she had been feeding. I answered her out of my own experience and practice. Instinctively, I gave her a many-faceted "holistic" answer to her question.

Step #1: Nutrition

First, of course, I talked about nutrition. If you have read this far you should know by now that I almost always begin with nutrition because it is foundational. As we have already seen, most of today's refined foods are laced with poisonous chemicals that aggravate and sensitize the delicate nervous systems of people and pets alike. I have met many pet trainers who have learned this same lesson and who advise their clients: "Get your pet on natural food, add some natural B vitamins, and above all get them off that over-stimulating junk formula that fries the brain. Try that for two weeks and then come back to me and I will see if I can unwire your pet's brain so it will function again."

Long ago the discovery was made that sick food results in sick livers. And a sick liver often leads to extremes of anger, anxiety and fear. I advised my questioner to be good to her pet's liver, and that of the feral cat as well. I suggested that she include liver-protecting foods such as a bit of raw grated beet, liver-building herbs, raw egg yolk (which is the colostrum of the baby chick), and even some raw organic liver.

Long ago the discovery was made that sick food results in sick livers. And a sick liver often leads to extremes of anger, anxiety and fear.

As part of basic nutrition I talked about a great "Super Supplement" that I sell in my office. This supplement contains whole ground flax seed, which is high in healing Omega 3 fatty acids. It includes ocean kelp and alfalfa for their unique mineral and nutrient properties—as well as many other healing herbs and concentrated natural ingredients. When the body is fully nourished, the result is a calmer and happier temperament.

Both people and pets feel more social when they eat right. This fact also fits the age-old advice: "The way to the heart is through the stomach!" I explained to her that this sage advice also applies to animals! But the healing food we recommend must be of a quality way above average! The goal is to feed the heart as well as to nourish the liver and the brain. Today's commercial junk food overloads the over-stressed liver and brain with toxins that feed that skittish sense of being disconnected and "on-edge."

Step #2: Natural Flower Essences

Secondly, I shared with her the advantage of adding a mixture of natural flower essences into daily bowls of food. Flower Essences are distilled from real flower petals. These essences are one group of nature's remedies for many types of emotional stress. The most famous are combinations of Dr. Bach Flower Essences. Other effective sources are also available. Check your local health store or natural health practitioner. Also many of these will one day be available on my website: www.mind-bodyministries.com.

The specific healing remedy I prescribed was called, quite appropriately, "Fear and Anxiety." Often I add another blend called "Calming." Sometimes

I also include "Vicious," which I suggested adding to the water bowl. Selecting the proper "flower essence," however, depends on identifying the individual personality type or emotional disturbance. Essences extracted from flower petals are gentle but at the same time powerful remedies. They balance the brain as well as the body and never do any harm. Did this feral cat have anything to fear from this particular woman? Of course not!

Step #3: Be Non-threatening

Thirdly, I recommended that she should move down to the cat's level. Leaders should be servants, right? I advised her to place the food at the safe distance of three feet and then simply to sit or lie quietly in a non-threatening manner. She should also avoid staring, as intense mental focusing in the direction of the animal would be perceived as threatening and an invasion of privacy.

Avoid staring, as intense mental focusing in the direction of the animal would be perceived as threatening and an invasion of privacy.

It is well documented that in the wild, after a lion has killed and eaten its prey and is satisfied, animals nearby will sense that there is nothing to fear. *Sometimes an antelope will graze within three feet of a satisfied lion when the lion's belly is full.* Does this amaze you, as it amazes me? Not that I am ready to practice that particular experiment! Personally, I will observe from a safe distance with binoculars. Yet every day I deal with dogs and cats with four sharp fangs, and that is a challenge I love and enjoy!

How do I deal with those sharp teeth in my office? Instead of installing a cold, stainless steel table, I position at a homey desk, use a simple desk chair surrounded with a comfortable rug or two. We have no cages and no kennel in my facility, meaning there are no barking dogs working up a commotion in the background. Add a soft touch, a quiet voice, within a non-threatening environment—and presto, we have established a routine that does wonders in creating a trustful atmosphere. In other words, we have created an atmosphere that is safe and inviting.

You see, my heart is to connect with animals. In the office my movements are unhurried and my voice is gentle. This creates that sense of safety. Rather than intrude in a hurried, business-like manner, I patiently wait until I am invited into the animal's space. Can you see my stretched out hand allowing *them to* ***first approach and touch me***? After I have won their trust, I can easily complete my exam with less stress or struggle. Isn't that the way it should be done?

This scene occurs only if we change our mindset from that of being a superior to that of being a servant. Our goal should be to cooperate with health rather than legislate our pre-determined will. Such an attitude requires a change of paradigms. A lasting companionship relationship is built only as we practice this new set of priorities. I try to model that atmosphere in my office.

Step #4: Let the animal make the first move

My fourth bit of advice to this woman was to suggest that she allow the feral cat to move into her space and not vice versa. One way of inviting companionship is with a delicate morsel of tasty tuna. This is similar to offering a nut to a squirrel or a crumb of popcorn to a hungry bird. Sometimes, by using these patient techniques, squirrels and birds will eat out of one's hand! But it takes quite a bit of practice and patience. And victory is unlikely if one has an ulterior motive. *Animals sense ulterior motives more quickly than most humans!* Therefore I suggest creating opportunities by building this more inviting space. Tasty food definitely helps!

Step #5: Use a neutral object to build trust

Next, I offered a technical idea, a technique I have used often in my office with a fearful animal. My hand is a part of me, which the animal may fear. But if I hold in my hand a pen or other long object that is an extension of me—but is not me—the animal often will view that object as something curious and safe. Invariably, the curious pet will extend its nose to "check it out." I then gently rub the object over its nose, face or whiskers, emulating a gentle message. The next thing that happens is a reflex response where the animal rubs back on the object; it is now responding to the attention! I have extended my space toward it, brought my field closer to it and established a respectful rapport. Often, almost as if by magic, trust strengthens and a safe although tentative bond is established.

My hand is a part of me, which the animal may fear. But if I hold in my hand a pen or other long object that is an extension of me—but is not me—the animal often will view that object as something curious and safe.

Step #6: Understand and use non-verbal communication

Finally, I explained that animals communicate by non-verbal communication. With animals it clearly is not the exact words we speak but the *tone of voice* we use. Even more than that, animals seem to respond to the *visual pictures* we project from our mind or heart. It is as though animals have the ability to "read" our pictures.

Here is how one dog trainer explained this phenomenon to me. He observed that a successful trainer "sees" the animal performing exactly what he or she is asking of the dog. The voice, tone and body language flow in sync with that visual command. If the trainer expects the dog to "sit" next to him, he will project, speak and motion that exact picture.

For instance, if the dog (that rascal!) is lounging on the couch and that is a "no-no," an inexperienced person will "see" in his mind's eye the animal *on* the couch and then scold in a disgusted voice, "Get off that couch!" The poor dog is absolutely confused! "He sees me on the couch and yet he is hollering at me! I don't get it!" The dog is puzzled, confused, and defiantly difficult to train. All because of an owner who fails to communicate in *dog language*!

The perceptive trainer does not picture the dog on the couch because he expects and "sees" the dog on the floor. This is a totally different approach to the problem—and the results are just as different.

How does this example apply to the undomesticated tiger cat in question? I suggested to this curious health professional that, while squatting on the lawn herself, to picture or see in her mind's eye the feral cat lying quietly nearby, relaxed, unthreatened and unafraid. She could also speak or hum in gentle, soothing tones. Very likely, the cat would soon relax, lie sideways or roll over and perhaps even glance off in another direction. I told her that if she maintained this quiet, comfortable and meditative mood, then likely after a few days the cat would start momentarily drifting into a "catnap."

This won't work, you exclaim? Assuming you get into the right frame of mind, I am willing to assure you that these methods will unlock miracles! In fact I spoke with this same woman a few weeks later. She told me, "I have not had time to apply everything you taught me, but already I can report great success!"

Become Like Children

Thousands of others have accomplished similar feats. I know a young lady who, when a horse or llama escapes and is on the run, is called in to help. Somehow she has developed a miracle connection with fearful animals. She walks toward the apprehensive animal very calmly, arm outstretched. And rather than galloping away, the animal walks toward her with trust. Onlookers are amazed!

I have noticed also that children tend to connect more naturally with animals than we more sophisticated adults. Somewhere along the way we lost it. That ability got cultured out of us by the sophisticated educational system of technology and conventional test-tube science. The only things stopping us are our mental blocks, our dominant attitude and our conventional cultural brain-washing.

I have noticed also that children tend to connect more naturally with animals than we more sophisticated adults.

We must again become like little children, with the heart and faith of innocence. Then I predict that you and I will be surprised and pleased with first-class results. And once we obtain our first results, it will have a domino effect into other areas of our lives. *We are called to have a supernatural connection with the creation.* Do you believe that? If that seems like a dream, I just taught you a narrative of how to begin "taming the tiger." Thousands have this ability. Remember the quote at the beginning of this chapter? "For every kind of beast and bird, of reptile and creature of the sea, is tamed and has been tamed by mankind." That was written some 2000 years ago. No exceptions, James noted. Mankind definitely has this ability, a gift from God. Genetically we have all been created with the ability to bring creation into harmony. It is time to awaken this latent ability deeply ingrained within our genetic code. Do the keys I presented make sense to you, for the animals in your life?

With certain adaptations, this approach might even work with fearful and apprehensive people! Why limit the project?

Summary

1. Animals have a natural fear of mankind.
2. Nature in its raw state is not nearly as violent as man!
3. Get your pet on natural food. Both people and pets feel more social when they eat right.
4. Add a mixture of natural flower essences into daily bowls of food.
5. Move down to the animal's level.
6. Let the animal make the first move.
7. Use a neutral object to build trust.
8. Learn to use non-verbal communication.
9. We are called to have a supernatural connection with the creation.

Chapter Sixteen

CAN A HOPELESSLY DAMAGED EYE BE RESTORED?

"*The light of the body is the eye*"

(Matthew 6:22; Luke 11:33)

"*The eyes of the blind shall be opened*"

(Isaiah 35:5)

I want to share with you a true story that is an example of a holistic approach to healing. Even though the final chapter of this story has not yet been written, the progress made in the meantime indicates that there truly is hope for the hopeless!

A right eye was severely damaged after accidentally being blasted with a paint ball gun from one foot away. The eye globe was ruptured from both sides, the viscous fluid exploding outward and draining all over the victim's face. In addition, some surrounding muscles and tissues were torn. As would be expected, the pain was excruciating.

The emergency physician frankly gave no hope for saving the eye. Infection was probable. Of course, the victim and his family wanted to save the eye, if at all possible. What would you do in this situation?

Here is the scene I painted, based on a real case. Remember that impossible cases require creative imagination that often will stray outside the box.

We all like to believe in restoration, don't we? Does that include restoration of the eyes, particularly one damaged this severely? The prognosis was zero to zero that the eye would ever see again. Those are pretty grim odds. If sight was restored, it would have to be judged as no less than a miracle. Were there things to try that might increase those odds?

The prognosis was zero to zero that the eye would ever see again. Those are pretty grim odds. If sight was restored, it would have to be judged as no less than a miracle.

Certainly, it was completely appropriate to rush to the emergency room and receive the best emergency care possible. Following surgery, treatment and repair, however, the prognosis still was that no sight would return to the eye. All the parts were there, but everything seemed damaged beyond repair. The victim faced a dilemma. Were there any alternatives? Was a miracle possible? What would be the Kingdom approach to this type of crisis, whether involving human or animal?

A week after the incident I was called in to consult because of my knowledge and experience in naturopathic and homeopathic treatments. Following is the list of specific treatments and therapies that I recommended. Keep in mind that the goal was to save the eye, if possible. The eye is the "light" of the soul. We all wanted a miracle!

Keep in mind that the goal was to save the eye, if possible. The eye is the "light" of the soul. We all wanted a miracle!

In planning our approach I considered everything both natural and spiritual that would facilitate the body's own repair mechanism. God created the body, and there are principles of repair inherent in every cell of the body. Understanding that principle, I carefully advised the following.

1. MSM (methylsulfonylmethane) is a natural sulfur-related compound extracted from trees, and normal to the physiology of every living plant. Applied as a liquid in the eye, MSM is a powerful anti-inflammatory, speeds healing of damaged tissues and helps to alleviate pain. I have used MSM frequently as eye drops for glaucoma and various other inflammatory eye diseases. In addition, we decided to add a homeopathic eye remedy to the MSM drops, a combination known to help facilitate eye injury recovery. I had used this synergistic combination in dozens of other situations ranging from glaucoma to cataracts and chronic infections, consistently with positive results. I suggested applying these drops in the eye 6 times daily.

2. Magnetic therapy has a history dating back thousands of years. North pole negative polarity magnetic therapy is known to increase the circulation of healing, decrease pain, suppress infection, and helping to bring nutrition into the eye by regenerating the circulation of healing to an injured area. Healing often occurs in half the normal time using magnetic therapy. There are over 4000 medical research papers supporting magnetic therapy in medicine. I had recommended this therapy for hundreds of cases previously, with no known adverse effects. Sometimes miracles were reported. Therefore I suggested holding or bandaging the flexible magnetic pad over the injured eye up to 10 hours daily; or a minimum of 3 times daily for periods of 20 to 25 minutes at a time.

There are over 4000 medical research papers supporting magnetic therapy in medicine.

3. Nutrition is *always* a key to healing. In this case we must consider the best nutrition specific for nourishing the eye. I have a product manufactured especially for eye damage that includes herbs, gland and eye tissue, and other specific eye nutrients, which I recommended taking twice daily. Next, I stressed the importance of drinking plenty of water, because the eye is over 90% water; dehydration was not an option!

Consumption of plenty of *raw* foods was crucial also, especially carrots and other raw vegetables and fruits known for vitamin A, C, E and other valuable medicinal nutrients. In addition I emphasized those essential omega 3 fatty acids (Olive oil, flax oil and Cod Liver Oil), all known to be anti inflammatory, anti oxidant, and essential for health and healing. Many herbs and spices also have specific anti-inflammatory properties that should be carefully considered. In my practice I use compatibility testing to decide which supplements best fit the specific problem. When the product fits the problem, astonishing breakthroughs can be expected.

*Consumption of plenty of raw foods was crucial also, especially carrots and other **raw** vegetables and fruits known for vitamin A, C, E and other valuable medicinal nutrients.*

4. Frequency, sound, music, laser and Rife hertz treatments are rapidly becoming more widely used and available worldwide. I have an economical class II cold laser that I have used for more than a dozen years. This is based on photon light therapy that is documented and supported in hundreds of scientific papers, including the NASA space program! Therefore I often apply laser therapy in my office. Sometimes I rent or sell this instrument so that the client can bathe the area with this safe healing light several times daily. This specific laser is safe enough to be applied in the privacy of the home.

These types of cutting-edge instruments are becoming more commonly used in both the orthodox and alternative medical community. I believe these types of therapies will become some of the primary healing modalities of the future. At the same time I predict that drugs and chemicals will gradually go into the background. *Stick around and I believe you will see a revolution in health care in the not too distant future!*

5. Laying on of hands. Remember that *touch* is one of the keys to healing. The hand has powerful healing vibrations that have been scientifically documented. Here is what I advised. Because the right hand is the hand of ministry and authority, lay the palm of the right hand gently over and around the damaged eye. The left hand supports this by placing it on the exact opposite side of the head, creating a complete electromagnetic field of healing. The hands are gently held in this position for a minimum of 7 minutes.

*Remember that **touch** is one of the keys to healing. The hand has powerful healing vibrations that have been scientifically documented.*

Often there is an intuitive sense of how long to hold the hands in that position. Physically, this can be detected by an *involuntary deep breath* on the part of the pet, the patient or the healer. Sometimes the area will suddenly become warm, then cool off again. Holding the hands there longer would be of no extra benefit. The body and the spirit both know when the time is up and both have a mechanism by which that is registered: the deep involuntary breath, a deep inner knowing, or both.

6. See. The mind is a powerful tool for healing. I ask participants to "see" what they are expecting. It helps to know anatomy. In this case, I instructed the patient to "see" the destroyed eye coming back to normal, to "see" it being restored inside the eye socket, reversing the process, until it is restored whole and complete. This picture should be held in the *eye of the mind* with hope and expectation. If we lose our focus by losing or forgetting the picture, the visual part of the brain is not participating in the healing process. *It is important to maintain the visual connection!*

We must engage every part of our being if we expect to win this battle. To decline to engage on every front is to admit disinterest, lack of desire, lack of authority and lack of applying every tool possible to win the war. Become your own prophet! See yourself whole just as God sees you. God does not look on the seen, but upon the unseen. We must do the same!

7. Speak. God created the world by His spoken word. He spoke and a whole universe came into being! Created in the image and likeness of the Creator, we also have the gift of voice and proclamation. ***Do we dare to speak health and healing over the impossible?*** There is an Aramaic proverb that says, "I create as I speak." To do that we must engage our heart with God's Heart, and speak as He Speaks. Jesus said He spoke only what the Father gave Him to speak. That is actually not spooky. At every moment Jesus was ready, engaged and connected to do the Fathers will. If the answer to the problem conforms to the letter (logos) and spirit (rhema) of God's word, and if God quickens you to speak in flow with the divine will—then be released!

Generally this type of inspired leading is confirmed by a gentle peace in the heart to speak forth something significant. Be sure you ask *permission* from the person in charge to speak. It is not wise to force yourself into a situation that is presumptuous. If what you feel to speak is truly from God, then He will also open the door using proper protocol.

Be sure you ask permission from the person in charge to speak. It is not wise to force yourself into a situation that is presumptuous.

When that door swings open, speak by faith and let the healing word flow from your mouth with power, conviction, sincerity, and authority. There is no need to scream or shout, of course. Quietness, sincerity and a tear with love have more healing power any day than working up an emotional hurricane. *Be led by peace.* And leave the results in God's hand—neither adding nor subtracting—because by using willpower and manipulation we cannot add an inch to our stature or change the color of our skin. By sharing those scriptural picture-words we are implying that *the conclusion of the matter must be left to rest in the hand of God by faith.*

8. Believe. Hebrews chapter eleven is the great chapter of faith. By faith common men accomplished uncommon feats that would have been impossible by any other means. That is because faith is a word containing real *substance* (see Heb. 11:1). Substance means that one has a foundation under his or her proclamation of faith. Faith doesn't shake or tumble down at every change of wind or doctrine.

By faith common men accomplished uncommon feats that would have been impossible by any other means.

In the "faith chapter" (Hebrews 11) kingdoms were conquered and dead persons were received back to life. That was kingdom reality—a reality that desperately needs to be restored in the world today. The Word states that the prophet Elijah was a man of "like passions" and battles just like every other person, yet dozens of powerful miracles were accomplished during his time on earth. And a "greater than Elijah is here," the resurrected Lord Jesus Christ, Creator of the Universe, the one who spoke the worlds into being! (see Jn. 1:1-3; Heb.1:2)

Remember, *belief is like a seed waiting to germinate.* We must plant it in the good soil of waiting hearts to grow. If a little mustard seed can grow into a giant tree, does not that also imply that our faith can also grow huge? Growth transpires as we nurture our faith in communion with the Creator of the Universe! We must absolutely settle that question in our heart. *Believers must believe.* Are you a "Believer?" If so, then your inner character will be to believe for things that would otherwise be totally impossible!

***

If some of these approaches sound strange or bizarre or "too complicated" to you, compare the above scenario with any similar case (pet or person) who goes forward or makes a request for healing prayer. Typically there is the hope that *someone else* will muster the faith to heal their suffering. At that crisis moment of faith the majority refuse to engage in any other steps of self-healing. "God will heal me," they imply. Or the doctor will heal me. Or the faith of my family or my pastor will heal me. And that is absolutely fine. No problem with that thinking at all. *However, what if Almighty God in His wisdom chooses to use spit, clay, nutrients, fig paste, touch, herbs or spices, including the wisdom and knowledge of a creative natural health practitioner, or maybe requiring the seeker to change abusive dietary habits—would there be the same readiness to comply?* That might require junking every ounce of addictive junk food! Any takers under *those* conditions?

What if, like General Naaman, head of the powerful Syrian army, God whispers to use some method which does not fit our puny concept of what we might "feel" willing to do? Fortunate for General Naaman, he relented, repented, and complied with what the prophet Elisha suggested as non-optional: dipping seven times in the *muddy* Jordan River—and was healed of his leprosy (2 Kings, chapter 5.) Do you believe openness to unusual revelation might be significant part of following the *biblical model*? I have seen dozens of healings take place by means of unusual approaches. And if that is so, what might be the sad result of stubbornly refusing to cooperate in your own healing?

I believe multiple healing principles should be applied to every case of injury, disease or abnormality. It is my absolute conviction that we must become participants in healing! We are called to consider each God created modality that might apply to our case. Always add *touch, vision, prayer and faith*. These are the ***powerful four***, that when added to the natural realm best ensure that healing will take place. *We must stop divorcing the natural from the spiritual realm as though they were unrelated.* I believe that both protocols taken together would improve the dismal healing rate in "impossible" cases from the typical 0 to 5% to over 50%. Miracles do happen, you know! *Become a participator in your miracle!*

I believe multiple healing principles should be applied to every case of injury, disease or abnormality. It is my absolute conviction that we must become participants in healing!

So what happened to the injured eye? First let me tell you that the total protocol was well received. Happily, the family as well as the patient complied with all of the recommended suggestions. Only six weeks after the emergency surgery, the surgeons and specialists were absolutely astonished at the degree of recovery. Externally, the eye healed so well that it appeared normal. In addition, partial vision had also been restored, again, to everyone's amazement.

Here are several questions to ponder in closing. Whether or not full vision returns to the injured eye—is that the only criterion that applies to this case? Isn't having a natural eye with partial vision better than having no eye at all? Is natural physical vision more important than spiritual vision? Is total vision more important than lessons learned? Could it be that sometimes there are other lessons waiting to be learned? In other words, is a failure (and this case was obviously not a failure) always a failure? Can lessons be learned even when there appears to be defeat, lessons that grow and prime our yet incomplete understanding concerning faith, nutrition, and other prudent involvements in healing? Could these lessons be used to prepare us for even greater miracles around the next corner of life?

Summary

1. God created the body, and there are principles of repair inherent in every cell of the body.
2. MSM is a powerful anti-inflammatory, speeds healing of damaged tissues and helps to alleviate pain.
3. Magnetic therapy has a history dating back thousands of years.
4. Nutrition is *always* a key to healing.
5. Frequency, sound, music, laser and Rife hertz treatments are rapidly becoming more widely used and available worldwide.
6. Touch is one of the keys to healing.
7. The mind is a powerful tool for healing. Created in the image and likeness of the Creator, we have the gift of voice and proclamation.
8. Belief is like a seed waiting to germinate. We must plant it in the good soil of waiting hearts to grow.
9. Always add *touch, vision, prayer and faith.* These are the ***powerful four***, that when added to the natural realm best ensure that healing will take place.

Chapter Seventeen

LYME DISEASE: THE UNRECOGNIZED EPIDEMIC

"Hope deferred makes the heart grow sick"

(Proverbs 13:12).

Since we're talking about the current health crisis in the west, here's a newsflash: *Lyme Disease is a tragic infection that has infiltrated 40-60% of the North American population!*

Kevin Trudeau, writing in *More Natural "Cures" Revealed,* notes, "Lyme Disease is very rarely diagnosed properly. People who have symptoms of MS, Fibromyalgia, chronic fatigue, etc. are never diagnosed as having Lyme Disease. Lyme Disease is prevalent in person after person after person. The percentage is outrageously high to the point of being epidemic."[29]

One reason for this is that the typical blood test is only 25-30% accurate at diagnosing chronic Lyme Disease. Another difficult factor is the insidious nature of this modern-day plague. Lyme Disease is hard to identify because it hides so well; some 350 different symptoms have been linked to the illness, making it very easy for it to masquerade as some other condition. Therefore, diagnosing Lyme Disease can be a real Pandora's Box. Because it is so easily misdiagnosed, it is often treated improperly if treated at all.

We're not talking about just a simple microbe here, but one that quickly evades its host's defense mechanisms and exhibits elaborate survival strategies. Lyme Disease penetrates deep into muscles, tendons, connective tissues and joints, as well as the nervous system. It can hide in the bladder, the gall bladder and even in the jawbone, including festering at the base of infected teeth.

All in Your Head?

Given its wide array of possible symptoms and its ability to masquerade as many diseases, it is no surprise to discover that Lyme Disease is the "cause behind the cause" of a large variety of illnesses both named and unnamed. Lyme Disease particularly likes to lurk behind any weakened or defenseless areas of the body. All of these factors together make Lyme Disease extremely difficult to cure. It is a hostile adversary requiring defeat at the deepest level.

I attended a seminar recently where Dr. Peter Kassner gave a lecture on autoimmune disorders. These are disorders where one's immune system does not recognize self as self and attacks one's own healthy tissue. Dr. Kassner presented a list of 147 autoimmune diseases that he believed were all misdiagnoses as to the real cause. He stated that although many of these diseases were named according to the different tissues affected, often the primary culprit proved to be Lyme Disease! I was fascinated!

As we listened to the lecture, my wife said to me, "Wow, I have all those symptoms! This sounds like me!" The amazing thing is that I had suspected for at least ten years that she was suffering from Lyme Disease—but every test had proven negative. Why the discrepancy? Why had everyone missed the diagnosis?

There was hope, however. We were encouraged by Dr. Kassner's description of a new antigen test developed by Bowen Labs that is much more accurate.[30] This new test was different in that it tested for the antigen rather than the antibody. When Jinnie took this new test, she tested Lyme positive at the highest level! Finally we were getting somewhere! Finally we had solid evidence of a specific diagnosable infection that lay behind much of her suffering, proving at long last that it was not all in her head!

This "all in your head" diagnosis, by the way, is the favorite scapegoat of half-baked modern medicine. If modern diagnostic methods can't find a physical cause then obviously the problem must be of a psychological, psychosomatic, emotional or mental nature, meaning, "It's all in your head!" *Lyme Disease, however, is the great mimicker of 350 symptoms, including every psychological diagnosis in the book and at least 147 autoimmune diseases.* It is *not* all in our head (unless it manifests in the teeth or the brain, of course).

A Tricky Invader

Why did the traditional tests miss Lyme? For that answer we must understand the intimate details of Lyme Disease. A quick web search for "Lyme

Disease" will yield a wealth of material including very traditional information as well as the latest cutting edge discoveries. You will read about worthless and sometimes dangerous treatments as well as highly effective treatments.

One of the keys to unlocking the mystery of Lyme Disease is to understand that it hides inside individual cells. It becomes intimately attached to self. About two weeks after infection, the subtle *spirochete* organism blatantly hijacks the cell and camouflages itself within so effectively that the standard antibody test often misses it. Consequently, the illness may be misdiagnosed as any one of dozens of other similar diseases.

One of the keys to unlocking the mystery of Lyme Disease is to understand that it hides inside individual cells. It becomes intimately attached to self.

Often the "final" diagnosis will be based on symptoms and sophisticated guesses and may even labeled "idiopathic," meaning that it is a "mystery" disease that perplexes medical science. Attaching a fancy Latin name to a puzzling condition may sound educated and impressive but it does little to alleviate—or cure—a patient's suffering. The prescribed remedy, of course, will be some *pharmakia* drug to suppress the predominant symptom or symptoms. Perhaps even three or four drugs will be prescribed, some of them no doubt categorically toxic. Some of these drugs may interact with each other, producing additional symptoms. This leads to an additional prescription of more drugs to control the toxic drug reactions—until the patient is under a handful of very powerful—and very dangerous—drugs. Some of these drugs may be prescribed for the physical symptoms and others for the psychological symptoms. But the *root cause* of the symptoms may be completely missed. Do you see something wrong with this cycle? I do!

Lyme Disease is epidemic in pets as well as people. It is time everyone realizes this veiled fact, from our highly trained professionals down to the grass roots John Q. public. Only as we clearly recognize the culprit, we will be able to strategize an effective campaign to totally eliminate this insidious epidemic disease!

In dogs we often label Lyme Disease as the "old dog syndrome." A young healthy dog may suddenly move, act and feel like it has aged ten years in a few weeks' time. Joints ache, appetite dwindles, depression rules, and the zest of life gets squashed. In endemic areas, observant veterinarians quickly suspect and immediately treat with antibiotics. That is appropriate in the early stages.

Veterinarians as a whole seem more aware of Lyme Disease than the average medical doctor. In fact, a recent veterinary journal told of a veterinarian who suspected Lyme Disease in several of her human clients, and it was her suspicion that finally got them headed toward a proper diagnosis and treatment program.

Understanding Your Enemy by Searching Outside the Box

When the diagnosis is totally missed, and the case turns chronic, we must reflect and experiment outside the box. By thinking outside of the box I have discovered that the greatest success with pets occurs when combining several of the following methods. First, I recommend several cutting-edge homeopathic remedies that are specific for Lyme Disease. Typically I next recommend large doses of buffered vitamin C. Vitamin C is a key in connective tissue integrity—the tissue most often attacked by the Lyme organism. Often I add colloidal silver, joint support formulas, immune support and, as always, a superior diet. I have been gratified to see some pretty hopeless cases bounce back and recover. A similar treatment also works well with horses.

Lyme Disease has a curious history. It was first diagnosed in Lyme, Connecticut, from which the disease takes its name. Initially only the deer tick was implicated as the cause. In truth, however, Lyme Disease can be spread by every species of infected blood-sucking insect, including ticks, mosquitoes, lice, mites and biting flies. Feces and bodily fluids such as urine and saliva are also transfer agents for the disease. This illness may very well be worse than the feared AIDS epidemic. Lyme Disease is also more insidious than AIDS because, even though it is not as likely to kill you, after years of suffering and misdiagnosis you may *wish* you were dead!

Once a diagnosis of Lyme Disease is made, treatment is simple, right? Wrong! Remember that this disease hides in the cells. You can't kill every cell! One strategy or secret, therefore, is to trick these spirochetes out of their safe hiding places by making them feel secure to advance their agenda, then hitting them hard for 2-3 days! They will quickly go back into hiding. (Sounds kind of like guerilla or terrorist warfare, doesn't it?)

Once a diagnosis of Lyme Disease is made, treatment is simple, right? Wrong! Remember that this disease hides in the cells. You can't kill every cell!

The next strategy is to back off the "big guns" temporarily and support the body and mind with daily nutrition, homeopathics, flower essences, cleanses and so on. Then hit them again! Be diligent, dangerous and demanding! Rotate this plan every 7 to 11 days. This is one effective strategy for winning this diabolical war.

At this stage, physicians are still learning. Occasionally it may be useful to use short-term antibiotics, sometimes by intravenous injection. This is most effective during the first 2-3 weeks of the infection. However, diagnosis that early tends to be rare. In humans, at least, 25 to 40% of tick bites result in an obvious red circle around the bite. This is a dead giveaway for Lyme and the most effective stage to begin aggressive antibiotics. In that case here is what I would do: if I noticed a red circle around the bite, I would consult with a doctor ASAP. Or if within days or a few weeks of tick bites I felt various atypical symptoms—I would get it checked out at this early stage!

In humans, at least, 25 to 40% of tick bites result in an obvious red circle around the bite. This is a dead giveaway for Lyme and the most effective stage to use antibiotics.

According to some of the latest research, reliance on antibiotics should be discouraged after the disease turns chronic. There are three reasons for this. First, antibiotics are usually not effective at the chronic stage. One study, in fact, showed *zero* effectiveness against *chronic* Lyme Disease. Second, antibiotics have various unwanted side effects. And third, natural treatments are usually much more effective at this stage.

One study compared 14 third-stage Lyme Disease patients in two groups. One group received standard antibiotic IV and supportive treatments while the other received a comprehensive program of herbs, enzymes, homeopathics, magnesium supplements, pH balancing and other supportive treatments. The group under standard care exhibited *zero* improvement. The group receiving the naturopathic program, however, averaged 85% improvement. Both groups were under the care of medical doctors.

It is results such as these that are prompting more and more people to seek treatment from licensed healthcare practitioners who do not use drugs and surgery as their only means of treatment.

Cutting-Edge Lyme Disease Treatments to Consider

Here are several of the primary treatments that cutting-edge natural healthcare practitioners are prescribing for treatment of Lyme Disease.

1. *Samento,* a rainforest botanical, is an extract of a Peruvian herb called Cats Claw or Uno de Gato. This product has received impressive reviews when used against Lyme Disease, as well as against several other chronic diseases.
2. *Medical quality colloidal silver* has been used both orally and, sometimes, by IV injection. Colloidal silver has a long history of use in a variety of infections, including viruses, bacteria, fungus and parasites infections.
3. *Vitamin C* in high doses is commonly recommended orally and sometimes also by IV injection. A powerful antioxidant, Vitamin C is a key player in repairing the connective tissue, joints and ligaments that Lyme Disease is programmed to invade, inflame and destroy.
4. *Food-grade hydrogen peroxide* has been recommended orally and sometimes by IV injection. Hydrogen peroxide (as well as ozone therapy) has a long and distinguished history of conquering various resistant diseases.
5. *Yew tree extracts, Aloe Vera Juice, Myrrh, and Olive Leaf* have often proven beneficial. All have anti-microbial effects and can be useful as part of a Lyme treatment program.

All of these products should be of medical-grade quality and used only under the care and counsel of a qualified health practitioner, someone who understands and has experience in treating Lyme Disease.

Nutritional Support

As with any other disease or health problem, proper nutrition is one of the strongest weapons for defeating Lyme Disease. In this regard, I refer you to the earlier sections on nutrition in this book as well as to my first book in this series, *We Don't Die, We Kill Ourselves!* A review of those materials will give you principles to help you get started on the right road to recovery. Let me also share a few other nutrition-related tips.

Remember that your body must be supported and nourished on a daily basis. For antioxidant support consider quality Noni, wolfberry, Acai or Goji juices. In addition, support your overall nutritional program with B vitamins, especially B6, and buffered Vitamin C ascorbates. Vitamin E with selenium (selenomethionine) may also be helpful.

Recently I spoke with several professionals concerning a new product on the market. Now undergoing study at Emory University, this product is a unique nutritional supplement that actually enters the mitochondria of the cell. This newly released polysaccharide product rebalances the ATP energy pathways by working at the cell level. By actually repairing the cell, it actually enables the cell itself to kick out viruses, fungus and the Lyme spirochete bacteria. Currently I am waiting for more verification of this new breakthrough. Stay tuned!

Here's another tip: alkalize, alkalize alkalize! To alkalize means to eat more alkaline foods. (Hint: Up to half your diet should be made up of a combination of dozens of fruits and vegetables.) It also means internalizing and bathing in alkaline emotions (Hint: Nurture joy, peace, faith, hope, love, reconciliation and forgiveness.) *Alkaline foods and alkaline emotions together create a prevailing environment where disease cannot thrive.*

Alkalize, alkalize alkalize! To alkalize means to eat more alkaline foods...It also means internalizing and bathing in alkaline emotions.

Consequently minimize acid foods. (Hint: Acid forming foods include most grains except millet, all meats and dairy, all junk foods, pastry, sugar and most drugs.) More specifically, pro-inflammatory foods include all the gluten grains, especially wheat, rye and barley. Corn, soy and dairy are also pro-inflammatory and acid forming foods. To read more on this vital subject read the first sections of my first book in this series: "*We don't die, We Kill Ourselves!*" And forget all bottled soft drinks! Pure water or water diluted half and half with100% fruit juice are far better alternatives. Likewise, avoid acid emotions. (Hint: Acid emotions include anger, anxiety, frustration, fear, hatred of others, self-hatred and all forms and levels of unforgiveness. Did you know that unforgiveness and anger are two of the most *toxic* emotions?)

Acidity at every level creates a sick environment that is conducive to every disease known to mankind. In *We Don't Die, We Kill Ourselves*, I share the secret of how to achieve optimum acid/base balance, so that everyone can live in vibrant health. Acid foods meet the specific criteria of being highly *pro-inflammatory*. Alkaline foods meet the basic criteria of being anti-inflammatory. *Anti-inflammatory is better*!

This leads to my next point. Lyme Disease is an extremely inflammatory and painful disease. It is for this reason that people and pets, and especially those who suffer from this disease, must avoid pro-inflammatory foods like the plague! This is absolutely essential if one desires to beat this disease permanently. Halfway measures will not win this dreadful war.

Commit to Positive Change to Achieve Your Miracle

Unfortunately, very few people are willing to self-create the required changes to make their lives better. There is something inherent in our society that absolutely requires a "quick fix." *"Somebody tell me what to do! Give me a pill! Baby me! Pay for my hospital bill! I'll be fixed by next week, right? Help me! Just don't require too much from me!"*

I'm sorry, but a pill by itself cannot birth permanent relief. We are talking about basic changes in attitudes. Ways of living and methods of coping must change. We are talking, of course, about personal involvement. We are talking about a new vision, a paradigm shift—taking personal responsibility for one's own health. We have screwed up big time! *It is time to reverse the mess we have created.*

Sometimes little changes birth big changes. However, where Lyme Disease is concerned, a mega-change is required if you hunger for your miracle. Usually that means a complete about-face, a 180-degree reverse in direction. Are you ready to commit to mega change? *Mega changes are required to birth mega miracles, and chronic Lyme Disease requires a mega miracle.*

Part of pursuing your miracle means addressing chronic acid emotions. This includes dealing with mental stress and emotional trauma. Do you realize that every thought, word and emotion has creative power? What we say, think, feel and believe create the very framework of our future reality. On the negative side, chronic hopelessness robs us of hope. "Hope deferred makes the heart sick" (Prov. 13:12). Lasting hope is the key to permanent victory.

In her book, *Your Body Believes Every Word You Say*, author Barbara Levine indicates that we ourselves are often the source of our own ailments. She writes:

> You may not want to recognize yourself as the source of your ailments. But until you do, you are not in the driver's seat and cannot begin to *think of yourself as the source of healing as well; you caused it, to some degree, and you can uncause it, to the same degree.* There is no self-blame intended in this statement. There are factors involved in any illness over which you have little, if any, control. Nevertheless, you can perceive or recognize that you do have some power over your health via your thoughts, your attitudes, your words, your actions and your behaviors."[31]

When we recognize our power and responsibility to participate in our personal healing, we obviously must consider also supporting our emotional and spiritual health. On the natural side of the equation this may include calming and healing nervine herbs and appropriate homeopathic remedies such as balancing flower essence remedies. *Natural remedies, of course, are for the natural part of the disease equation, whereas spiritual help is for the spiritual side.*

When we recognize our power and responsibility to participate in our personal healing, we obviously must consider also supporting our emotional and spiritual health.

Balance is Another Key to Your Miracle

So many people are out of balance in today's society. Extremes are the thrust of the day. As a result many humans err on the side of over-emphasizing the all-natural side of the equation. Their *god is naturalism,* which includes the many natural and drug cures offered by enterprising vested interests of the many-sided commercial conglomerates.

On the opposite side of the pendulum, some people reject the natural altogether and spiritualize everything, relegating all disease and other problems strictly to the emotional and spiritual realms. Self help, emotional healing, prayer lines and positive thinking are their usual answers. "*Don't feed me that natural stuff, they chime—that's unspiritual!*" Unspiritual or not, this extreme errs on the side of refusing to take care of their natural body. I meet these people all the time, like the person who tried to convince me of the philosophical truth that it doesn't make any difference what we put into our mouths; the key is to be spiritually tuned. Great—that is a half-truth. We shook hands. Folks, it is past time to wake up! Both extremes are way out of balance. *Either one will keep you from your miracle.*

Recently I discovered a line of emotional remedies that are the most innovative to date. These remedies *combine* cutting-edge nutrients, professional potency homeopathic remedies, flower remedies and herbs, all synergized together in a powerful water-based blend. Several of these remedies are specific for Lyme Disease. Consider remedies like these that address emotional fatigue, empower healthy genetics, boost healthy immune function, and help to balance the mind as well as and body. Ask your health care provider for specific advice. *Please insist on treating your emotional health in the most natural way possible.*

Synergistic and combination remedies empower the body at many levels all at the same time. You and I have a life to live, and I for one don't want to live my life as a slave to dozens or hundreds of different supplements, extracts, drugs and pills! Keep your program as simple as possible.

Find a Qualified Health Coach

Anyone with chronic degenerative Lyme Disease needs a qualified health coach. By now I'm sure this whole program sounds complicated. Well, it is! But this is war! In reality, however, the principles follow common sense guidelines and are actually quite simple. A health coach will help you survive the ups and downs of the mountains and valleys that are part of the usual first 3-9 months required for recovery. After that it may require 1-3 *years* of daily attention to build the immune system for permanent victory. *Don't underestimate the enemy. The enemy is tough. The battle is engaged. Don't give up in the middle of the fight. Take back your health!*

At the same time, definitely engage yourself in this battle 100%. Can I assume that your desire is to be crowned a winning champion? Then commit yourself to taking a full year to apply yourself to gaining back your health! Be consistent! Be angry, in the *right* sense! When the smoke and sound of the battle finally clear and you have your health back, you will then be able to dedicate yourself to fulfilling the many unfulfilled dreams in your life.

Can I assume that your desire is to be crowned a winning champion? Then commit yourself to taking a full year to apply yourself to gaining back your health!

Lyme Disease must be stopped NOW. It is scattering globally at this very moment. Lyme Disease is one of the most insidious pandemics in history and yet it is barely on the radar screen of modern medicine. Dr. Peter Kassner says that Lyme Disease gets him really angry! It makes me angry too. Maybe if we get angry enough, motivated enough and educated enough we might discover the secret to stop this epidemic dead in its tracks. In the meantime, if you or some member of your family falls victim, begin taking your life back with hope and vigor.

This subject is not just theoretical for my family. My wife Virginia is presently engaged in this epic battle. Just knowing the enemy has given her immense relief. The same is true for my father-in-law. I fought and won it a few years ago! Fortunately, therefore, we already have significant experience with this particular enemy. We have engaged several health care practitioners who are standing with us and giving guidance. We enjoy prayer support from people who love us with a non-judgmental attitude. I say non-judgmental, because those are the only kind of friends that stick with you when the going gets rough. Who needs fair weather friends?

Therefore, we are together fighting this battle at each level of body, soul and spirit. As a family we are committed to winning this war. We are already experiencing significant answers and wining our first victories!

Lyme Disease is presently a global battle. I invite you to enter the battle in your own corner, with your own family, and for your own home, garden and field. Do you know someone who has symptoms compatible with the Lyme Disease syndrome? Will you be one who answers his or her call for help?

Help others potentially suffering from Lyme Disease by getting this important information into their hands. Knowledge and desire are the first steps to freedom. Next comes the diagnosis and finally, the treatment. *Above all, reach high for the faith, hope and authority required to beat this beast back into the background of bacteria-land history!*

Summary

1. Lyme Disease is a tragic infection that has infiltrated 40-60% of the North American population!
2. Lyme Disease is the great mimicker of 350 symptoms, including every psychological diagnosis in the book and at least 147 autoimmune diseases.
3. Use of short-term antibiotics is most effective during the first 2-3 weeks of the infection.
4. As alternative Lyme treatments, consider samento, medical-quality colloidal silver, Vitamin C in high doses, food-grade hydrogen peroxide, yew tree extract, aloe vera juice, myrrh and olive leaf.
5. Maximize alkaline foods and minimize acid foods.
6. Take responsibility for your part in achieving your miracle.
7. Strike a proper balance between the physical, mental, emotional and spiritual dimensions.

ENDORSEMENTS FOR CHAPTER EIGHTEEN

Hey this is great; the analysis of the different people groups is so great that every one from my own part of the world (Africa) would be encouraged to know that they are uniquely created and gifted with a gift and a purpose. Thanks for sharing this with me. I appreciate that and have been blessed and encouraged by reading it.

— Samuel P. (Nigerian who lives in South Africa),
businessman, media consultant and missionary

Roger: I have read what you have sent and, with your permission, was so impressed I would like to share it with others. The vision of what you "see" as God's purposes and plan for the nations and cultures I also "see," and share wholeheartedly. I have always believed that the different cultures were designed by God with a specific purpose and unique contribution to mankind, and so I especially appreciate the information regarding the Hopi Indians and the Colors. The sentence, "We must regain humility, servanthood and community as biblical values that guide our motives and powerfully shape our mission initiatives," and the content of the paragraph wherein it is contained is, I believe, a key paradigm shift which needs to occur in order to precipitate the unfolding of God's purposes as you have described.

—Ben Konkle, pastor

Roger: I really resonated with what you wrote. I will never forget the Hopi prophecy concerning the unique gifts of each of the four races. This was VERY INTERESTING. I can only say, WOW, YES, Yah, and THIS IS GREAT!

—Dr. Perrin H.

Hello Roger: You have revived many old memories. During the 1950s, 60s and 70s, I owned and operated a store that specialized in handmade American arts and crafts. Buying trips took me to most of the Indian Reservations in North America. Also, parallel with that time period, I was born again. Of course, I immediately received a burden and interest in the spiritual state of the Indian people. *Generally, all but four tribes in North America had lost their original languages and religions.* The four that still had some understanding of their original spiritual beliefs were the Iroquois Nations in New York and Ontario, the Navajo in the Four Corners area of Arizona, New Mexico, Utah and Colorado, the Zuni in New Mexico, and, the tribe with the most intact traditional beliefs, the Hopi of northern Arizona.

Due to their remote location in a desert area with absolutely no resources attractive to Anglos, the Hopi had the least contact with the Americanization of the west. They also maintained their original language, which is the number one key to passing the beliefs of their original religion on to each new generation.

I became good friends with many Hopi craftsmen (potters and silversmiths) and had the very rare experience of being invited into Hopi Kivis to see several Hopi religious ceremonies. It was all most impressive. My reaction at the time was the observation that the Hopi greatly fulfill Romans 1:20, "For the invisible things of him are clearly seen by the things that are made..."

Most Indians have a closer relationship and awareness of nature, but the Hopi, due to their being farmers in a desert environment, learned to depend upon God for so many natural needs. Like the Tribes of Israel, which had seven feasts that coincided with planting and harvesting, the Hopi also maintained a series of dance ceremonies collated with planting and harvest. It was some of these ceremonies that I witnessed. Most of the other North American Indian tribes were basically hunters, whereas the Hopi were primarily farmers.

Another unique feature of the Hopi that parallels Israel is that just as Israel is a small but very sophisticated nation surrounded by nomadic tribes of backward Arabs, with whom they have constant land disputes, the Hopi Tribe is a small but very sophisticated nation completely surrounded by the backward and nomadic Navajo, with whom they also have constant land disputes.

I believe God has a special purpose for the Hopi and has kept them isolated for these thousands of years. I have special place in my heart for the Hopi.

—Tom Jones

Chapter Eighteen

THE JOYS AND BENEFITS OF DIVERSE CULTURES WORKING TOGETHER

"There is neither Jew nor Greek, there is neither slave nor free, there is neither male nor female; for you are all one in Christ Jesus. And if you are Christ's, then you are Abraham's seed, and heirs according to the promise"

(Galatians 3:28-29).

"For as the body is one and has many members, but all the members of that one body, being many, are one body, so also is Christ. For by one Spirit we were all baptized into one body—whether Jews or Greeks, whether slaves or free—and have all been made to drink into one Spirit"

(1 Corinthians 12:12-13).

"So we, being many, are one body in Christ, and individually members of one another"

(Romans 12:5).

During our years deep in the jungles of Colombia, we worked with various cultures in a spirit of total equality. All in all ten teaching farms came into existence, the largest comprising around 200 persons, and the cultural mixture in each one was incredible. Americans from the north, south, east and west mixed with Colombians from the cities, towns and jungle villages. A few were highly educated but many more had no more than 1-2 years of schooling.

Those with the least amount of formal education had the vital experience of surviving and thriving in a dense jungle on the upper Amazon River. Colombians, Mexicans, Chinese, Indians, black and white all worked together. Even the eldership and leadership contained representatives of every color and every level of education. We made all our decisions on the principle of consensus rather than by majority vote.

Although seniority and wisdom obviously carried more influence in these budding inter-cultural communities, *every* voice counted. Major decisions were based on unanimous agreement rather than position. Of course, in the daily life of the farms and communities, anyone leading an area had the freedom to make daily decisions. And any person in each workgroup enjoyed the freedom to voice his or her opinion. Our goal was to do the best work possible, in the best way possible, in the best spirit possible. The guiding principle we followed always was not who was right or wrong but on finding the best solution to whatever problem or challenge we faced.

Does this sound like a farfetched utopian dream? Actually, it worked surprisingly well considering the obstacles of human nature, the diversity of cultures and many extreme personal differences. The uniting factors, of course, that overrode all the others, were common goals derived from a common faith.

The Judge was Shocked!

One day a Colombian judge came to visit the farm and remained for several days. He had socialistic leanings and was part of a communist front organization. After he had seen what we had accomplished in the jungle, turning forest into fields and fields into gardens, he put his arm on my shoulder and wept. He said, "*In all my dreams I have never experienced anything so beautiful*! This is what *we* are trying to accomplish! You have already done it, except this is better than I ever imagined!"

Needless to say, I was shocked as well as a bit uncomfortable. Here he was, a communist leaning judge, crying on my shoulder. Much yet remained to be accomplished. I knew that we were *far* from perfect. Like anyone else, we all had the normal human struggles. Even more, however, I knew that together we had a higher vision than what this judge could see with his natural eyes: a vision that each individual's purpose was to represent Christ in the midst. Jesus prayed in John 17 that His people might be *one* even as He and His Father were *one*. This judge was witnessing with his own eyes an answer to that prayer. However imperfect our unity was, as judged by ultimate truth, it went far beyond anything this judge had seen anywhere before.

This judge was witnessing with his own eyes an answer to that prayer. However imperfect our unity was, as judged by ultimate truth, it went far beyond anything this judge had seen anywhere before.

The previous evening the judge and I had engaged in a long discussion about human nature. This led to a discussion about America, including its strengths and weaknesses. The communist party in Colombia was decidedly anti American, of course, so the judge was shocked that I recognized the weaknesses of the United States as represented by its current political structure and worldwide financial and military power, which sometimes led to corruption.

Years earlier I had read a book titled, *The Ugly American*, and knew that the image that America presented to the world was not always positive. By the world beyond our borders we were often seen as proud, materialistic, dominating and superrich. This attitude resulted in a perception that America was milking the rest of the world dry to satisfy its own opulent way of life. Many were angry by what they saw and, frankly, some of that anger was justified.

When the judge realized that I was not political and that our mission had no nationalistic goals of domination and expansion, he became quite thoughtful. The more he heard and saw that our sole purpose was to represent the Kingdom of God and not North America and western culture, the more his defenses softened. What amazed him the most, I believe, was the fact that the Americans in these communities did not "run" the farms; that we got our hands dirty and worked like everyone else. "This is not what I expected at all," he mused. "What you are doing in Colombia is good for Colombia. This is very admirable. I am impressed."

*Diversity **can** work if it has the proper moral and spiritual underpinnings!*

A Hopi Indian Prophecy Concerning the Oneness of the Human Race

A good case can be made that God speaks to dissimilar people, both believers and unbelievers alike. God is no "respecter of persons" (Acts 10:34 KJV). If God can (and did) speak to influential agnostic kings like Pharaoh, Nebuchadnezzar and Cyrus, revealing truth by dreams, surely God's voice and revelation can touch any people anywhere on the face of this earth. Peter himself was shocked to learn that God spoke to and accepted Gentiles as Jews. But Peter *did* learn it: "*I now realize that it is true that God treats everyone on the same basis. Whoever fears him and does what is right is acceptable to him, no matter what race he belongs to*" (Acts 10:34-35 TEV). Would you agree?

Let me be upfront and tell you that this chapter is not intended to be a theological treatise. In fact, the viewpoint expressed in the following paragraphs could probably be called risky. One person who previewed this material suggested I was walking a fine line. Even so, I believe many will resonate, as did this person. I have taken a new look at the "box" and have decided that we are in grave danger today, as was the first-century church—of creating a "boxed-in" theology—a theology that well may be blasted into smithereens when reality arrives! So yes, I am pushing the envelope a bit. You are free to agree or disagree.

That said, let me proceed.

The Hopi Indians have teachings that go back to the time of creation. One of their teachings has to do with the formation of the nations and the four colors, from what they call their "Original Teachings." These prophecies foresaw great civilizations coming forth, and great struggles that would encircle the globe.

Each color, which developed over time, was given a particular responsibility, called a "*Guardianship.*"

To the Indian—the red people of North, Central and South America—God gave the guardianship of the earth.

More than any other group they would understand the cycles of the earth, the foods that should be eaten, the herbs that heal, and so on. Guardianship of the earth would be their driving and unique responsibility. When, in time, the four colors came back together as one, each was to share its knowledge with the others for the benefit of all. It is interesting to note that, according to an article in the Times, that 8 out of the 10 foods that people worldwide eat today were developed in the western hemisphere as a result of that guardianship.

In an article appearing in the February 2007 edition of ACRES U.S.A., Allan Balliett reports remarkable new archeological findings in the vast rainforests of the Amazon. The article, "Magic Soil of the Lost Amazon," outlines some of the amazing agricultural advances achieved by the local Indian tribes.

Archeologists have discovered manmade "Terra Preta" soil two feet deep in sites varying from 50 to 865 acres in various areas of the American continent. This soil is some 2000 years old, with high levels of organic material, enhanced fertility and embedded with clay pottery. The soil is so rich it produces 800 percent more than adjoining rainforest soils! Papaya and mango grow "about three times as rapidly as on surrounding infertile soils."[32] *It is speculated that these amazing soils were associated with heavily populated towns using intensive farming methods far superior to their European counterparts.*

"What these creative Amerindians lacked, unfortunately, was resistance to the European diseases....Several waves of deadly diseases swept through the Americas after Columbus' first visit. By the mid-1500s, most of the indigenous Americans had died as a result of these epidemics, and the Amerindian society began to collapse...just 50 years later....populated by small bands of scraggly natives."[33] Only now are we beginning to understand how advanced some of the Indian populations were in North, Central and South America.

At a time when the earth has been raped, drugged and sucked dry of its nutrients, a time of reckoning is at hand. "The land is defiled," (Lev. 18:25a). The land is crying out against us. Will the nations of the earth listen to the wisdom of our red brothers? Today, even precious few of them understand their true calling, having also been raped, drugged, herded onto reservations and sucked dry of their original teachings. Before it is too late, we need a revival of scriptural stewardship, a renewal of the guardianship secrets that have been long lost. *I have met Indians who still remember.* The land must be healed. The strength of the earth must be restored. Our red brothers must rise up and help us achieve that healing.

"The land is defiled," (Lev. 18:25a). The land is crying out against us. Will the nations of the earth listen to the wisdom of our red brothers?

To the yellow race of people God gave the guardianship of the wind.

The yellow race was called to learn about the sky, the wind, breathing and how to use those principles for natural and spiritual advancement. We note that many health exercises include proper breathing, deep breathing, oxygen, moving in flow and so on. A good singer must learn how to breathe not from the chest but from the abdomen. Those of us in the western cultures tend to be shallow breathers. We run too fast, breathe too fast, and seldom take time to relax and clear out the carbon dioxide!

Breath symbolically has to do with spirit, the "ruach" of the original Hebrew writings, and the "pneuma" of the Greek New Testament. Both words relate to wind, breath and spirit. Although it is true that this guardianship has degenerated within a culture that has a strong propensity toward superstition, occult practices, eastern mysticism and dragon gods, that propensity does not detract from the fact that they have been endowed with unique insights, gifts and understandings. The underlying truths must be restored! Each culture must be redeemed and purified!

What has been lost in the first Adam is being restored in the second Adam, Jesus Christ. It is our prayer that our yellow brothers might find great freedom to move into their highest cultural calling. The world needs a revival of wind and spirit to softly blow over all nations. Is spirituality only found in the West? That would be narrow-minded and bigoted thinking. Would you agree with that statement?

What might happen if the true power of Christ was unleashed in a culture already gifted with an inherent spirituality that much of the West lacks? Is it possible that one part of our answer lies deep in the spirit of our Asian friends, to be released when purified by revival winds as they blow across the Far East? We all desperately need their spiritual release. I am not advocating occult oriental practices. I am contending that every culture has a Kingdom calling that when fully purified will benefit mankind as a whole. Only then will the creation benefit from all that was originally intended by our All-Wise Creator.

Is it possible that one part of our answer lies deep in the spirit of our Asian friends, to be released when purified by revival winds as they blow across the Far East?

To the black race God gave the guardianship of water.

The black race was called to learn the teachings and secrets of water. Water is one of the chief elements of both the earth, over 70% of which is covered by water, and of the human body, which is made up of over 70% water. It is interesting to note, then, that the black race primarily inhabited the tropics and rainforests. In line with this, oddly enough, they also seem to drink more and sweat more than most other races. In fact, perhaps their ability to detox because of profuse sweating may be one of their secrets of surviving under great odds. The importance of water, the flow of water and how to understand water was given to the black people to appreciate and to teach others, according to our Hopi friends.

According to the World Health Organization, pure water will be the great challenge of the next several decades. Globally, water has become contaminated at every level, from the acid rains from the sky to the winding streams, the underground rivers, the farm and city reservoirs and even the seven oceans. There are places in Africa, Haiti and other poorly-developed nations where people must walk miles to obtain drinking water. Even then, most of that water is unsafe and contaminated. It is time for our black brothers to step up to the plate, not only for themselves but also to help us all solve this critical global problem! *We need their help!*

It is time for our black brothers to step up to the plate, not only for themselves but also to help us all solve this critical global problem! We need their help!

Water also represents the Word of God, not so much on an intellectual level but on a heart level. Perhaps this is one reason the black race, when they are connected and not caught up in other agendas (political, cultural, religious, etc.), tend to have a unique understanding of the Logos (letter) and Rhema (spirit) of God's Word. It is interesting that *water is a type of the Word of God* as it cleanses, purifies, refreshes and teaches (see Eph. 5:26; 1 Cor 3:6). Thus the black race often has a simplicity, freedom and flow that the intellectual Western church does not easily comprehend. The day must come when every nation, tribe, tongue and people come together to worship the one true God. *The black people must be represented at that table as equals!*

To the white race was given the guardianship of fire.

Fire is at the center of many things the white race does. The white race was given the guardianship of energy, explosions and power. In the natural this includes the light bulb, engines, spark plugs, electronics, nuclear power and so on. It also includes guns, bombs and fearful inventions that could easily destroy the earth. All these are devices that can be used wisely for the benefit of mankind or foolishly for the destruction of mankind.

Much of the white race's knowledge has been twisted to the wrong use. This does not mean these inventions are wrong; just that many of them have been misused and abused. Put to the proper use, and shared with the other races for good, this guardianship was originally meant to benefit all mankind.

Fire also represents authority and godly judgment. The white race has been gifted with influence and power to help bring the different races together.

Perhaps this was the genius of the "melting pot" that took place in North America. The melting pot represented an equal opportunity for everyone.

The American Constitution represented an opportunity in life with equality and righteous judgment based on the Torah legal principles given by revelation to Moses. These founding principles also under girded English "common law." Both of these laws are the basis of constitutional law that binds the States into a *republic form of government.* In recent decades these laws have come under constant fire, been watered down and often rendered powerless.

It is the responsibility and destiny of the white race to lay aside any attitude of superiority. Each nation must return to its foundation, in the spirit of Christ, and do its part in inviting all the races to sit in equality at the same table, each sharing their guardianship for the benefit of all. Will the white race heed the call?

It is the responsibility and destiny of the white race to lay aside any attitude of superiority...Will the white race heed the call?

John Dawson addresses this very issue in his book, *Healing America's Wounds*: "America has inherited the wounds of the world. Our large cities are the greatest collections of cultural diversity every seen. In them Turk and Armenian, Arab and Jew, Russian and Pole, Serb and Croat, live side by side in sometimes uneasy proximity. Could the healing of these wounds be America's assignment?"[34] A thought-provoking question!

Great Shakings and Imperialistic Empires Have Built Walls Rather than Bridges

The "Original Teachings" foresaw times of great shakings on the earth. Mankind as a whole would lose sight of their guardianship, of their responsibility to learn and to share. Out of fear they would build walls rather than bridges. When there was a need to solve global problems, different groups and colors arrogantly would exclude, conquer or take advantage of others. Great misunderstandings would arise. Agreements and compromises would be made, although seldom with the proper intent. *The spirit of nationalism, gain and greed would rule over the spirit of oneness in Christ.*

Therefore, great empires would arise. These empires included the Nazis, responsible for 100 million deaths worldwide. It included the rising sun of the imperialistic Japanese Empire. It would include another 100 million exterminated under communism's advances. It included the misuse of fire where lives would be destroyed by atomic bombs. The evil of *radiation* would further contaminate the earth. Instead of lasting peace, continual wars would erupt. Nation would rise up against nation, often for reasons that defy common sense.

As a result, colors, tribes and nations lost interest in learning from one another. Selfishness reigned rather than the common good. Conflicting interests blocked the inclusion of certain key groups. For instance, the red Indian nations of North America have always been blocked from being included at the world table. One sad result is that the nations as a whole have been speeding in the wrong direction regarding guardianship of the earth. As I said before, even most of the Indians have lost their understanding. This has brought the world to the edge of great calamity and suffering. *Half of the world goes to bed hungry every night.*

The Indian prophecies foretold World Wars I and II and foretell a World War III that is yet to come. They foretold the discovery of telephones, the manned landing on the moon and other significant events in world history.[35]

Personally, I resonate with much of this prophecy. That viewpoint gave me a new appreciation and respect for every color and race, each race having a calling of unique purpose and destiny. The Spirit of God is again moving on nations and tribes as well as on individuals that they might fulfill their destinies on this planet. A shift in perception is taking place globally. The way is being *prepared* for a "new heaven and a new earth." Each race and people must learn to co-labor with the Creator as that new day approaches.

The Spirit of God is again moving on nations and tribes as well as on individuals that they might fulfill their destinies on this planet.

You may ask, "Is this really that important, this unity of the races where each finds its unique expression in Christ?" My reply is that if the earth is to survive (and it *will* survive!), the walls of prejudice and intolerance must soften and dissolve. Only when those walls are gone will we ultimately learn from—and deeply appreciate—each other's gifts, guardianship and uniqueness.

It is ludicrous to suppose that one group of people, or one color of people, will have all the answers. In Christ there is no color, no rich or poor, no Jew or Gentile, no male or female. We are all one in Christ. To become one requires that every semblance of jealousy, prejudice, vindictiveness and superiority must go to the cross. Only by giving and receiving what God so generously invested in each individual will oneness be birthed and come to maturity. Only as we see the value of the creation, and the value of each member of that creation, will peace be possible. *Will it take another global war before the warring factions will beat their swords into plowshares?*

To become one requires that every semblance of jealousy, prejudice, vindictiveness and superiority must go to the cross.

God Moves in All the Nations and People Groups of the Earth

Two thousand years ago the message of the angels was, "Peace on earth, and good will toward men." Amazingly, the message of this "gospel of peace" was not given to the entrenched rulers of the day. Peace was the last thing they thought about. They were looking for a King who would throw off the Roman yoke by force! Against all protocol their coming King was born in a dirty stable rather than in a mansion or a palace. And the first to know of this significant birth were humble shepherds!

The second to know of the birth of this coming King were "wise men" from the Orient. Those men also happened to be wealthy kings. Asians generally have been more open to the signs of the heavens (the sky and the heavenly realm as divine revelation) than have their Western counterparts. These men of wisdom apparently had a better grasp of the significance of the plan of God than did the leaders to whom the covenant and the law had been so graciously given!

The misled rulers of that day (the Pharisees, scribes and Sadducees) were so thoroughly enveloped in sterile rules and regulations that they totally misunderstood their true meaning. Truth in the person of Jesus walked in front of them day after day and the life and Spirit that were in Him totally contradicted everything those leaders believed in. His life and actions elicited jealousy, anger and rage rather than humility and self-examination. Yet, the common people received him gladly.

Rather than opening their own hearts, the local rulers moved in the killer instinct. They did not understand that the wisdom of God is always different from secular theology. Yet, the kings of the Orient understood! Isn't that amazing? (Could the reason for their openness may be related to their calling as guardians of the wind?)

Throughout history God has moved uniquely in the different tribes and skin colors. Moses' wife happened to be an Ethiopian woman, a women of the black race. To Moses, "*black was beautiful!*" Her father at one point spoke the wisdom of God into Moses' hectic life; a man we think of as a pagan priest—yet *he* heard from God! In the New Testament, Philip was sent to explain the

Scriptures to another Ethiopian, a man with a high position in the pagan court (Acts 8:26-40). Philip was able to explain to the eunuch's satisfaction a puzzling chapter in Isaiah that prophesied the coming of the Messiah—after which the man asked to be baptized as a believer.

There are records indicating that the first-century gospel penetrated deep into the Orient as well as south into Africa. Historical records from the Indian tribes of both North and South America relate creation accounts strikingly similar to that recorded in the Book of Genesis. Also recorded are stories of a worldwide flood and a huge boat that rescued the human race from destruction. Five major world cultures have records of an extra long day dating from around the time of Joshua, when the "sun stood still" (see Josh. 10:12-13).

Historical records from the Indian tribes of both North and South America relate creation accounts strikingly similar to that recorded in the Book of Genesis.

Whereas many cultures were polytheistic, the majority of the red-skinned Indian cultures believed in one God, whom they called the "Great Spirit." I have been told that among the local Cherokee tribes of North Carolina the name of God in the local tongue is striking similar to "Yahweh," the Hebrew name of God. Obviously, there must be common links! Many of their patterns of worship also resembled the patterns given to Moses. *The Bible reveals that God created "one race of men on the earth" and that He placed in the heart of every nation and tongue a void that would seek to be filled by the one true God.* He did this so that each culture and individual might "seek and find" their common Creator.

Color Blind and Culture Blind

Something inside me is breaking. I see the day coming when we will become "color blind" as well as "culture blind." We will lay down our prejudices and ingrained customs in order to humbly learn from one another once again. Paul tells us in First Corinthians 12 that the body of Christ is one body consisting of many members. One of Satan's most effective strategies against us has been to deceive us in ways that have split the human race into thousands of splintered sects, schisms, denominations, colors, flags and nations. Under that kind of deception oneness is *impossible.*

The day is coming when every knee will bow and every tongue confess that Jesus Christ is Lord (see Phil. 2:10-11). All redeemed humanity will be under one flag and one confession. That confession will not be limited to superficial words, as words alone can be insincere. Above all, oneness will be a confession of the inner heart—a place where love and humility have an opportunity to reign supreme. *The Spirit of God in each race is destined to express itself uniquely. Guardianship will be restored. Purpose will be restored. Honor and respect will be restored. A new age will be upon us.*

As dark as it appears in this present hour, a new day is dawning. My friends, we must remember that the darkest hour occurs just before the dawn. Are you preparing your heart for the awesome resurrection of life that is destined to take place?

The Scriptures tell us that "great tribulation" will precede resurrection. Resurrection will be followed by a worldwide kingdom of peace. When that resurrection life breaks forth, it will arrive suddenly, like a dramatic flash of lightning, flashing from the east and streaking to the west. (see Mt. 24:27ff.) Great light will suddenly pierce the present darkness. The light at the end of the dark tunnel is *about* to give way to the fullness of heavens light!

Of course, "about" could be similar to a "twinkle" (1 Cor. 15:52). If a "day" in the sight of God is like a thousand years (2 Pet. 3:8), then a "twinkle" could be 30 years! We cannot rush or predict a definite time. That would be foolish.

If you are expecting a neat theological package on this subject as I draw this section to a close you will surely be disappointed. *My goal is not to prove my point of view as much as challenge the status quo.* Proof texts are nearly useless because they can be taken out of context and forced into an interpretation that destroys their true meaning. Some theologians argue aggressively over the nuances, word meanings and theological significance of isolated words and verses, to their credit. Seldom, however, have theological debates resulted in a joining of minds and hearts.

This chapter is therefore a message spoken from my heart to yours. If I presented my thoughts against your will, even if persuasive, I will not by argument alone win your heart! You will either see the heart of this issue or you will not. Quoting multiple verses might or might not help. Either way, the conclusion is that a great new day is ahead! A wise person prepares for what is coming. Does not that probability quicken something in you—a quickening that suggests that we must all prepare NOW?

A Massive Shift is about to Break Forth

Do you ever feel bewildered by the massive changes and shifts that America and the world around us are undergoing? Have you ever wondered how these changes, both good and bad, impacts how we interpret the ageless message of the gospel?

Exploring and understanding the redemptive plan of God becomes critically important, especially as our global community becomes more and more a part of our daily lives. The *plan of God* for the present generation is designed to inform and equip believers to become global Kingdom thinkers. We must be a people who are willing to discern the "signs of the times." Only with that perspective will we be able to live bold and courageous lives both within and outside the "box" of the American/Western church.

A new awareness of our connection to the *global church* must arise worldwide if we are to fulfill our prophetic destiny as followers of the good news of Christ. We must be willing to end the exportation of our western ideals, structures and methodologies in the name of evangelization (advancing the kingdom) while at the same time welcoming the contributions of the diverse communities God created. We must regain humility, servant-hood and community as biblical values that guide our motives and powerfully shape our mission initiatives.

A new awareness of our connection to the ***global church*** *must arise worldwide if we are to fulfill our prophetic destiny as followers of the good news of Christ.*

A Missionary Incentive for All Cultures

At one time America and Europe sent missionary teams around the globe. America and Europe are now by and large secular and cold toward the gospel. As a result, the mission is being reversed. Today less than 10% of the population of Europe consider themselves Christian. The shoe has changed to the other foot. A recent poll suggests that in China, Russia, India, Africa and South and Central America, 25,000 people are becoming "believers" every 25 minutes. In the prosperous west, 9 out of 10 of our youth reject the faith of their fathers. At the same time, one million adults leave the church every year—never to return.

Because the west has largely rejected Christianity in both belief and principle, the cloud has moved south and east. Another way of looking at this is what a professor I heard at a conference some 40 years ago call the "westward movement of Christianity." He theorized that the direction of movement of Christian evangelization has always been in the same direction as that of the sun. The movement that began in Jerusalem and the Middle East moved primarily westward into

Europe. Centuries later it progressed to the Americas. Accordingly, the *next great move* should be to the billions of souls living in the Orient. And now, 40 years later, that is precisely what appears to be happening!

With great signs and miracles, millions are accepting the "good news" in China and other parts of Asia. Estimates are that there are between 100 and 200 million Christians in China alone, with the number increasing rapidly, even in the face of periodic and sometimes terrible persecution. One elderly house leader, with scars on his body, is intent in bringing the gospel full circle. He states that believers from Asia can easily mix and witness among those of the Middle East, where the gospel first began. One day soon, he believes, the witness for Christ will shine brightly once again in the place of its original birth. In other words, the gospel will have come *full circle*!

Whereas Americans and Europeans are suspect, considered "soft" and stand out as targets in the Middle East, Asians are accepted, "hardened" and prepared under years of intense persecution. Therefore, Orientals will be those who can best carry the torch back to the lands of Islam, secular Judaism and the entire Middle East. This persecuted underground house leader might be right!

I believe a great awakening is at hand. The final result will be likened to a brilliant flash of lightning, lighting the entire spiritual skies from east to west. Then every tongue, nation, color, gender and tribe will recognize the benefits and blessings that follow becoming one with our common Creator.

For oneness to take place there must be reconciliation between all races. Every race must release every other from the debts that have accrued over the generations. *God is calling forth a Jubilee, where debts are cancelled, and those held in slavery are set free!*

For oneness to take place there must be reconciliation between all races. Every race must release every other from the debts that have accrued over the generations.

For those of us living in the west, a *spiritual poverty* and slavery have subtly enveloped our still prosperous cultures. We have been cajoled into *secular slavery* based on the doctrines of false material strongholds. Either willingly or unknowingly, we have fallen victim to the "kingdom of self." Wars have been fought and multitudes of lives have been destroyed in the name of that kingdom. *Does this not wrench your gut, when you fathom the injustice of mankind against his neighbor?*

But what can we do? How can we put the pieces of this puzzle together? We were each created with blind spots that only our brother can supply. A man was created to need a helpmeet! A woman was created to be respected and loved. And every race has a purpose and a destiny!

Twelve Personal Points to Ponder in Moving Toward Oneness

1. *Prefer and esteem your brother and neighbor.* How might this look in daily life in your sphere of influence? Can you esteem someone even if you disagree with him? How?
2. *Be willing to ask questions as well as to listen and learn.* Are you a good listener? Have you listened and learned from someone you disagreed with in the past week?
3. *Give honor to whom honor is due.* Can you define honor? What is the basis of honor? Should honor be nurtured in all directions? Would it be wisdom to honor someone with less age, less education and less experience than your self? Why or why not?
4. *Be open to those who are completely different.* Those of you reading this book are probably among the 1% of those on the globe with a high school or greater education, one car or more and a bank account. Would you feel comfortable with those less fortunate? How might that comfort be facilitated?
5. "*Judge not, that you be not judged*" (Mt. 7:1). But when judgment is required there must be "righteous judgment" resulting in true justice. Do we have a Biblical model for solving conflict? What is that model?
6. *We must be very practical.* We all know the problems. The question is, what are the answers? Do you have answers at both the practical and governmental levels? If we are called to be kings and priests, does that have anything to do with government? In what way? Does that scare you or challenge you?
7. *The right answers hinge on asking the right questions.* Tough and appropriate questions may require tough and appropriate answers in order to be relevant. Are we willing to take that risk? What might be the outcome of risk taking?
8. *We must pray for revival, especially for the revival of understanding, true creativity and of knowing God in new ways.* Can true answers manifest apart from revival? Do you have any ideas how to prepare the way for radical revival?

9. *We have been called to move from glory to glory.* That highest glory is prophesied to cover the entire earth. What does glory mean? What does glory look like? How do we move into that glory?
10. *Restoration and restitution are not optional as a part of reconciliation.* Is this true? If so, how might this be achieved in ways that are fair, equitable and liberating for every individual and all races? What kind of spirit is necessary in order for there to be true reconciliation?
11. *Discipleship, training, and empowerment are keys to extend to those who have been downtrodden.* How would this look in a Third World Country?
12. *Everyone must deal with bitterness, resentment, anger and blame.* Unforgiveness is the result, and that only divides and leads to racism, which is crippling. If this is so, is forgiveness then optional? Do you have any clue how to deal with the deep wrongs of the past in ways that lead to healing? What would you do if the roles were reversed?

Summary

1. Diversity can work if it has the proper moral and spiritual underpinnings!
2. To the Indian—the red people of North, Central and South America—God gave the guardianship of the earth.
3. To the yellow race of people God gave the guardianship of the wind.
4. To the black race God gave the guardianship of water.
5. To the white race was given the guardianship of fire.
6. The Spirit of God is again moving on nations and tribes as well as on individuals that they might fulfill their destinies on this planet.
7. The day is coming when we will become "color blind" as well as "culture blind."
8. A new awareness of our connection to the global church must arise worldwide if we are to fulfill our prophetic destiny as followers of the good news of Christ.
9. For oneness to take place there must be reconciliation between all races.

Chapter Nineteen

SPOKES AND WHEELS: A STUNNING WORD-PICTURE OF OUR CREATIVE CALLING IN CHRIST

"*It is evident that an acquaintance with natural laws means no less than an acquaintance with the mind of God therein expressed.*"

—James Joule, British Scientist.

"*The more I study nature, the more I stand amazed at the work of the Creator.*"

—Louis Pasteur, chemist & biologist.

"*If you are able to believe, ALL THINGS are possible to those who believe*"

Mark 9:2

Recently I hosted an impromptu discussion group at my home. The nine of us were discussing the land and our responsibility to be responsible stewards of the creation (which is, of course the theme of this book!). As you undoubtedly are aware, whenever an impromptu group gets going, vigorous perspectives can fly at a dizzying rate. If the situation is right, cross-pollinated ideas can become downright radical!

We began with the presupposition that the land and the soil are definite parts of God's original mandate for man. All of us were in agreement on this point. As our discussion proceeded, various ones offered their individual insights as to what our mandate includes. Someone said that invention is a part. Another mentioned science as critical to the plan. Still another emphasized love as indispensable.

"Where does Christ fit into all this?" asked my 84-year-old father-in-law, an energetic gentleman who still travels in the pastoral ministry.

And so the discussion went. As I sat there listening to the different ideas being tossed around, a seed thought germinated in my mind and gradually expanded as the discussion continued. I began sketching out a "word-picture" to represent the creation mandate as it was shaping itself in the discussion. What I saw in my mind's eye was a wheel, a spoked wheel, as on a wagon. The hub, or center of the wheel had to be where God fit in. He is the very center of all things. That seemed obvious.

What I saw in my mind's eye was a wheel, a spoked wheel, as on a wagon. The hub, or center of the wheel had to be where God fit in.

Now the question was, how many spokes are on this wheel? What did each spoke represent? What did the rim of the wheel symbolize? Several thoughts fell quickly into place. Then I thought of Ezekiel's "wheel within a wheel," a dynamic living wheel! This had to be an expansive, powerful, *Scriptural word-picture* if it was to make any sense. When I felt the moment was right, I shared what I had drawn. "Yes, that works," agreed my friends, as they each then began to expand the original insight from their own individual perspectives. What power there is when spontaneous sharing turns into creative discussion!

Later that evening I completed the missing parts in the spokes. During the discussion I had proposed twelve spokes because it sounded just right. In biblical numerology, twelve speaks of completeness or perfection of government: twelve tribes, twelve gates, twelve apostles, twelve angels. Also, each of the spokes had to be in harmony and balance. No weak links. Each spoke must be identical in importance and strength and all must fulfill their respective roles together. In addition, each spoke must be attached firmly to both the hub and the rim. Every part of the wheel must work in harmony and balance—or it would not work at all.

What words or phrases could adequately describe those twelve factors that signify *man's involvement in the creation—with God as the center—reaching out to the world?* Because of our subject, I listed agriculture and animal husbandry first, followed by health and nutrition. I recognize that these might be personal prejudices, but they nevertheless fit perfectly the picture presented in the first three chapters of Genesis, at least in my mind. Here is the list that evolved in the end:

1. **Agriculture:** Mankind as stewards of plant life and tilling the land.
2. **Animal Husbandry:** Mankind's husbandry and dominion of the categories of animals listed in Genesis 1:28.
3. **Nutrition:** The full understanding, teaching and application of health and dietary principles at all levels.
4. **Geography:** The proper understanding of the world, its borders, products, minerals, reserves, purposes etc.
5. **History:** The study of history is truly the study of: "His-Story," God working out the redemption of people and nations, including the redemption of the total creation.
6. **Government:** All the types and levels of government that rule in both the natural and spiritual realms.
7. **Religion and spirituality:** This includes everyone's relationship with the Creator and His creation. It must include the covenants, the Torah, the Logos (Word), and also the Rhema (breath and spirit) of God's eternal purposes.
8. **Arts & Music:** Art and music are some of the most powerful expressions of mankind in worship and service. In fact, all of creation is a vivid and harmonic expression of creative art. Every person, star and atom, every bird, cricket and frog, participate in their own musical outburst for attention, song and creative effort!
9. **Science:** The various sciences include mankind's ability to understand and apply knowledge that results in creative inventions to serve mankind. True knowledge, and its appropriate application, result from the integration of both sides of the brain as well as the insights of heart and spirit.
10. **Language skills:** Communication skills include speaking, writing and understanding the tongues and expressions both of men and of angels. Candid and careful communication results in community harmony at all levels of the creation.
11. **Mathematics:** Math is the study and application of numbers and principles, which represent order in the creation. Higher mathematics, geometry and physics catapult us into realms that are still being discovered. The Creator constructed everything in the creation by

the Word and work of His majestic rule. Everything in the creation seems to be built on the basis of intricate mathematical principles. This indicates, of course a Master Architect of remarkable creative skill.

12. **Social Skills:** Social skills, rules and ethics are the underpinning of cultural and family inter-relationships and bonding. Love is the highest social skill! Divine love is the bottom line of everything meaningful at the social level.

As I mentioned before, the hub around which everything revolves and must connect to is Christ in God. In order to achieve spiritual balance, everything also had to be relevant to the earth and the natural realm. Christ is the wheel in the middle of the wheel—the creative force that empowers and holds everything together. This wheel is SELF-POWERED!

Christ is the wheel in the middle of the wheel—the creative force that empowers and holds everything together.

Numerous Scriptures in the New Testament affirm that the Lord Jesus Christ was and is the Eternal Word, Yahweh in the flesh, the One who created the world—and presently holds it together by the Word of His power (see Jn. 1:1-3, 14-18; I Cor. 8:6; Col. 1:15-20; 2:9; Hebrews 1:2-3)

Finally, the outer rim of the wheel intimately connects with the earth, the minerals, and the soil. As such, the rim touches and interacts with the earth and the world. Heaven always touches and influences the earth, just as the sky meets and interacts with the ground with its life-giving light and oxygen. *Therefore, the wheel, as it turns, gives opportunity for each spoke to exert its influence on the earth.* All in all, I found this entire image to be an elegant, refreshing and meaningful concept that enabled me to express tangibly a philosophy that had been brooding inside my being for decades! Examine the two figures included here and you will get a concrete idea of the concept.

***Word Picture #2**: Artistic drawing to illustrate dynamic creativity at all twelve levels. On the right is a magnificent tree illustrating fruit for all seasons, animal husbandry, and note two happy fish in the river! Beginning on the left is a geography class, a music section with trumpets and a harp, dancers involved in the arts, a group engaging in social skills, a group involved in government, followed by a class in science, math and history. The purpose is to illustrate the integration of creativity in every aspect of human endeavor. The wheel with 12 spokes signifies a multi-dimensional involvement with the Creator—reaching out in stewardship to a world requiring mankind's positive guardianship. (Drawings by Bill Rankin, Texas)*

Let's try for a few moments to stretch our spirit for an even more magnificent picture. If we study the "living wheels" of Ezekiel 1:15-16 and 3:13, and their context, we end up attempting to describe a dynamic living entity that blows our minds!

> [4]*Then I looked, and behold, a whirlwind was coming out of the north, a great cloud with raging fire engulfing itself; and brightness was all around it and radiating out of its midst like the color of amber, out of the midst of the fire.* [5]*Also from within it came the likeness of four living creatures. And this was their appearance: they had the likeness of a man.* [6]*Each one had four faces, and each one had four wings....* [10]*As for the likeness of their faces, each had the face of a man; each of the four had the face of a lion on the right side, each of the four had the face of an ox on the left side, and each of the four had the face of an eagle....* [15]*Now as I looked at the living creatures, behold, a wheel was on the earth beside each living creature with its four faces.* [16]*The appearance of the wheels and their workings was like the color of beryl, and all four had the same likeness. The appearance of their workings was, as it were, a wheel in the middle of a wheel.* [17]*When they moved, they went toward any one of four directions; they did not turn aside when they went.* [18]*As for their rims, they were so high they were awesome; and their rims were full of eyes, all around the four of them.* [19]*When the living creatures went, the wheels went beside them; and when the living creatures were lifted up from the earth, the wheels were lifted up.* [20]*Wherever the spirit wanted to go, they went, because there the spirit went; and the wheels were lifted together with them, for the spirit of the living creatures was in the wheels* (Ezekiel 1:4-6, 10, 15-21).

Note that in Ezekiel there were 4 wheels. Isn't that interesting! Four represents the four corners of creation, the four winds, the four colors or families of mankind and completeness or perfection in the realm of created things. Four also represents stability.

Ezekiel's wheels within wheels also represent four living creatures. "The spirit of the living creatures was in the wheels" (Ezek. 1:20). However we understand this vision (and there are many interpretations), most scholars agree that the four faces represent the following:

1. The face of a *man* represents redeemed mankind created in the image and likeness of God.
2. The face of the *lion* represents *authority and kingship.*
3. The face of the *ox* represents the *servant,* one who bears the burdens of others.
4. The face of the *eagle* represents *flow, understanding and power in the heavenly realm.*

Can you see that everything is intimately connected? I believe these symbols represent the totality of the calling and ability of God's sons when they walk and move in their highest creative calling! "*And this was their appearance: they had the likeness of a man*" (Ezek. 1:5b).

Do you sense the power and the awesomeness of Ezekiel's vision? This is *word-picture* that blows apart small thinking! Notice the brilliance of God's glory as it emanates vivid light and pure pulsating power. Feel the rush and electrical voltage of this strange picture that travels like a "flash of lightning." There is whirlwind of activity, billowing clouds and refining fire. Everything speaks of creative direction and purpose under the authority and command of God. Yet the involvement of man is implicated as he with confidence moves into his calling as King and Priest of the Most High God. Notice that the heavens and the earth are harmonically related by the earthy symbols of faces, wings, wind, creatures and the number four!

These sketches represent my "revelation" and express a mental image that has fired up my Creation Mandate passion. Is this your passion also? If you have read this far, then I certainly hope that by now it is. Do you "see" what *could be* if the sons of men became the *sons of God*, powerfully fulfilling their destiny as they move daily with authority and humility in the image and likeness of their Creator? Does this picture pulsate in you the way it does in me? As far as I'm concerned, the potential is light years beyond awesome! Would you care to be a part of this awesome calling? If so, consider the following prayer. Let it become your request—and your commitment—to God.

Do you "see" what could be if the sons of men became the sons of God, powerfully fulfilling their destiny as they move daily with authority and humility in the image and likeness of their Creator?

A Prayer to be internalized and preferably read out loud daily:

God, Your ways are way above my grandest imaginations. I had no idea that I could participate and actually qualify at the dimension and level that I now see. I am asking that You download into my heart and spirit the kind of thinking that takes me beyond myself into Your throne room. I have read that "eye has not seen, nor has ear heard" the wonderful things You have waiting for Your people. What I am hearing and seeing blows my mind. You will have to show me what this is all about. I am willing. I understand that You will have to refine me and teach me so that I can be a part of this creative calling. Right now I bow before You as the Lord of my life. Please extend Your royal scepter toward me. I confess that I am totally unworthy. I understand that I am totally worthy as I get connected to You through Your Son, Jesus Christ. Please connect me right now. Deliver me from my self-imposed boxes and inabilities. Help me to abide in Your presence 24/7. Amen!

Chapter Twenty

CREATION MANDATE: CONCLUDING THOUGHTS

"Wisdom calls aloud outside; She raises her voice in the open squares. She cries out in the chief concourses, At the opening of the gates in the city, she speaks her words: 'How long, you simple ones, will you love simplicity? For scorners delight in their scorning, And fools hate knowledge'"

(Proverbs. 1:20-22).

"*Making heaven on earth is our business.*"

—William Booth, founder of the Salvation Army

As we move toward the conclusion of this admittedly "radical" presentation of our Creation Mandate, I would be remiss in failing to acknowledge that my views have been challenged candidly and honestly on several occasions by persons whose sincerity and integrity I have no reason to question. Some of this correspondence, along with my responses, may be found in Appendixes 1-3 that follow. In this final chapter, however, I want to give a general response, share a "Creation Mandate Worldview" as a summary—and then offer a few concluding thoughts.

In this final chapter I want to give a general response, share a "Creation Mandate Worldview" as a summary—and then offer a few concluding thoughts.

The only correspondence I have received challenging my premise of a Creation Mandate reflect, in my opinion, belief systems based at least in part on *defective* perceptions of reality. The most common challenge relates to the charge or suspicion that my views are linked to the occult. A number of credible theologians, pastors and medical doctors believe that any modality that has to do with energy, or the movement of energy, is of the occult and therefore of the devil. Their list is long but includes all forms of homeopathy, western (and especially Chinese) herbs, chiropractic, all forms of bio feedback, light therapy, massage, reflex analysis, acupressure, iridology, foot reflexology, lymphology—and the list goes on and on. One person even told me that anything that ended in "ology" was demonic and of the devil. (What about *the-ology*?)

I would like to plow up some sacred ground here. Must we fear and reject every new or unique discovery that comes down the pike simply because it is new and different? Is the devil really the creator of *any* natural modality, no matter what its source? Or is he the great counterfeiter, an imposter, the hijacker of every good and valid resource? Just because we don't understand something, does that mean it is occult and of the devil?

Must we fear and reject every new or unique discovery that comes down the pike simply because it is new and different?

Unfortunately, that "knee-jerk" response seems to be the system of though of many. If that static opinion reigned throughout history—and in some places it has and still does—we would still be in the Dark Ages! We would still be living in a world celebrating a flat earth, devoid of microscopes, telescopes, cars, airplanes, telephones, electricity, computers, x-rays (many of them forms of energy flow) or any other of our modern conveniences. Don't forget that at one time, the Copernican "theory" that the earth orbits the sun was condemned by both the Church and established science as heresy!

Everything man can dream up may one day be possible. The problem is not the dream, the discovery or the invention, but the *uses* to which they are put. At the time of the Tower of Babel God confused human language to "prevent" man from discoveries that would destroy him. Mankind had lost their covenant and connection with their Creator. They were bent on building a *kingdom of man* that exploited everything evil.

The only language that has the possibility to restore the land and guide us to healing is the language of true love. Do you believe, as I do, that God is restoring that language in Christ? Although it might not look like that on the evening news, a deep global groan is welling up, a worldwide cry for genuine answers. Let us stop fearing what man can do and get on with the task of bringing the authority of Christ into *every area of need on this planet*! That is *our* job description!

No single person has the gift or the ability to fulfill that job description alone. Only as we corporately lay down our pride at the cross, allowing our ego and self-will to be crucified, can we prepare for global renewal that is beginning to sweep this planet. We are called to be "repairers of the breach." We are called to disciple nations. We are called to reconciliation and *restoration* at every level of need.

We are called to be "repairers of the breach." We are called to disciple nations. We are called to reconciliation and restoration at every level of need.

If Christ is coming for a perfect bride, "without spot or wrinkle," then should we not as believers prepare ourselves at every level of service, authority and stewardship? Otherwise we won't be ready whenever and however He comes.

Here's a question to ponder: Is it our eternal goal to be swept away into heaven, a place somewhere beyond the sky, as our final and eternal destination? Or is the kingdom of Heaven destined to be planted on this planet, having something to do with this earth? What did Jesus mean when He prayed to His Father, "Your kingdom come, Your will be done *on earth*, as it is in heaven?"

Your response to these and similar questions will determine how you live and prepare yourself *on this earth*! General William Booth, founder of The Salvation Army, proclaimed: "Making heaven on earth is our business!" If that statement is true (and I believe it is), should we not, like Jesus, be about our Father's business?

Creation Mandate: A Worldview Worth Considering

My unapologetic worldview is based on several presuppositions. I have condensed it below into twenty brief but practical statements with which you may agree or disagree. All of these statements are based on solid biblical precepts as I understand them. In this format they also serve a secondary function of summarizing briefly the primary points of this book. So I hereby submit for your consideration this *"Creation Mandate Worldview" and summary.*

1. God created *everything*. Satan created *nothing*.
2. Everything God created serves both *transitory* (seed) as well *ultimate* (fruit) purposes.
3. God created mankind to be caretakers of this earth, to take authority over the earth, to exercise dominion over it and to be fruitful and *multiply*.
4. *Everything* under our management should also *multiply* noticeably as we serve the creation.
5. All experience, knowledge, wisdom and understanding each person gains is to serve, uphold and benefit mankind as well as the plants, the animals, and the creation as a whole.
6. We as humans were inbreathed (Heb., *ruach*) with God's own likeness, image and nature; therefore God's likeness, image and nature should be revealed through every advance, discovery and step that we achieve.
7. As believers we are destined to rule and reign with Christ. On earth we are the church, the *ecclesia*, the body of Christ, who is the Head of this corporate body of believers. Remember that the church is *not* a building but consists of every believer who walks in true unity with the Creator.
8. As we move in our true nature we will be a *blessing* to the creation, always showing the way of peace—as we follow the Prince of Peace. All nations are to be *blessed* by our presence, work ethic, ingenuity and common sense—which ultimately are based on a radiant and biblical worldview that illuminates and energizes our purpose on earth.
9. Our battle is not with sword, gun or bomb, but by the Spirit of God. We wage spiritual warfare by speaking a creative word, by intercessory prayer and by manifesting a profound faith based on Scriptural principles and promises. This subtle but effective warfare is mighty enough to break down controlling strongholds of deception at every level, whether religious, social or civil government—any control that is opposed to the Creators intent.
10. This does not mean that governments do not bear the sword. The Scriptures tell us that civil government is ordained of God in this present age, and "does not bear that sword in vain." As we pray for those in governmental authority, and set an example at every

level, our light should shine as salt and light into every society. Salt and light must be powerfully restored in a world out of control, where diabolical plans and agendas are presently destroying the fabric of society at the most rapid pace in history.

11. We are to reveal the pure character, nature and personality of the Creator in everything we do, create, think or express. How is this possible? Because in Christ we have the "DNA"—the very nature—of our spiritual Father dwelling in our spirit. His nature is deep inside us, waiting to be revealed for the benefit of humanity and the entire creation, which "groans" daily for deliverance: "For we know that the whole creation groans and labors with birth pangs together until now" (Rom. 8:22). The Greek word for "groans," *sustenazo*, means to moan *jointly*, to experience a *common* calamity; to groan *together*. The basic root word, *stenazo*, means to weep silently, to cry as a child, to sigh, to be in grief, distress and anguish.

12. God Himself is the author of the great diversity of human characteristics. This diversity is expressed in the various nations, cultures, colors, and ethnic groups as well as in every star, rock, snowflake and fingerprint. We must *embrace* rather than fear this diversity.

13. Each diverse gift has the power either to control and destroy or to serve and heal. We are called to serve and heal.

14. Every misuse, abuse and disuse of God's creation must be redeemed and restored to its proper use. To *not* be involved is to confess unbelief, fear and failure.

15. Every modality and invention has a good and proper use. We are called to redeem, renew and revive the appropriate use of everything on this planet, from minerals and mining, to agriculture and healing, to the arts and music, to the sciences and every creative invention!

16. The fullness of the creative intent will not be realized before the kingdom of God arrives in its fullness. Nevertheless, we are called to "occupy," to build and prepare for that coming day: "And he called his ten servants, and delivered them ten pounds, and said unto them, Occupy till I come (Lk. 19:13 KJV). The Greek word *pragmateuomai* (occupy), means to busy oneself with something; to engage in business, to buy and sell.)

17. As that "great and terrible (awesome) day of the Lord" (Joel 2:31) approaches, sin will become more sinful, the darkness will become darker, yet the righteous will become more righteous, and the light will become brighter. In the end, God wins and the devil and the flesh loses. It's in the bag.

18. Even as we wait for the physical, visible, bodily, external return of Christ, we must also let Him work from *within us.* After all, Jesus said, "The kingdom of God is *within* you" (Lk. 17:21b). We must let Him restore our heart, our spirit, our calling and our creativity so that when He comes we might hear the words, "Well done, good and faithful servant," because we have invested wisely in our individual and corporate talents. In Jesus' parable, only the servant who *buried* his talent was judged harshly. The others received crowns and great rewards (see Mt. 25:14-30).

19. There are answers for every plague, disease, mental dysfunction, crime, war, and rampant toxic pollution—*thousands of answers that we are currently missing.* Why are they missing? Why do we not have better answers? Have we failed on our watch? Must we as a generation admit defeat, daily bogged down in non-answers and non-participation regarding healing the *wounds* of society? Or is there another approach, a better approach, a higher approach—that we are somehow missing?

20. Let us be faithful on our watch. A new era is blowing in. Will you and I be caught napping? Are we ready for the greatest challenge and opportunity any generation has ever been given? If so we must be a people of vast faith, people of prayer and vision, with a dynamic heritage that can't be robbed. Can we say with the apostle Paul: "*...not that I have already attained.... but I press on*"?

Do You and I Have the Authority Required to Restore and Replenish the Earth?

Man-made religion and culture have demolished true authority. How much authority did Adam have before the Fall? Virtually unlimited, as far as the earth was concerned. How much authority was restored in Christ? He restored everything Adam lost—and more. How much authority do we have in Christ? The same authority He had on earth. Remember, we are the ones that Jesus said would do the same works He did and *greater works.* Are we seated in heavenly places with Him? Yes, according to Ephesians 2:6. Then what is our problem? Very simply, *unbelief.*

There are individuals and groups who possess far greater talent than I. Please don't beat a trail to my door; I too am a searcher. But I have a vision, a bold and hopeful picture of the future that I have nurtured over dozens of years. More than that, I also bear good quality fruits in my own life that declare the reality of that vision.

Without a vision people perish (Prov. 29:18). My purpose is to sow a paradigm, a vision and a dream. This dream is based on reality and has been partially attained by many different individuals, by different people groups, even by different leaders and nations at unique times in history. Today we are merely scratching the surface. Research the *positive* stories of history and you will be encouraged. Every nation has those stories woven into the very fabric of its culture. Search until you find.

This dream is based on reality and has been partially attained by many different individuals, by different people groups, even by different leaders and nations at unique times in history. Today we are merely scratching the surface.

Be encouraged. Be part of the renewal. Continue to grow in your corner. Stretch deep, wide and high. Look up! Search the Scriptures! As we each keep knocking, the *doors will open* and *seekers will find* (Mt. 7:7-8). That is God's promise!

Therefore, in spite of our individual and corporate tribulations and differences, our hope burns bright. Have you been sensitized by God to take up this *torch of hope*? If so, grasp it tightly and let us run this relay race together. As a people of diversity, color-blind and filled with a vision of hope, let us *run as one*, because the prize is huge as we together plunge toward the *final quest*!

> *Those from among you will rebuild the ancient ruins; You will raise up the age-old foundations; And you will be called the repairer of the breach, The restorer of the streets in which to dwell* (Isaiah 58:12 NASB).

> *God...reconciled us to himself through Christ and gave us the ministry of reconciliation* (2 Corinthians 5:18 NIV).

Application

Any belief or agreement must be tested. Ask yourself: "Am I believing or confessing agreement to any of the above points?" *A positive confession is nothing more than a mental game unless it is matched with action.* "How deep does my agreement go? Do I have responsibility to be a steward, a caretaker of some aspect of our creation? Am I open to valid areas and methods of creativity that others reject? Am I willing to take responsibility for my own body, mind and spirit?" If your response is deep enough to say "yes" in your heart, then the *fruit of application* should follow.

Ask yourself: "Am I being all I am capable of being in Christ? Am I called to be part of the renewal process to help reconcile the creation back to its original intent? Do I need further training, discipleship or study in any area to help me fulfill my destiny? Which areas? What kind of training? What are the steps I can take to help prepare me for my next step in life?"

Please answer the following questions to help focus your personal goals in life:

1. What are several training, self-study, projects or discipleship steps that could help me fulfill the calling on my life? ______________________

   ____

2. What steps (reading, study or projects) will I commit to this week or this month that will help jump-start my dream? ______________________

   ____

3. What other long term or future steps would help prepare me to fulfill my destiny? ______________________________________

   ____

4. Reconciliation is not cheap. It may cost me everything: "*If anyone wishes to come after Me, he must deny himself, and take up his cross, and follow Me.*" (Mt. 16:24 NASB). Am I willing to take up my cross daily to follow my calling? ______________________________________

   ____

Model Prayer of Repentance

"*If my people, who are called by my name, shall humble themselves, and pray, and seek my face, and turn from their wicked ways, then will I hear from heaven, and will forgive their sin, and will* ***heal their land.***"

2 Chronicles 7:14, emphasis added.

If the Holy Spirit convicts you of falling short of your calling, please consider the following prayer as a model. This is a prayer of repentance, so approach it with an attitude of humility, as is appropriate for all prayer. If you believe restitution is required, do not hesitate to make things right. This can be either a personal or a corporate prayer. Make it as personal as possible, perhaps even writing out the parts that fit you and tacking it up somewhere as a daily reminder. In one way or another, each and every one of us needs to repent individually of our own sins and corporately for those of our generation and of our forefathers.

> *Heavenly Father, You created the earth and its fullness. You own the earth and gave it to Your people to manage, nurture and cultivate. We have failed to fulfill Your command. We as a people have sinned by filling the earth with violence. We have ignored Your laws and moved in selfishness rather than responsibility. We have treated the earth and its people like garbage, ignored their feelings, cursed and lied. We lost interest in walking as a steward and became a slave to our own lusts. We have broken covenant with You and with Your creation.*
>
> *Now that we and the earth are at such a low place physically and spiritually, we recognize that we have misjudged our place in the creation. We have acknowledged You as Creator but failed to care for the creation You made. We have set a terrible example by harming our own bodies, the world around us, and the land that You created.*
>
> *Father, I ask You to first heal our hearts and minds. Please heal the hurts we have inflicted on others. Our spouses and children have suffered much. I now ask forgiveness for the way I have treated all the creatures around me—myself, my neighbor, and even the smallest invisible microbe—that in self-defense have turned against us. We hear reports of sharks, stingrays, beasts of the earth, bacteria and the earth itself having lashed out at our people. We have deserved this judgment.*
>
> *In repentance I now bless everything around me. I worship You as Creator. I commit myself to move in harmony with nature and the land. I hand over my life to One greater than myself, that I might be empowered to bless and curse not. I now renounce every area of my life where Satan has taken ground in my life, as manifested in my actions, attitudes and motivations. Lord, I want to please You and now offer You my heart that I may from today on build pure, proper and holy relationships with every creature on this earth. I give You the glory for what You are about to do in my life as*

I restore my relationship with You, with my fellow humans, with the animals, with the plants, and with the land! Please help me, Holy Spirit, to be truly loving, truly forgiving, and forgiven. Thank You for forgiving me and for restoring me. Come into my heart to live and abide always. Amen.

Appendix One

RESPONSE TO A PASTOR IN MAINE

The following is a letter I prepared in response to a pastoral analysis of my previous book, *We Don't Die, We Kill Ourselves: Our Foods Are Killing Us.* One of his parishioners loved the book and passed it on to him, thinking he would be blessed. Unfortunately, he was quite belittling and wrote a sharp letter of criticism in response. Surprised by his response, this dear lady passed the letter to a mutual friend who then passed it on to me. What follows below is my response to them and, indirectly, to their pastor, addressing his critical analysis of my book. I have included this correspondence as an appendix to this book because there are still many people who share the same or similar attitude (misguided in my opinion) as this pastor.

Let me preface my response by sharing some of the adjectives this pastor used in his letter. He declared that I was "irresponsible," "inconsistent," "unbiblical," "simplistic," "hard to respect"—and those are just a few. Of course, I believe his analysis came from, frankly, a very limited and biased theological perspective.

He feared that my book may be causing *confusion.* This is certainly possible. Defending and balancing every statement would require writing multiple volumes, and then nobody would read it. I could have soft-peddled some of my statements, but then they would have had minimal impact. Challenging people to climb out of their ruts nowadays requires a bulldozer and shock treatments—-and even this, realistically speaking, may not work in our secular, pampered and fun loving society. *But a giant iceberg is dead ahead.* Therefore I purposefully used crisp and strong language.

Is it possible to write an apologetic without being defensive? The purpose of this reply is to benefit others who might have similar questions. I structured this reply as a "teaching forum." I trust the reader will find my answers satisfying, biblical, balanced and charitable.

Here then is the text of my response:

Dear C. and C. (names withheld):

Thanks for forwarding the letter from Pastor S. (name withheld.) His evaluation of my book, *We don't Die, We Kill Ourselves* was very well verbalized as well as very provocative. He was modest and brutal at the same time. Of course, I disagree with him concerning his own exegesis of the Scripture on all three of his major points, as expressed below. His are very traditional viewpoints, which, as I discovered in due time, viewpoints that were subtly blended into the church by the gradual fusion of Hellenistic (Greek) and Gnostic philosophy into every-day Christian thinking. Thus the simplicity of first century Christianity has been notably undermined. Rationalism crept into the church. Unbelief has become rampant and unparalleled. One form of rationalism that is prominent in modern society accepts "sickness as normal" and somehow acceptable. This philosophy, prominent in his letter, smacks with a "form" of godliness—in my view—but unquestionably lacks the power to effect deep personal and cultural change.

One form of rationalism that is prominent in modern society accepts "sickness as normal" and somehow acceptable.

First I should explain that I once believed the way he does. Thirty five years of being a pastor and teaching in various fellowships, as well as my 12 years of experience in Christian and agricultural missions in the deep jungles of South America, not to mention my 40 years in clinical practice dealing with medical, nutritional and emotional/spiritual issues, gradually convinced me that: I WAS WRONG.

I was wrong first because I was a product of a limited cultural and religious education that did not prepare me for the realities of life. Medically I was taught palliation and suppression of symptoms—with drugs—rather than the discovery of root causes leading to treatments and potential cure. Prevention was *talked about*, but was generally drug- or vaccine-oriented. Thus we must ask the question: does orthodox medicine have a "cure" for diseases like chronic arthritis, heart failure, cancer or diabetes? After billions spent in research, the answer is an unfortunate "NO!"

Let's ask other questions: have all of these same serious problems been sometimes been cured by conquering the nutritional, emotional and spiritual ROOTS INVOLVED? And secondly, have I personally witnessed those types of *cures* in both people and pets? The answer to both of those questions is "YES!"

Theologically, I was educated that the key to the gospel was the salvation of the soul. This salvation was basically two fold: being saved from sin, then getting a "ticket to heaven" when we die. Neither the medical, educational nor the religious systems taught us our *overall* biblical responsibility while here on earth. They rarely taught the Genesis 1:26-28 mandate concerning our responsibility and heritage in Adam of stewardship, husbandry and dominion.

And secondly, it was seldom mentioned and never emphasized that in Christ—the Second Adam: 1. His sacrifice included not only salvation from sin but also, within the very nature of the Greek word, it included healing for our body. (I will share more on that point later) 2. Way beyond that, the price paid included the redemption of the *entire creation (Greek "cosmos").* 3. Furthermore, the debt paid for salvation included not only of our soul and spirit, but also included healing of negative emotions within our body (resulting in peace, joy etc.). 4. Finally, that salvation was not just a futuristic someday-in-heaven, in the sweet-by-and-by, but includes our life today...right *now* here on this earth.

The Lord's Prayer poignantly demonstrates this fact when we petition: "May thy Kingdom come, may thy will be done ON THIS EARTH as it already is done in heaven." That was a *kingdom prayer.* That kingdom prayer includes such mundane items as our daily food, deliverance from sinful temptation, and deliverance from *evil.* That 2000-year-old prayer is just as applicable today. Why pray that awesome prayer? Because it reminds us of all benefits of the Kingdom, benefits directly available to a covenant people as we walk in faith and victory—ON THIS EARTH.

This larger message is the message of the *Gospel of the Kingdom.* We must dramatically upgrade our understanding of this gospel—the "Good News." This Good News is that people everywhere, nations and the entire creation, can be set free in every area of body, soul and spirit. It only remains for us to APPROPRIATE THAT FREEDOM. And that happens when and *if* and as soon as we BELIEVE and APPROPRIATE the fullness of that Kingdom message!

Let me share an overview of my personal perspective on the three points the pastor strongly disagrees with as being so obviously unbiblical. He concludes that:

1. Teaching health is definitely NOT the responsibility of the church.

2. Scripturally, the Torah laws are NOT valid in the New Testament—the unclean is now clean; we are free to eat anything we desire.
3. *Pharmakia* does NOT mean drugs and pharmaceuticals; that is a misinterpretation of the Greek meaning of that word.

POINT ONE. As far as the premise that the "CHURCH" HAS A RESPONSIBILITY to lead the way in health at every level, I stand by that premise. Not only is it biblical, it is based on every right core foundational premise of taking care of our body as the "temple of the Holy Spirit." The medical system is certainly not healing us. Just a few days ago an Associated Press report in the *Washington Post,* by AP medical writer Lauren Neergarrd, reported: "Drug Errors Injure More Than 1.5M." The first sentence states, "Medication mistakes injure well over 1.5 million Americans every year, a toll too often unrecognized and unfought, says a sobering call to action." The report goes on to say these problems are grossly *under-reported.* It also reports that both the government and the AMA are turning a deaf ear to this grave problem.

"Medication mistakes injure well over 1.5 million Americans every year, a toll too often unrecognized and unfought, says a sobering call to action."

Dr. Julian Whitaker MD wrote in *Health and Healing,* Vol. 16, No. 8: "More than 2.2 million adverse drug reactions are reported every year among hospitalized patients, and more than 106,000 of them are fatal. It is difficult to get exact figures on how many drug-related deaths and injuries occur outside hospitals, but estimates are in the *millions.*" Who will stand up to defend the poor, the widow and the fatherless in this situation where they apparently have no other defense?

Defenseless people and pets are dying on our watch. The system is responsible and the church has its head buried in the sand. Could it be that some of us, as teachers, pastors and leaders, will have to answer to our Creator someday for this travesty of justice? James 3:1 states that teachers will receive heavier judgment. We are required to "get it right!"

Some of those hurt and dying are our families, our friends, and our people! In ignorance or in fear we have complacently avoided the issue. Is it not time to hold up a higher standard and become an enhanced source and resource of truth in BOTH the spiritual AND the natural realm? After all, God is the creator of both heaven AND earth. Our physical body is derived from the dust of the earth. Our stewardship includes the animals in, under and above the earth. We are mandated to serve the creation, having "dominion…..over *all* the earth." (Genesis 1:26) Do humans deserve less? Have we forgotten how to be salt and light? Have we been moving in default rather than salt and light?

Of course the modern church IS currently and actively teaching in the areas of physical health. Here are the standard messages, by default: First it has taught and is teaching that we should pray over our food and then we are free to subsequently eat anything we want to. Secondly, some obviously teach that it is God's will to be sick, that God has a plan for sickness—and sometimes God wants Christians sick. But if there is a crisis, it thirdly teaches we should go to the medical doctor for solutions, that the secular medical doctor is obviously God's provision for the church. *I disagree with all three teachings*. All three are directly or indirectly responsible for the present sorry state of health care as practiced worldwide. It is way past time to shift gears and become more Biblically responsible as pastors, parents and leaders.

Yes, of course we have "FREEDOM" to eat what we want to. The Scriptures are clear on that one. In my book I quoted Paul in Romans defending that principle! *We also have freedom to put water, oil or vinegar into our gas tank as an alternative fuel.* Or we could put diesel fuel into a gasoline engine. Any of those fuels would be unintelligent and uninformed, however. I believe Christians are just as unintelligent and uninformed when they teach and believe that we can put *any fuel we want to into our mouths*—because we have the "freedom to do so"—and assume that somehow God will bless and cover that decision.

Why is it we take more responsibility for our automobile than we do for our Temple of the Holy Spirit? It's all fuel for some system of energy, right? What's the difference? The difference is in the type of engine! The human engine was not created to run on the devitalized, hydrogenated and artificial fuels people are consuming in excess, and that includes the "unclean" fuels outlined by Moses through revelation. Read the owner's manual!!!

Eating whatever we want to, however, is an argument I commonly hear from sincere Christians—well, many others also for that matter. *But where is the proof that this theology is working*? Sorry, the argument doesn't hold water. And I would hope the pastors are few and far between who would conscientiously teach their people, as this pastor apparently does, when he teaches, "Maybe God wants you sick."

The guidelines of what are the proper fuels for the human body have already been outlined in the Scriptures, beginning in Genesis 1:29, to which we may add hundreds of other guidelines taught throughout the Scriptures. Why do we have our "head in the sand," in that we discount the hundreds of other Scriptures that deal with health, disease, agriculture, mental health and so on? *I am shocked at the resistance of the typical biblical "scholar" to recognize common sense, historical precedence and first covenant wisdom*!

I am shocked at the resistance of the typical biblical "scholar" to recognize common sense, historical precedence and first covenant wisdom!

Here is another problem. Fully 30% of chronically sick people have been proven to nurture their own illness. Psychologically, their disease is their crutch. Very few are willing to radically adjust or transform their *addictive lifestyle*. Am I not correct in that statement? So this pastor would tell these precious folks their sickness is maybe from God, to the saving of their soul? *That type of reply should be ranked with pure unbelief*, in my opinion. Sure, one can take a few Scriptures out of context and make a case for that position. But the vast bulk of the Scriptures clearly teach that God through Christ is our HEALER. He wants us well! So let's not build our doctrine on a few out-of-context exceptions.

The pastor mentions "self-control." Why not anticipate and pave the way for the church to actively teach "self-control" and wisdom in regard to *food*? Obesity and early death is ONE OF THE PRIMARY PROBLEMS of our Western, pragmatic, opulent and affluent culture. Should not parents, pastors and leaders apply the Scriptures to *daily life*? And to the *modern context*?

For many, the weakness of the flesh is the belly, which the Bible calls gluttony and gluttony is called sin. That weakness alone *should* keep every pastor and spiritual adult on his knees seeking daily deliverance from corpulence. Obesity statistically will cut 10-13 years from the normal life span. **"Why die before your time?"** That is chapter one, page one and verse one in my book, *We Don't Die, We Kill Ourselves*! Slow suicide with our knife and fork! How many Scriptures do I need to defend this point?

In that context, where is the inspired pastor, deacon or teacher who would step out and teach the truth that the world system has led us down an erroneous prim-rose path of nutritional suicide? If this well-disguised truth is left to individual self-discovery, there will be very few who will find the narrow path. No…rather as I state forcefully in my book, that responsibility belongs to the fathers in the faith, the leaders of the local and worldwide *ecclesia*, the called-out ones.

Called out from what? Called out from the system of slavery to our own lusts, whether that lust be junk food, promiscuous sex, gluttony or lack of self-control—all of which are "works of the flesh." And by implication, also "called out" from junk food *addiction*, Babylonish carnal thinking, secular trash music, and the misuse, abuse and over-use of pharmaceutical poisons!

The problem is there are very few true "fathers" left in the church—a painful problem that Paul lamented over in the *ecclesia* of his day. But who will *dare* touch this issue? Most pastors would be afraid to! My God, let us weep over the terrible deception mankind is in and let us care enough to teach the correct path at *all* levels. Let us empower those within the church who DO HAVE ANSWERS. If not the pastors, then some other para-church leaders, deacons, nurses, nutritionists or teachers who connect with the truth and have the respect of the people!

The pastor used Paul as one of his arguments. He wrote: "This premise (that God's people should "lead the way" in health) is unbiblical. Look at Paul, who healed others from their sickness....*it was God's will for Paul to have an ailment for God's glory.*"

Let me comment that because Paul's "thorn in the flesh" was directly related to a "*messenger from Satan*" to buffet his flesh, that particular phrase leaves tons of room for speculation. Could it have been a spirit of anger? Remember, Paul was previously a very angry man, angry enough to kill people! Was that carnal zeal totally in control? Paul was a single man; could it be he was weak in that area and had to fight a daily battle with a spirit of lust? We don't know for sure.

However, the authentic answer probably lies in the very context of the Scripture quoted by the pastor. 2 Corinthians 12:9-10 reveals that God's "power" would be revealed in the midst of "insults, with distresses, with persecutions, with difficulties." And then it concludes, "...for Christ's sake; for when I am weak, THEN I AM STRONG!"

What was the weakness? Enduring great affliction and suffering for Christ's sake! Throughout Paul's writings he confirms the accuracy of Ananias's Word from God concerning the, "great things Paul would suffer" for the sake of the gospel (Acts 9:16). What direction did that suffering take? The Word tells us! It included shipwrecks, hardships, being "beaten times without number", imprisonments, sleeplessness, hunger, in danger of robbers, the sea, rivers, the Gentiles, even from his own countrymen! That was more than most human are "asked" to endure either emotionally or physically for the sake of the gospel. Could you or I have handled that level of suffering? Yet Paul was in "all these things more than a conqueror!" Buffeted in the flesh but not conquered. Wow!

In that weakness of "flesh," God's GRACE (preserving power) proved sufficient! Gal. 4:13-15 mentions that Paul preached in spite of a "physical infirmity," and that was the trip that followed immediately after having been stoned and left for dead. Indeed, Paul must have looked like mincemeat after that ordeal! Probably his body as well as his face and eyes were badly swollen, fractured, and perhaps infected. And yet, concluding that Paul had a *chronic* God-induced eye infection from this particular set of verses is a stretch. Why? Because if we interpret this Scripture in the context of the culture in which it was written, it was a *common Middle Eastern proverb* to tell someone that you would "*give them your eyes.*" It meant something similar to the American statement, "*I would give you my right arm.*" When these brethren saw Paul so beat up, their appreciation for his ministry was so profound, that *symbolically* they would have plucked out their eyes or right arm, happily and willingly—if that would have helped Paul.

We miss so much when we Westerners try to interpret Scripture from our Western mindset. No, we must study and interpret the Bible in the light of the culture of that era in history. Therefore this Scripture is no proof at all of Paul having a chronic physical infirmity, or that God gave it to Paul because "God wanted Paul sick." That interpretation is totally inconsistent with the nature of God.

We miss so much when we Westerners try to interpret Scripture from our Western mindset.

The pastor's personal conclusion was that the word "flesh" meant physical sickness. I realize that is a common interpretation. I believe it is a misinterpretation. As we have demonstrated, however, "flesh" not only may mean CARNAL THOUGHTS, such as anger, envy, strife and every other fleshly battle. It also likely includes the many assaults that Paul experienced in city after city as he heroically advanced the gospel. Yes, Paul definitely had some "weakness" that kept him on his knees. But as we look at the context and totality of the Scriptures, the argument that "God wanted Paul sick" to bring God glory is an argument that does not convince me. Dr. Michael W. Hulsey, M.Th., D.D. in *Healing...The Children's Bread...Understanding Your Covenant Right To Be Healed* (see chapter 6: "Paul's Thorn, Paul's Eye Disease, and the Man Born Blind") is not convinced either!

POINT TWO. I may not be a biblical Scholar. Is the pastor? How is it that I passed these themes through a dozen or more pastors for their constructive evaluation, pastors from various denominational backgrounds, and not one even one pastor advised me that I was misinterpreting the Scriptures? Perhaps they recognized the balance that I achieved? Nor did I ignore the passage from Colossians, from which the pastor challenged my uprightness. In fact, I quoted and referenced several Scriptures from Corinthians and Romans that teach the same principles.

I have a relationship with several Messianic rabbis and have an ongoing discussion with them over some of these same points! In my opinion, many of them put too much emphasis on the law, on the Torah, on tradition, and to them *eating pork is sin.* However, it is not *sin* to *my* understanding of the New Testament Scriptures. Unwise fuel for the human body, yes. There are many reasons why this latter position is scientifically accurate and defendable. But a *sin* (which affects our eternal salvation) to eat pork? I made it clear in my book that *eating pork is not a sin, meaning a sin that affects one's eternal destiny.* Where is the confusion? But there is a *huge difference* between what we are **free** to do and what is **wisdom.**

One of my research projects 20 or so years ago was a study concerning the unclean foods. I obtained a research paper from a senior medical scientist and oncologist from the John Hopkins cancer center who was also a Hebrew scholar. He wrote a paper in a theological journal describing how he imported dozens of unclean meats by air on ice from around the world and tested them against the clean meats in regard to toxicity. He discovered and proved scientifically that 100% of the unclean meats he tested were of equal toxicity to the toxic blood of cancer and schizophrenic patients at the John Hopkins medical teaching hospital. On the other hand, "clean" fish and meats, as delineated by Moses in the Torah, were either neutral or of positive benefit. There are many other scientific reasons that unclean meats are *unwise fuel* for the human digestive system.

100% of the unclean meats he tested were of equal toxicity to the toxic blood of cancer and schizophrenic patients at the John Hopkins medical teaching hospital.

I will emphatically stand by the fact that the health laws of Moses had and still have something to do with human health, just as much as cleanliness, burying excrements and the other health laws that Moses prescribed for an uninformed people are *still valid* in the world today. Yes, it is true that washing your hands won't "save" you. Burying human excrement won't save anyone's soul either. Both could help prevent local and worldwide plagues and epidemics, however. And ignorantly consuming unclean "toxic" meats could definitely pave the way for dozens of chronic and acute diseases. (I treated a poodle once that was given a helping of Christmas ham. This holiday treat was followed by gran-mal epileptic seizures. Removing smoked ham from the diet "cured" the problem.) God used Moses, by revelation, to codify these and many other health laws for the wisdom of following generations. In my opinion, we are exceedingly foolish if we discount this wisdom and teach contrary precepts.

It may be unpopular to teach this type of truth, because this subject is touchy and interferes with custom, taste and modern religious belief at its very core. Probably I won't convince the pastor either, even if I listed a dozen other facts, because if he was disturbed by the clear message of my book, then I doubt if a few more facts would shake and realign religious beliefs. Nor would I try to convince him. Each must be persuaded in their own heart. That is the awesome freedom we have in Christ!

But there are more than a few reasons why *I stand firmly by my premise.* None of these reasons were learned at the theological seminary from which I graduated. They were learned as hard lessons in the university of life, as I slowly got delivered from my previous suicidal interpretations of the Scriptures.

And above all the pastor totally misinterpreted the *obvious interpretation and application* of Peter's vision. That vision had nothing to do with debunking 3000 years of wisdom and health principles. Peter's vision was specifically figurative and symbolic. By giving Peter this vision, God was graphically painting a picture with a dramatic and visual clue that God's redemptive plan included all gentile nations. *This was a bold revelation to a pre-programmed and resistant Jewish mind. Nor did Peter immediately get the impact of the message.* But when the gentiles suddenly received the baptism of the Holy Spirit—spontaneously and without coaching—Peter immediately perceived that God was doing a NEW THING. This was mind boggling to Peter, way beyond his boxed in grasp of reality.

The vision had absolutely nothing to do with food, diet changes or a new change in the health principles—revealed principles that taught wisdom relevant to *freedom from disease.* It was strikingly a figurative vision given to prepare Peter mentally for a major psychological breakthrough. *To interpret this vision any other way defies every rule of logic and basic biblical exegesis.* Yet Biblical scholars by the thousands fall before this error, and so teach others. And I am accused of mishandling the Scriptures!

I would say this passage is just one example of misapplication and misinterpretation by our pastor friend who claims to be a biblical scholar. But is he interpreting this vision by *letting the Scriptures interpret themselves*? The interpretation is right there in the context!

Or has our pastor friend fallen into the common trap of capitulating to a pre-programmed viewpoint? I have discovered that those who hold this interpretation are neither easily dissuaded nor convinced. Like an addiction, in this case a *conviction addiction,* it is a rigid interpretation that is not easy to get delivered from. This interpretation seems to be a "sacred cow" in much of the fundamental Bible-believing community—an interpretation that has been subtly seeded into theological consciousness over many generations. It is a mindset that got carved into cement and woe is to the one who challenges it…let his name be mud!

The pastor says, "I must say to Dr. De Haan, what God said to Peter, 'What God has cleansed, no longer consider unholy.'" In reply to that I would say that when God cleanses any person, whether Jew or Gentile, they are holy. *That is the clear Scriptural application.* But in regard to unclean animals, I do not consider them unholy, just unhealthy.

POINT THREE: *PHARMAKIA*. I have studied, written and published papers on the meaning and application of the Greek word *pharmakia* for over 20 years. I am quite aware of the technical nuances of word usage and its multiple meanings. I have shared my personal conclusions on this subject with various Christian medical doctors and teaching pastors, besides referring to Greek lexicons. Again, I stand 100% behind what I said. It was not my purpose to greatly expand or defend that point. I have done that elsewhere. My goal was merely to share the word and explain its basic meaning in a style and context that was unmistakable and recognizable to the interested student of Scripture.

Nor was it my purpose in *We Don't Die, We Kill Ourselves* to support my statements through historical and exegetical proofs. The only ones who do not "see" this prophetical application are those who do not or cannot understand the powerful influence of a very influential and pervasive spirit. Isaiah prophesied that a cloud or "veil" had been spread over "all nations." Revelation teaches that "all nations have been deceived" by this merchandizing spirit. Good people, good medical doctors, and good Christians have been profoundly deceived. For many years I too was deceived.

Good people, good medical doctors, and good Christians have been profoundly deceived. For many years I too was deceived.

Gradually I began to realize the power of the damage I was doing—when there were far better answers. Does the pastor realize that a minimum of 769,000 people *die every year* in America *directly caused by properly prescribed drugs, properly done surgeries, and other life-threatening reactions to orthodox medical treatments?*[xxxvi] *Dr. Whitaker, quoted above, also says in the same article, "But as I've pointed out time and again, the pharmaceutical industry is the most dangerous industry in the history of civilization."* Sorry, this is a medical high priesthood of death, not of health. They call them health clinics. A better word would be institutions of high risk. I am just one of thousands of "insiders" who are waking up to this universal problem. But millions are still blind leaders of the blind.

Hitler specifically sought for a *pharmakia* drug to control the German nation, so that the national mind would be dulled and more easily controlled. What was his answer? A poisonous drug called FLUORIDE, which was subtly introduced into the German drinking water prior to WW II.* (*Source: *Minerals for the Genetic Code*, p xi to xix by Charles Walters, ACRES USA, www.acresusa.com) With the evidence available today, anyone who still believes fluoride slows tooth decay has bought into a deception and misinterpretation of rigged scientific studies. Big money is behind this industry. The majority of the American public has unhappily bought into this theory. Several European nations have already outlawed fluoride in the public drinking water. Several have also outlawed mercury fillings in the mouth.

*Hitler specifically sought for a **pharmakia** drug to control the German nation, so that the national mind would be dulled and more easily controlled. What was his answer? A poisonous drug called FLUORIDE.*

IF merely mentioning this information causes a defensive attitude from any person, pastor or leader, then they too may be operating under the cloud of confusion that has engulfed all nations. (As the pastor said earlier, if the shoe fits, wear it, else don't; though he confidently stated he *did* believe the shoe fit me, as his own personal judgment against my book.) That veil unfortunately includes the American Dental Association, the AMA, the FDA and the USDA, which are all under the direct influence, control and manipulation of big business and the pharmaceutical and chemical conglomerates. Did I claim that any one of the doctors, dentists or drug salesmen were evil? No I did not. Everyone that I have met are seemingly decent persons. What I am implying is that there is a worldwide sincere belief and deception that is somehow intimately joined to the *secular* system of big government, big business, and powerful corporate control, financial power and greed. Does this surprise anyone?

Both fluoride and mercury are two of the most toxic elements on the planet. Both are cancer-causing, immune-suppressing, enzyme-destroying and brain-toxic in extremely low amounts. Both are behind much of the suffering on this planet. But like the historic defense of a flat earth, or the old belief that dirty and filthy hands could never spread disease— modern science is not about to change from its entrenched position and love of *pharmakia* poisons. Huge financial and legal interests are at stake! They are dug-into this position and will resist and defend it vigorously till the end. Fortunately the end is in sight.

Other points to consider:

Salvation in the Greek ("*sozo:*" save, make whole, heal, deliver from danger) has a very wide application. In fact, the Greek word *soma*, translated "body," is used 146 times in the Greek New Testament, and is derived from the root *Sozo*. (See Strong's # 4982, 4983, 4990, 4991.) Both words are intimately related and both have physical as well as spiritual meanings. It is time to restore the *full meaning* of *sozo* to the body of Christ.

I want to emphasize again that the word "salvation" in the original Greek includes freedom from spiritual, emotional *and* physical sickness. This is not a way-out application. It includes the plagues and diseases of Egypt, as well as all the modern plagues and diseases! *Or if not then the Old Testament covenant was better than the New!*

The word "salvation" in the original Greek includes freedom from spiritual, emotional and physical sickness.

How is that freedom effected? That freedom is the result of applying God's principles and commandments at all levels. This includes walking and living in the natural laws of the physical creation—(gravity, mechanics, sowing seed in the proper season, the laws of sowing and reaping, etc)—as well as applying the practical principles of basic biblical *nutrition*. It includes the emotional level whereby there are specific laws and principles that govern the healing of our emotions (the Book of Proverbs, Phil 4:8, 2 Tim 1:7 etc.). And then it includes the various laws that govern spiritual health (forgiveness, faith, love etc.).

The pastor teaches that *everything* in the Old Testament was fulfilled in Christ. That is partly true. I agree that the *ceremonial and* temple laws were fulfilled in Christ. But the *whole* body of the Scriptures was given for our instruction, for our correction and for our wisdom. Paul makes that abundantly clear in his letter to Timothy. Perhaps that is the root of our disagreement.

If I were predisposed to nit pick, biblical scholars tell us only 1/3 of the Law and the Prophets were fulfilled by the first coming of Christ—when He arrived as the "suffering servant," the "Lamb of God" slain before the foundation of the world. Two thirds have yet to be fulfilled, when He returns as the Lion of the Tribe of Judah, the reigning King! Much more could be said on this subject. Therefore my book is a very incomplete, on-the-surface response to a very complicated subject. Or at least, mankind has made it complicated.

It is interesting that the first covenant taught that if we follow the Torah commandments the result would be: "*none of these diseases*!" The new Covenant was a "*better covenant*" based on "*better promises.*" So now God wants some of us sick! Whoa! Did the pastor really mean that? IF that is what pastors teach their people, maybe that explains why Christians have the same level of disease, cancer, mental breakdowns, bankruptcy etc. etc. as unbelievers. Is that teaching not a wishy-washy gospel built on unbelief—devoid of both power and promise? Has orthodoxy become the bastion of unbelief in regard to health? God forbid!

In my book I purposely and consciously chose to *not* enter into a discussion shielding against the position taken by this pastor. *That was not the purpose of my book.* True, my goal was to be theologically correct. But *We Don't Die* was definitely not purposed to be a theological treatise. It was not even purposed to present a perfect balance—even if that were possible. My deeper purpose was to *touch the heart and soul of the reader* with just enough documentation to satisfy the average interested reader. *If* we were both on the same wavelength, the heart to heart message would hopefully inspire the seeking heart to stimulate momentous and meaningful change.

As far as interpretation of the Scriptures, my editor was a pastor and a graduate of a Southern Baptist seminary. I asked him if he had any theological disagreements with how I interpreted the Scriptures. He told me he was in full agreement.

You will note the general endorsements from a dozen or so pastors who read the book and sent me comments before it was published. They were from every walk of life. They included conservative Baptists, a retired Methodist pastor, two Presbyterian clergymen, a Church of God Bishop, a Four Square Gospel pastor, several charismatic pastors, a Messianic Rabbi, and a former Jesuit priest. I did that on purpose in order to obtain a cross section of biblical scholars. Not one of them pointed out the fallacies this pastor did. All of them were apparently not yoked to that limited perspective.

I was surprised, of course, because I expected to run into resistance, challenges, and disagreement. But iron sharpens iron. And that was my purpose. I am not out to deceive or mislead anyone. Thus I was supplementing my own years of study and meditation of the Scriptures, believing that "in the mouth of two or three witnesses" there is safety. Did I do my homework? Others will have to judge. But I do think it is good to clarify that I was not "shooting from the hip" in total theological ignorance.

Sadly, most people have no clue how to eat. The system has failed them. Disease is epidemic. The average medical doctor has no clue either. "Eat a balanced diet," we are told. People are dying on "balanced diets" because the average diet IS NOT BALANCED!

"Eat a balanced diet," we are told. People are dying on "balanced diets" because the average diet IS NOT BALANCED!

And just to whom does the responsibility fall to teach these things? Do we continue with the status quo? I would like to know Pastor S's answer! Fatalism? It's God will for you to be sick? Go to the doctor?

My answer is that health care instruction definitely falls under the auspices of the five-fold ministry of the New Covenant called-out Ecclesia. At least part of that responsibility falls on the "teachers." (That might include private schools, youth meetings and adult education classes.) Anything less is irresponsibility. As Dr. Hauser pointed out in his endorsement, the church has been negligent and irresponsible in this area of non-teaching. He told me: "Pour it on—convict pastors!"

This area of instruction could be an area relevant to the modern deacon, as this ministry is responsible for caring for the physical needs of the church. It matters not which leader or teacher fulfills the burden of guidance and instruction, as long as God anoints them and the church is open to hear. But unless instruction prevails we fail.

I attended a Christian school growing up. I learned reading, writing and math. I learned typing, business math and driver's education. I received catechism instruction and headed youth subscription drives. But hardly a word on diet, nutrition and how to stay healthy! Why this glaring absence of taking care of our natural body, the temple of the Holy Spirit? We should be the best of the best, the healthiest of the healthy!

This entire topic should be under the auspices of the apostles, prophets and elders or pastors of believing congregations. In my opinion we have been derelict in our God-ordained duty. I give the biblical basis of this in my upcoming book, and cannot go into detail here.

Christians have lost much of their testimony at nearly every level of society. We live in post-Christian America. We have no convincing message because our bodies are as sick as our neighbors. 80-90% of our children leave the church out of boredom because they are not convinced either. Culturally, we are no longer the salt of the earth. Economically, the squeeze is on. Traditional Christianity is in retreat. It is documented that 1,000,000 people leave the church every year. It is partly because the church has lost the message of the everlasting gospel that touches and transforms the spirit, the soul, the BODY and the creation at all levels of *stewardship*.

It is a statistical fact that Christians die of the same diseases as agnostics and atheists. Medical doctors die, on the average, years younger than those who never received a medical education. That is a message in itself! So far the best health odds documented are among the Seventh Day Adventists, Orthodox Jews, and several societies who live in areas of traditional diets and highly mineralized soils. That should give us other CLUES!

I was surprised this concerned pastor overstated so may of my viewpoints, and took others out of context. He says, "Eating well is important but it cannot be a universal solvent." That is one of my foundational points. We agree!

"What about environmental causes of sickness?" Ditto again. I don't understand the basis of the criticism.

"DeHaan toward the end of the book recognized that not everyone will be helped by his method but he says to just continue on anyway until they do help." What I obviously meant was to *continue* to eat properly, then *build* on that foundation at all other levels. Did Pastor S. read my conclusions? Did he read how nutrition, unresolved emotional issues and unforgiveness are ALL INTERTWINED? Did he somehow miss my points where I drew everything together? Did he miss chapter 18 in the Mind/Body connection concerning weeding our spiritual garden, and the priority of worship, Word and prayer as it relates to health?

Consider this: If one reads the book of James, one would get an entirely different perspective of the gospel than one would get from studying John or Paul. Does that mean James missed it? Did John miss it? Or did Paul miss it? Obviously, none of the above. God was using their particular life experience to plant a different but complementary aspect of the gospel message. My life, experience and training are MY MESSAGE. Each individual chapter is only one part of that message. Only God and time will be the judge of my book's effectiveness. But we *can* benefit from each life, each chapter, each book and each life experience, if we choose, and taken together they synergize and help bring a mature balance.

And if we read between the lines of what James or John or Paul wrote, actually they were all saying the same thing—just in different words. Thus in many aspects, the pastor and I are actually also saying the same thing. However our conclusions are different! The pastor chose to pick several of my points apart, dissecting them from their complete context. Perhaps he was skimming the book too lightly, or perhaps he was sidetracked by the three points to which he so vigorously disagreed? Interesting questions.

Thus in many aspects, the pastor and I are actually also saying the same thing. However our conclusions are different!

CONCLUSIONS. From the overall tenor of his letter I would say Pastor S. is a fine man. He sincerely tried to focus on what he personally believed to be false teachings. He is defending the folks under his charge against what he believes are unmistakable deceptions. Good men can disagree. I disagree with both his observations and his biblical conclusions as he analyzed my book, *We Don't Die, We Kill Ourselves.* I believe *he* is the one causing confusion.

At the same time, in my book I endeavored to walk in charity and in balance, always giving careful attention to the original sense of the Scriptures. I wrote the book as a teaching forum, *aiming at the heart rather than the left-brained intellect.* With this pastor, evidently I failed. Others with that same perspective might be less charitable, more ruthless—possibly calling me a false prophet or worse. I have read "exposé" books like that. Therefore, I was impressed, in the closing sentence, that brother S. said he was *open to correction* if any of his points were judged "unfair" or "unfounded." It might require several books to prove that. Even then the Holy Spirit would have to do the convincing. It is His job to correct hearts and minds. Mine is to teach, being faithful in the teaching ministry to which I am entrusted. Still, the attitude expressed at the end is a dramatic saving point—and I trust that same charity and openness will be expressed both ways in the future—as we all endeavor to come into the unity of the faith, unto a mature man in Christ.

I wrote this rather quickly. I hope when I look back I will not be surprised or shocked by what I wrote! Therefore in advance please forgive me for any misunderstandings that I may have gleaned from the letter, and therefore for any offensive comments on my part.

May Christ be lifted up every day and in every way,

Roger L. De Haan

A RESPONSE TO A CHALLENGE REGARDING THE LEGITIMACY OF HOMEOPATHY

The following is the text of a letter I wrote to a father in response to correspondence he had received from his son regarding the son's research into—and skepticism about—homeopathy. The father is a dedicated Christian while his son is a "searching" intellectual agnostic.

Hi B. (name withheld)! I read your son's review on homeopathy. Interesting. Of course, I have read reviews like this for years. Some of the information seems useful, some of it very slanted. Even the section quoted from the homeopathic medical doctor is slanted, although he also made some good points.

One can find almost anything on the web nowadays. Some of the most convincing information claims to be impartial "scientific research" that PROVES this or that is UNSCIENTIFIC. Most of that information, if the truth were known, is bought and paid for by the medical and pharmaceutical establishment. Almost anything passes as science nowadays, as long as it has some PhD name and a university study behind it. Guess who pays for those studies? Guess how many studies never see the light of day? Guess how many studies conveniently delete the information that does not fit the purpose of the study? Sadly, the majority of them.

The tenure and pay scale of the average university professor depends on him producing precisely what the investors paid for. Lots of politics goes on behind the scenes. Did you know that? I know that first hand. One tenured oncologist told me personally he could not prescribe nutritional supplements at the university or it would damage his professorship. Since he believed in nutrients, his alternative was to send his clients requesting nutritional advice and counsel to me for adjunctive treatment.

Do you know how homeopathy really got shut out in America? By 1 vote in the US Congress around the turn of the century, by the high-powered influence of the AMA, one of the most powerful lobbies in history. They shut out homeopathy from the medical school curriculum, made it nearly illegal, a medical laughingstock, and it was forced underground till recently. One of my wife's great uncles was a medical homeopath with oversight of the New York State health program in the public schools. That was before political pressure from the AMA destroyed the reputation of homeopathy. Its revival is due to the serious questions, mistakes and lacks within the modern medical system. Subscribe to www.mercola.com to get another view of the world of medicine. Mercola is a medical doctor. Subscriptions are free.

When the swine flu epidemic hit and some 50,000,000 (yes 50 Million) died worldwide in 1918, over 50% of those treated by the orthodox medical profession died. Those under the care of homeopathics experienced under a 3% death rate. Why the difference?

Recent statistics demonstrate that 769,000 good people DIE EVERY YEAR *just in America*, due to a combination of properly and improperly prescribed drugs, botched or unnecessary surgeries, over-the-counter drugs, including bleeding to death from Aspirin overdose and so on and on.[37] 769,000 thousand is equivalent to a jumbo jet crashing and killing everyone on board every day for 365 days of every year. (This does not include the millions seriously affected, bed ridden, work lost, invalided or weakened who did not die. Neither does this include the deaths and injuries occurring in over 100 other countries on the rest of our planet.) Some claim the official numbers are GROSSLY UNDER-ESTIMATED. This is one of the best-kept secrets. Napoleon said, "*When it comes to the judgment day, doctors will have to account for more lives lost than even us Generals.*" They think homeopaths should be sued? A good case could be made that the entire medical system should be sued!

There has never been a single death attributed to homeopathy. Is homeopathy perfect? Of course not. Yet to infer that most of its positive effects are placebo is nonsense. Animals do not show the placebo effect. I can attest to hundreds that have been helped, including lives saved, with homeopathy. I treated a cat years ago that came to me in kidney failure, skin and bones.

Nothing I did helped much. Then the owner visited a homeopathic veterinarian. A month later I saw that cat again and it was totally healthy and cured. I was both shocked and pleased. Since then I have witnessed dozens of results like that. Can't tell me homeopathy doesn't work.

Name calling homeopathy as occult is an old trick. Say it enough and people will believe a lie. I won't go much into that. But look at the other side of the equation. If you go into the history of the Greek word *pharmakia,* and pharmaceutical medicine, that type of medicine is clearly and historically ***sorcery***. *Pharmakia,* for hundreds of years translated, "sorcery," is the profession involved in chemicals, pharmaceutical drugs and toxic poisons that are destroying our ecosystem. *Every drug is a poison, by the way.* I learned that in Pharmacology 401.

I am sure you are aware of the 5 specific references in the Greek New Testament where *pharmakia* is used, including Revelation 18:23? Personally, I believe that latter Scripture reveals a significant key. Not that doctors are evil. Not that every drug is evil. Of course not! But the *merchandizing* of *pharmakia* drugs is an international cartel based on profit, slick advertising and *very poor science*. Look at all the drug companies getting sued recently. They KNEW the risks, yet the hid the facts, even from doctors, in the name of greed and profit. Scary AND unethical.

It is true the reason homeopathy works is not well understood by modern science. Well, the last I knew they haven't figured out how gravity works either. Neither have they discovered how or why a cat purrs. That doesn't stop gravity from working or a cat from purring, however. Some of our most brilliant minds tell us mankind only knows about 1% of what is to be known. We are not as smart as we think.

Some of our most brilliant minds tell us mankind only knows about 1% of what is to be known. We are not as smart as we think.

But there is now solid research that water is a universal carrier of energy imprint information, much like a tape records sound and music. Now if you play that tape one can elicit lots of valid scientific responses in plants, people, milk production in cows, even the number of eggs a chicken will lay. Good classical music rates the highest. On the other hand, hard metal rock discordant music has been shown to stunt and sometimes kill plants, decrease milk production in cows, and can even be a form of torture in humans.

But if you carefully and scientifically analyze the chemistry of the tape in a test tube, one would have to conclude *both* the classical music tape *and* the hard metal rock tape have the *same chemical composition.* But when played on a recorder there would a total difference in biological response. What is the difference? The electrical/magnetic imprint! And, well, also the positive or negative effects on the well-being of people, pets and plants. And what is homeopathy? An electrical magnetic (energetic) imprint!

Over 20 years ago I took two weeklong courses in homeopathy and health. The very basic presupposition is that the bottom line of everything in the universe of nature is energy. *Einstein expressed that in e=mc squared.* All "mass" can be converted into "energy." Energy is wavelength and frequency. The bottom line of EVERYTHING in nature is frequency and resonance. All mass and biological systems can be reduced to frequency and resonance i.e. energy.

The bottom line of EVERYTHING in nature is frequency and resonance. All mass and biological systems can be reduced to frequency and resonance i.e. energy.

Now the very bottom line of homeopathy is that biological molecules are transmuted into energy wavelength molecules. It is true, there is no biological matter left in the homeopathic solution after the 30th dilution. Today I personally used a 10M dilution to help ward off the flu. *10M means 1 followed by 10,000 zeros!* Powerful stuff! BUT, the very process of homeopathy changes or transmutes the mass into energy—and each dilution raises the energy frequency to a higher level. From *mass to energy.* Kind of like an atomic bomb—if one knows the secret of how to release that energy. Why is that so hard to understand?

Every disease, cell, mineral and chunk of matter has a specific scientific frequency. It is well known that any frequency can be CANCELLED OUT by an opposite sine wave or frequency. Modern sound squelchers are based on this phenomenon. Send in a counter wave and the incoming wave disappears. The same principle is true with disease. Cancel out the disease frequency cycle and the disease begins to melt and disappear. NASA and all cutting edge medical technology is aware of this. (Star Trek technology!) But today's modern family physician is still "practicing" on humans under the cloud and constraints of a 19th century medical model.

Believe me, the medicine of the future will be based on a superior and far safer technology. Creation and everything within it was created by the Word—

the energy and creative frequencies, the spoken creative Word of Yahweh Elohim. *No, God didn't use homeopathy.* But homeopathy is based on and expresses that very principle. Homeopathy is a step in the right direction! And homeopathy is based on energy frequency signals, not poisons! And here we are in the 21st century muddling around trying to heal with poisons and drugs. Totally anti-scientific, anti-God, and anti-health as a true healing profession, in my opinion. Why are we so dense? Or can this rut be explained in trillions of dollars and cents, pride and greed?

Most of the animals I treat are fall-outs from orthodox veterinary medicine. Many come with blood test values off the chart. They come in "sick as a dog!" Why is it that I can put them on homeopathics and often within weeks the blood tests rebound toward normal, the pets energy returns, at least in the majority of cases, and the clients are ecstatic? Sorry, I don't buy the overt political "occult, occult" name-calling, nor the placebo claims.

By the way, the homeopathic medical doctor "exposing" the lack of significant benefits using homeopathy practiced *classical* homeopathy. He limited his practice and teaching career to *orthodox outdated methods,* which significantly reduce results. Even Dr. Hahnemann used higher potencies and multiple dilutions before he died. He found the classical approach worked well in Germany, his land of birth. When he retired to Paris, France, in the midst of complicated disease situations and higher toxicity due to luxurious and toxic high society living, he was unable to obtain the same wonderful results. He discovered the situation was far more complicated in Paris. It was there that Dr. Hahnemann perfected his LM potencies and also combined multiple remedies. Finally, he was getting results again. The guy was brilliant. However, due to retirement much of that later research was lost—but has recently come to light.

Let's accurately define occult. The historical definition of "occult" is the use of hidden or invisible (occult) *negative* spiritual powers. By definition the occult practices operate under the guise of hidden but harmful spiritual powers. The actual definition depends somewhat whether one is judging it from chemistry or a spiritual standpoint. Using the latter spiritual definition we are obviously defining the involvement of subtle (but hidden) demon powers, white magic, or spirit connections as somehow involved—not so different from the various forms of witchcraft.

Because homeopathy is not well understood, it is so easy to lump it with the occult. However, for true occult powers to function one must be in some measure into the occult and therefore connecting with these "hidden" occult powers. *Just because something is invisible or poorly understood does not make it occult.* Otherwise, gravity and a host of other invisible rays, frequencies and wavelengths would also have be classified as occult. Am I making myself clear?

The historical definition of "occult" is the use of hidden or invisible (occult) negative spiritual powers. By definition the occult practices operate under the guise of hidden but harmful negative spiritual powers.

From a purely etymological standpoint, homeopathy is neither toxic nor poison, nor is it based on any hidden, direct or indirect influence from the spiritual realm. Therefore the accusation is false. I discovered over 20 years ago that homeopathy got the same results whether a believer or unbeliever dispensed the remedies. Nothing magical, nothing occult—just *physiological.* I guarantee that homeopathy will one day be fully justified and explained scientifically. The people who lambaste homeopathy live with a flat earth mentality.

Probably my answer raises more questions than it answers. Argument and facts alone will not satisfy most people. It was 10 years after I first saw a dog who came into a clinic that could not walk, and left walking following an acupuncture treatment, before I was finally convinced, and finally mustered enough guts and courage to train in and practice acupuncture. Of course, I also was convinced that homeopathy was placebo and occult in my earlier years. But then I ran into cases and witnessed responses that I could not explain any other way. So to use the old adage, "Now I are one!"

You asked for a response. I hope this helps some.

Roger

Appendix Three

A RESPONSE TO A QUESTION CONCERNING "ORIGINS" OR "FIRST USE"

The following is a letter I wrote in response to questions I received regarding the origins of alternative medicine and therapies. Many people still are confused or suspicious about the source or origin of these different modalities.

The Origin of Things, Their Proper Use and Significance

I am glad you brought up the question of the "first use" or origin of a modality. That is a very old argument. Sometimes it is valid, other times it is an excuse. Often, one does not go back far enough into the origin of a subject to get to the true tap root. Yes, the origin can give us a key.

You wrote: "*New info indicates that the Origin of some of the holistic stuff is what makes it bad. I guess because it is often traced to Orient with some of the energy stuff. I heard one person say that Jesus was born in the East, so that can't be the problem. But have you any rebuttal about the origin of things, whether that is a valid point to judge something by or not? Not sure where that came from, but the origin of all things is God, a polluted version is created by the enemy. What say ye?*"

Let me suggest other ways to look at this argument. Personally, I ran into this dispute years ago when I began to consider the use of herbs and applied kinesiology in my practice. That was a favorite argument artfully aimed against all forms of holistic medicine—against anything that departed from the "orthodox standard." Guess who used it most? Those in the medical establishment!

The purpose was obviously to discredit chiropractic, acupuncture, herbology, applied kinesiology, homeopathy and more. Several prominent and effective books were written by Christian medical doctors debunking all holistic practices. They went into the occult *origins* of every modality. They found something suspicious about each modality, of course. If the founder was in some way involved in the occult, in their estimation, and the way *they* defined occult, the entire modality was occult. "Run the other way!" So went the argument.

Of course, I understood enough about the origin of the medical profession to know that poisonous drugs and pharmaceuticals were classified as sorcery for over 1500 years. In the 13th century, with the birth of alchemy and chemistry, a negative word gradually took on a respectable meaning. This NEGATIVE word "*Pharmakia*" was translated as both "sorcery" and "witchcraft" in the Greek New Testament. As the world was evolving out of the Dark Ages, alchemy and chemistry became classified as "sciences." *Pharmakia* became respectable again! After thousands of years of herbal and natural medicine, the "sorcerers" were suddenly casting stones at those who used natural or non-drug medicine—out of a newly achieved position of social respectability.

I don't find much if anything in the Bible against herbs, spices, chiropractic, massage, use of magnets, homeopathy and the like. What I do find is an absolute warning against sorcery. Sorcery in the New Testament is derived from the English word translated from the Greek word *Pharmakia.* Both Strong's and Young's Concordances clearly define *pharmakia* as the use of drugs and poisons. Of the 5 negative uses of that word in the New Testament, Revelation 18:23b most clearly defines the problem: "....for thy merchants were the great men of the earth; for by their sorceries (Greek: pharmakia) were ALL NATIONS DECEIVED." Babylon the Great's international merchants, salesmen, sorcerers and spin-doctors are all grouped together. If we study out the true meaning of that Scripture, the context and the word origins, it should shake some sense into us.

Does that mean the New Age philosophy is free of error? Unfortunately there has been a subtle hijacking of natural modalities, which has often resulted in serious perversion, abuse and misuse nature's medicine. *The reason is that many New Agers have worshiped the creation rather than the Creator.* And because New Age has perverted what God created, both religious and medical orthodoxy had taken the pious position that sorcery (modern pharmaceutical medicine) is a blessing of God and the "occult" natural stuff is of the devil.

Wrong! Sorcery needs to be rejected. And natural medicine needs to be redeemed from New Age occult practitioners who have hijacked what God created for our use. Let us again take authority and dominion over what God created, as STEWARDS and Husbandmen over the natural aspects of the creation also.

Let me explain some of the misguided rational of those who use the argument of origins.

The origin of China dishes is China. China is saturated with the occult. Therefore, China dishes must be occult, right? But most wouldn't go quite that far. The following are better examples.

Dr. Palmer, who reputedly discovered chiropractic, was a magnetic healer, therefore (by some definitions) into the occult, therefore chiropractic is occult. Yet chiropractic principles were around long before Palmer. The origin therefore was not Palmer. God created the body.

Dr. Hahnerman, a brilliant German medical doctor and scientist, a man who spoke over a dozen languages fluently, was the father of *modern* homeopathy. The "sorcerers" found something in Hahnerman's past that smelled of the occult. Therefore, homeopathy is occult. Yet the principles of homeopathy go back thousands of years before Hahnerman. Hahnerman did not discover homeopathy, did not father it, but merely recognized it, documented it, expanded it, and got the credit. The principles go back to the dawn of creation.

New Age folks are deeply into herbs, the earth, and mother earth. Many of them are sincere, caring and conscientious people. They use herbs. No matter, herbology is still therefore new age and occult. Seriously, that is what these Christian medical doctors write. Yet we read about herbs and spices in the Bible, nearly always in a positive light. God created herbs and spices!

Let's take a different twist. Those who use the argument of origins get a blank look when the following are explained:

Lucifer was the cherubim of music, long before man was created. Therefore, is *all* music satanic? Several "Christian" groups believe that. Yet music goes back to the beginning of history. King David and the Tabernacle of David symbolized music at its highest earthly level. The Tabernacle of David and its music will be one day restored according to biblical prophecy. But the "first use" of music had to do with Lucifer. But who created Lucifer? *Music pre-existed Lucifer.*

The first use of the harp and organ, of brass works, and of herding cattle were originally under the fathering of those in rebellion against God's plan. For instance, Jubal was the "father" of the harp and organ, in the line of Cain, the son of Lamech, an apostate. (Genesis 4:19-24) Are the harp and organ therefore evil in origin? Some believe that!

Jabal his brother was the "father" of cattle herders. Does that mean cowboys are therefore automatically in apostasy? We could go on with other examples. You see, the argument can get ridiculous.

Does God inspire only the righteous? Or does He pour out good things on anybody willing to receive? The "rain" of inspiration, creativity and ingenuity falls on the just and the unjust alike, according to the Scriptures. Obviously, the righteous *should* be the ones who use their gifts and talents for the greatest benefit of humanity; whereas the unrighteous are more likely to abuse them. But sometimes the righteous are not very righteous, and sometimes the unrighteous are wiser than the sons, again according to the Scriptures.

You are right: God is the Creator and Author of everything in nature. That includes gravity, electricity, solar energy, and every form of *energy* principle that is known and unknown, both understood and not yet understood. God created energy; He spoke and everything came into being. And now He "holds everything together by the word of his power." It is interesting to find words in the Scriptures that can be translated *energy* and *dynamite*!

It is not so much what it is the origin, because everything originates from Yahweh Elohim (LORD God) as Creator. The real key is HOW any modality is PUT TO USE that makes it acceptable or suspect. Gunpowder can be used to feed the family or kill one's neighbor. Is gunpowder therefore evil? Or is it how the gunpowder is put to use, and the motive behind its use?

Holo is a Biblical Greek New Testament word, first used by Dr. Evers, a Christian medical doctor, who coined "holistic medicine" in the 60s. He coined the word from its use in the Bible, where the apostle John wished his readers would be *holo* (whole, complete, healthy) in body, in soul and in spirit. The origin of the word "holistic" is therefore biblical and Christian—not New Age, occult or Oriental. Few understand that. *Misunderstanding is at the origin of so much confusion when it comes to health, religion, philosophy and belief systems.*

Therefore the problem is seldom where something came from, meaning its *supposed* origin. The real questions are: "Who told you, *Who is guiding you*? What is your heart in the matter? Is this a proper use or an abuse of the modality? What is your motive?" If your motive is *not* right, DON'T TOUCH ME!

In other words, are you doing whatever you do because *God opened the door? Is what you are doing* for an honorable and ethical use? Are you worshiping the Creator or the modality? Is your god "gain or godliness"?

And finally and ultimately we must ask, WHAT IS THE FRUIT? Are the fruits health, joy, freedom, thanksgiving and worship of the true Creator? Or is the fruit increased: depression, amplified illness, and annihilation of the heart toward God?

It is true: the devil created nothing. His expertise is the Pollution of every good thing. *Sin is adding leaven, a lie, a twist, or a falsehood to the original purpose.* Let us not throw out the baby with the dirty bath water of falsehood as defined by imaginary orthodoxy. Are we after cultural acceptance and being a man pleaser? *If* we are to please God and bring healing to a sick creation, surely we must be open to cutting-edge creativity, inspiration, change and empowerment that may sometimes cause questions, rebuttal and even crucifixion. That is a path that few are willing to follow. But following that path could well bring us to the true ORIGINAL INTENT, and open doors that the faint hearted will seldom dare to open, much less enter.

To conclude, generally the argument of origins is espoused by those supporting the status quo. That argument is filled with circular reasoning. That argument leads to stagnant thinking, a flat world, and lack of creativity. It is often intellectual and mental in origin, the worship of rational thinking, meaning Greek philosophy, and a "worldview" that has a westernized, left-brain flavor. It leads to the stagnation of true spirituality, to manifest legalism, and a "form" of religion rather than true liberating power.

Not sure why the question. This is my approach to a reply. Does this help?

Blessings,

Roger L. De Haan

Appendix Four

CREATION MANDATE SCRIPTURES

The Scriptures present over 1700 verses that mention or speak of the land. The land is important to God. God loves the land simply because he loves, as the Creator, everything that he has created. Everything has a *purpose*, and His desire is for that purpose to be fulfilled. It has been almost impossible for believers to express their appreciation and love for the land without being labeled as radical. This must change. For God Himself is radical! And we are His sons!

We must get it into our heart and conviction that there is nothing political about concern and appreciation for the land. God gave the land for man to manage. We will have to account for our stewardship of the land! Psalm 115:15 proclaims, "The heaven, even the heavens, are the Lord's; But the earth He has given to the children of men." God gave the earth to us because He is the rightful owner. Psalm 24:1 says: "The earth is the Lord's, and all its fullness, The world and those who dwell therein." In Leviticus 25:23, God declares: "The land is Mine!" God will never give up ownership of the land. But we have been given *jurisdiction and authority* over the land.

Rank disobedience is the reason mankind has relinquished his responsibility and guardianship of the land. The land itself is looking for relief. The pressures of defilement are the result of unfaithful stewards. We can blame the devil if we wish. However, as rightful stewards we hold far more authority than either angels or devils. There is a whole lot at stake here!

God is the owner. We are stewards. Our stewardship is generational and is passed from one generation to the next. It is time the rightful stewards claim their place in this generation, so that our light due to appropriate stewardship might shine mightily once again! Isaiah 60:1-2 declares: "Arise, shine; For your light has come! And the glory of the LORD is risen upon you. For behold, the darkness shall cover the earth, And deep darkness the people; But the LORD will arise over you, And His glory will be seen upon you." Is it not time to arise and walk in that promise?

Usually when we read or hear promises that God will bless and *heal our land*, we think He means He will *heal our people.* The primary benefit of repentance definitely is to restore people! But as you read the following sets of Scriptures, it will become clear that these are also *environmental and ecological verses*! When we sin, the very ecology and environment suffer! "Cursed is the ground because of you," God told Adam. The very soil is affected by our sin. So when it says God will heal our land, it means just that: He will HEAL OUR LAND!

Heaven should be the model for our life and ministry. This gives new meaning to the Lord's Prayer: "As in heaven, *so on EARTH.*" Jesus lived out this principle by doing only what He saw His Father doing. Learning to recognize the Holy Spirit's presence and how to follow His lead in every area of life will enable *us* to do the works of Christ. Healing and deliverance must become the common expression of this gospel of Kingdom power once again.

The problems in the world cannot be solved unless there is a massive return to responsibility and morality. A breathtaking awakening is required. Could it be that the assaults on this planet, engineered out of our ignorance and wrong ideas of how to heal this planet, could be the final stimulus for massive change? Could it be that God is on the move, a move that transcends mere human effort and humanism, to bring creation to the point where we will once again recognize that neither religion, nor agnosticism, nor atheism have the correct answers? But that only a massive return to the God of creation, through repentance, will bring the needed answers? I believe we need massive REVIVAL. We need revival on such an enormous scale that the world will never again forget that we humans are *NOT* "THE MASTER OF OUR FATE, THE CAPTAIN OF OUR SOUL!"

Above all, it is time to recognize that *salvation is global in dimension.* Are we not called to help deliver the very creation around us from its daily anguish? I agree that we only see "in a mirror, dimly, but then face to face" (1 Cor. 13:12b). Nevertheless, we are called to move from the current glory to greater glory. We are called to establish one level of glory now, to pave the way for the greater glory! We are called to express God's heart on this earth. **If you really want to heal the land, begin with the land of your own heart, and cry out to God for His mercy on our poor and broken creation!**

Unless otherwise noted, the Scriptures below are taken from the *New King James* version of the Bible.

Mankind's was given an awesome responsibility in creation

Dominion: "You made him ruler over the works of your hands, you put everything under his feet" (Ps. 8:6, NIV).

Ruling and Subduing: "Be fruitful and increase in number; fill the earth and subdue it. Rule over the fish of the sea and the birds of the air and over every living creature that moves on the ground" (Gen 1:28, NIV).

Cultivate and Keep: "Adonai, God, took the person and put him in the garden of Eden to cultivate and care for it" (Gen. 2:15, Complete Jewish Bible). "Cultivate" is also often translated "till" or "serve." "Care" is also often translated "keep" or "preserve."

Image Bearer: "Let us make man in our image, in our likeness" (Gen. 1:26, NIV).

Caretaker: "What is man that You are mindful of him, And the son of man that You visit him? For You have made him a little lower than the angels, And You have crowned him with glory and honor. You have made him to have dominion over the works of Your hands; You have put all things under his feet, All sheep and oxen—Even the beasts of the field, The birds of the air, And the fish of the sea That pass through the paths of the seas" (Ps. 8:4-8).

Righteous Caretaker "A righteous man cares for the needs of his animal..." (Prov. 12:10a, NIV).

Creation Delivered: "The creation waits in eager expectation for the sons of God to be revealed. For the creation was subjected to frustration, not by its own choice, but by the will of the one who subjected it, in hope that the creation itself will be liberated from its to decay and brought into the glorious freedom of the children of God" (Rom. 8:19-21, NIV).

Total Harmony: "The wolf also shall dwell with the lamb, The leopard shall lie down with the young goat, The calf and the young lion and the fatling together; And a little child shall lead them. The cow and the bear shall graze; Their young ones shall lie down together; And the lion shall eat straw like the ox" (Isa. 11:6-7).

The Creatures Suffer because of Mankind's Lost Dominion

Creation groans: "For we know that the whole creation groans and labors with birth pangs together until now" (Rom. 8:22).

Animals groan: "How the animals groan! The herds of cattle are restless, Because they have no pasture; Even the flocks of sheep suffer punishment" (Joel 1:18).

Land mourns: "....There is no truth or mercy, Or knowledge of God in the land...Therefore the land will mourn...With the beasts of the field And the birds of the air; Even the fish of the sea will be taken away" (Hos. 4: 1, 3).

Food fails: "'Yes, the deer also gave birth in the field, But left because there was no grass. And the wild donkeys stood in the desolate heights; They sniffed at the wind like jackals; Their eyes failed because there was no grass.' O LORD, though our iniquities testify against us, Do it for Your name's sake; For our backslidings are many, We have sinned against You" (Jer. 14:5-7).

The Consequences of Lost Dominion on the land and earth.

Carelessness: "The whole land is desolate and no one cares" (Jer. 12:11, TLB).

Pain: ""For we know that the whole creation groans and labors with birth pangs together until now" (Rom. 8:22).

Wasted: "I will make the land desolate because they have been unfaithful, declares the Sovereign Lord" (Ezek 15:8, NIV).

Empty: "The LORD *is* King forever and ever; The nations have perished out of His land (Ps. 10:16b).

Land vomits: "For the land is defiled; therefore I visit the punishment of its iniquity upon it, and the land vomits out its inhabitants...Keep my statutes....lest the land vomit you out also when you defile it, as it vomited out the nations that were before you" (Lev. 18:25-26, 28).

Desolation: "I will bring the land to desolation, and your enemies who dwell in it shall be astonished at it" (Lev. 26:32).

No rain: "Lest the Lord's anger be aroused against you, and He shut up the heavens so that there be no rain, and the land yield no produce, and you perish quickly from the good land which the Lord is giving you" (Deut. 11:17).

Deserts: "For the land is full of adulterers; For because of a curse the land mourns. The pleasant places of the wilderness are dried up. Their course of life is evil, and their might is not right" (Jer. 23:10).

Destruction: "The nations were angry, and Your wrath has come...that You should reward Your servants the prophets and the saints, And those who fear Your name, small and great, And should destroy those who destroy the earth" (Rev. 11:18).

Defilement: "The earth is also defiled under its inhabitants, Because they have transgressed the laws, Changed the ordinance, Broken the everlasting covenant" (Is. 24:5).

Plagues: "Locusts shall consume all your trees and the produce of your land" (Deut. 28:42).

Weeds: "If my land cries out against me, And its furrows weep together....let thistles grow instead of wheat, And weeds instead of barley" (Job 31:38, 40).

Pollution: (They) shed innocent blood, The blood of their sons and daughters, Whom they sacrificed to the idols of Canaan; And the land was polluted with blood" (Ps. 106:38).

Desolation: "They have made it desolate; Desolate, it mourns to Me; The whole land is made desolate, Because no one takes it to heart" (Jer. 12:11).

Waste lands: "The field is wasted, the land mourns; For the grain is ruined, The new wine is dried up, The oil fails" (Joel 1:10).

Deserted fields: "I will take up a weeping and wailing for the mountains, And for the dwelling places of the wilderness a lamentation, Because they are burned up, So that no one can pass through; Nor can men hear the voice of the cattle. Both the birds of the heavens and the beasts have fled; They are gone" (Jer. 9:10).

Land Mourns: "There is no faithfulness, no love, no acknowledgment of God in the land...Because of this the land mourns, and all who live in it waste away; the beasts of the field and the birds of the air and the fish of the sea are dying" (Hos. 4: 1, 3, NIV).

Ground Cursed: "...Cursed is the ground because of you...It will produce thorns and thistles for you...By the sweat of your brow you will eat your food..." (Gen 3: 17-19, NIV).

Human Guilt: "The earth dries up and withers, the world languishes and withers, the exalted of the earth languish. The earth is defiled by its people; they have disobeyed the laws, violated the statutes and broken the everlasting covenant. Therefore a curse consumes the earth; its people must bear their guilt" Is. 24:4-6, NIV).

Earth spoiled: "The earth will be completely laid waster and totally plundered..." (Is. 24:3, NIV).

Land Mourns: "How long will the land mourn, and the herbs of every field wither? The beasts and the birds are consumed, For the wickedness of those who dwell there..." (Jer. 12:4).

No Pasture: "How the animals groan! The herds of cattle are restless, Because they have no pasture; Even the flocks of sheep suffer punishment...And fire has devoured the open pastures" (Joel 1:18, 20b).

Pasture Restored: "Do not be afraid, you beasts of the field; For the open pastures are springing up, And the tree bears its fruit; The fig tree and the vine yield their strength" (Joel 2:22).

Animals become vicious in response to man's mutiny

Today, as throughout history, wild beasts violently kill humans: note daily reports of sharks, killer whales, sting-rays, bears, wolves, lions, poisonous snakes, killer dogs, killer army ants, killer bees, etc: who viciously kill or mutilate humans as well as other animals.

Killer Beasts: "I will send wild beasts among you, which shall rob you of your children, devour your livestock, and make you few in number..." (Lev. 26:22a).

Beasts predicted: "... I will also send against them the teeth of beasts, with the poison of serpents of the dust" (Deut. 32:24b).

Righteous delivered: "You shall laugh at destruction and famine, And you shall not be afraid of the beasts of the earth...And the beasts of the field shall be at peace with you" (Job 5:22-23).

Men like Animals: "I said in my heart, 'Concerning the condition of the sons of men, God tests them, that they may see that they themselves are like animals" (Eccles. 3:18).

Babylon judged: "But wild beasts of the desert will lie there, And their houses will be full of owls; Ostriches will dwell there....The hyenas will howl in their citadels, and jackals in their pleasant palaces..." (Is. 13:21-22).

Babylon confirmed: "Therefore the wild desert beasts shall dwell there with the jackals, And the ostriches shall dwell in it. It shall be inhabited no more forever, Nor shall it be dwelt in from generation to generation" (Jer. 50:39).

Nations judged: "It shall be a habitation of jackals...The wild beasts of the desert shall also meet with the jackals...Also the night creature shall rest there...There the arrow snake shall make her nest and lay eggs...There also shall the hawks be gathered...Not one of these shall fail..." (Is. 34:13-16).

Killer animals: "And I will appoint over them four forms of destruction...The sword to slay, the dogs to drag, the birds of the heavens and the beasts of the earth to devour and destroy" (Jer. 15:3).

Jerusalem judged: "So I will send against you famine and wild beasts, and they will bereave you" (Ezek. 5:17a).

Temple beasts: "So I went in and saw, and there—every sort of creeping thing, abominable beasts, and all the idols of the house of Israel, portrayed all around on the walls" (Ezek. 8:10).

Judah destroyed: "....the one who is in the open field I will give to the beasts to be devoured, and those who are in the strongholds and caves shall die of the pestilence. For I will make the land most desolate...because of all their abominations which they have committed" (Ezek. 33:27-29).

Judah restored: "I will make a covenant of peace with them, and cause wild beasts to cease from the land; and they will dwell safely in the wilderness and sleep in the woods" (Ezek. 34:25).

Nebuchadnezzar shamed: "But when his heart was lifted up, and his spirit was hardened in pride...Then he was driven from the sons of men, his heart was made like the beasts, and his dwelling was with the wild donkeys. They fed him with grass like oxen...till he knew that the Most High God rules in the kingdom of men..." (Dan. 5:20-21).

Men as beasts: "But these, like natural brute beasts....speak evil of the things they do not understand, and will utterly perish in their own corruption" (2 Pet. 2:12).

Lions mouths shut: "Then Daniel said to the king, 'O king, live forever! My God sent His angel and shut the lions' mouths, so they have not hurt me, because I was found innocent before Him; and also, O king, I have done no wrong before you'" (Dan. 6:21).

Paul fights beasts: "If, in the manner of men, I have fought with beasts at Ephesus, what advantage is it to me? If the dead do not rise, 'Let us eat and drink, for tomorrow we die!' Do not be deceived..." (1 Cor. 15:32-33).

The Land is blessed when the People are Righteous

Crops: "I will raise up for them a garden of renown, and they shall no longer be consumed with hunger in the land, nor bear the shame of the Gentiles anymore" (Ezek. 34:29).

Rain: "I will give you rain in its season, the land shall yield its produce, and the trees of the field shall yield their fruit" (Lev. 26:4).

Healing: "If My people who are called by My name will humble themselves, and pray and seek My face, and turn from their wicked ways, then I will hear from heaven, and will forgive their sin and *heal their land*" (2 Chron. 7:14, emphasis added).

Covenant keeping: "For I will look on you favorably and make you fruitful, multiply you and confirm My covenant with you" (Lev. 26:9).

Fruitfulness: "But you, O mountains of Israel, you shall shoot forth your branches and yield your fruit to my people Israel, for they are about to come" (Ezek. 36: 8).

Productivity: "Then I will give you rain in its season, the land shall yield its produce, and the trees of the field shall yield their fruit. Your threshing shall last till the time of vintage, and the vintage shall last till the time of sowing; you shall eat your bread to the full, and dwell in your land safely" (Lev. 26:4-5).

Peace: "I will give you peace in the land, and you shall lie down, and none will make you afraid; I will rid the land of evil beasts, and the sword will not go through your land" (Lev. 26:6).

Blessing: "For the land that soaks up frequent rains and then brings forth a crop useful to its owners receives a blessing from God" (Heb. 6:7, Complete Jewish Bible).

Deliverance: "I will make a covenant of peace with them, and cause wild beasts to cease from the land; and they will dwell safely in the wilderness and sleep in the woods" (Ezek. 34:25).

Fullness: "If you be willing and obedient, You shall eat the good of the land" (Is. 1:19).

Safety: "And they shall no longer be a prey for the nations, nor shall beasts of the land devour them; but they shall dwell safely..." (Ezek. 34:28).

Protection: "When there is famine in the land, pestilence or blight or mildew, locusts or grasshoppers; when their enemy besieges them in the land of their cities; whatever plague or whatever sickness there is...then hear in heaven Your dwelling place, and forgive, and act, and give to everyone according to all his ways..." (1 Kings 8:37, 39).

Final Judgment: "The Goyim raged. But now your rage has come, the time for the dead to be judged, the time for rewarding your servants the prophets and your holy people, those who stand in awe of your name, both small and great. *It is also time for destroying those who destroy the earth*" (Rev. 11:18, Complete Jewish Bible).

The land is to be given a rest, just like its people

Fruit trees rest: "When you come into the land, and have planted all kinds of trees for food, then you shall count their fruit as uncircumcised. Three years it shall be as uncircumcised to you. It shall not be eaten" (Lev. 19:23).

Poor benefit: "When you reap the harvest of your land, you shall wholly reap the corners of your field....You shall leave them for the poor and for the stranger: I am the Lord your God" (Lev. 23:22).

People benefit: "Speak to the children of Israel, and say to them: 'When you come into the land which I give you, then the land shall keep a sabbath to the Lord" (Lev 25:2).

Fields rest: "In the seventh year there shall be a sabbath of solemn rest for the land, a sabbath to the Lord. You shall neither sow your field nor prune your vineyard. What grows of its own accord of your harvest you shall not reap, nor gather the grapes of your untended vine, for it is a year of rest for the land" (Lev. 25:4-5).

Land rests: "Then the land shall enjoy its sabbaths as long as it lies desolate and you are in your enemies' land; then the land shall rest and enjoy its Sabbaths" (Lev. 26:34).

Nature responds to the voice of a genuine husbandman:

Wind obeys: "Who can this be? For He commands even the winds and water, and they obey Him!" (Lk.8:25).

Animals teach: "But now ask the beasts, and they will teach you; And the birds of the air, and they will tell you; Or speak to the earth, and it will teach you; And the fish of the sea will explain to you" (Job 12:7-8).

God's Goodness: "You open your hand and satisfy the desires of every living thing" (Ps. 145:16, NIV).

Animals praise, bless and somehow connect with their Creator!

Animals honor: "The beast of the field will honor Me, The jackals and the ostriches, Because I give waters in the wilderness And rivers in the desert, To give drink to My people, My chosen" (Is. 43:20).

God's animals: "For every beast of the forest is Mine, And the cattle on a thousand hills. I know all the birds of the mountains, And the wild beasts of the field are Mine" (Ps 50:10-11).

Animals praise: "Praise the Lord!...Mountains and all hills; fruitful trees and all cedars; Beasts and all cattle; Creeping things and flying fowl...Let them praise the name of the Lord...." (Ps. 148:1, 9-10, 13).

Animals talk: "Who teaches us more than the beasts of the earth, And makes us wiser than the birds of heaven? There they cry out, but He does not answer, Because of the pride of evil men" (Job 35:11-12, emphasis added).

Covenant all-inclusive: "I establish My covenant with you and with your descendants after you, and with every living creature that is with you: the birds, the cattle, and every beast of the earth with you, of all that go out of the ark, every beast of the earth. Thus I establish My covenant with you: Never again shall all flesh be cut off by the waters of the flood; never again shall there be a flood to destroy the earth" (Gen. 9:9b-11).

Creation mirrors Creator: "For since the creation of the world His invisible attributes are clearly seen, being understood by the things that are made, even His eternal power and Godhead..." (Rom. 1:20).

Animal harmony: "And the beasts of the field shall be at peace with you" (Job 5:23b).

Appendix Five

CREATION MANDATE DEFINITIONS

FARMER: We must enlarge our concept of farmers and farming! More than one who cultivates the land, the plants, and animals, a true "farmer" is one who manifests stewardship and guardianship over every aspect of our magnificent creation. Are you gifted in pottery, in painting, in music, writing, or invention? Potters use clay, painters use paint, musicians use instruments, writers use paper and pen, and inventors shape inventions. The farmer is a steward of everything natural within the creation. He accomplishes this by drawing on the resources of his heart and spirit to serve and worship the Creator as well as serve the creation. The true farmer has his feet on the earth, his hands involved in a worthy endeavor, and his mind, heart and spirit seeking to use every talent and gift in a way that brings honor to the Creator of both heaven AND earth!

CREATION: Creation includes everything created. This includes heaven and the spiritual as well as the earth and natural realm. Creation includes every principle of energy, harmonics, reproduction, beauty, sound, and light in both the seen and unseen realms. It includes things above, on and below the earth. It includes the sun, moon, and stars, along with space and the galaxies. It includes past, present, and future. Creation presupposes a Creator. A Creator presupposes being creative, creating new things, shaping new forms, or causing something to exist in new or different forms. "In the beginning God created the heavens and the earth" (Gen. 1:1). "God created man in His own image" (Gen. 1:27). "Create in me a *new* heart" (Ps. 51:10). "We are his workmanship, created in Christ Jesus" (Eph. 2:10). "Behold I create a *NEW* heaven and a *New* earth" (Isa. 65:17).

STEWARDSHIP: The Bible presents over 1700 verses that mention or speak of the land. The land is important to God. He loves the land! We have been given stewardship over that land. Stewardship means managing another's affairs or property. What a high honor we have been given. That honor includes giving accounting for the management of HIS properties!

Stewardship is generational and carries forward from one generation to the next. Stewardship is a face to face relationship with the owner of the land. We have access to His presence. Without presence we have lost connection. We can only fight for the land if we know who we are and who God is! God is a warrior, a God of battles. As stewards we also must be warriors, as we battle to cleanse and redeem the land that has been robbed from its rightful owner. "It is required in stewards, that a man be found faithful" (1 Cor. 4:2).

GUARDIANSHIP: Guardianship is a term akin to stewardship. The word indicates an office where one is chosen to guard, protect, preserve, defend and look after something placed in his or her care, to protect it from injury, loss or attack. We are to guard our homes, our families, our property, our good name, and the land and animals placed under our care. Like David, we may have to figuratively kill the lion and the bear, as well as the Goliath that hampers our destiny. Guardianship is fulfilling our God-endowed responsibility to maintain oversight over both the natural and spiritual aspects of creation. This is both an individual and corporate responsibility.

REDEMPTION: Redemption is the long-term plan of God for any part of creation. Every part of creation has a purpose, sometimes many purposes. The simple element calcium has over 300 known functions in the human body! Every element, every cell, every organism has a purpose! Every virus, mosquito and lizard somehow fits into that plan! Therefore, redemption includes more than just the souls of men. Christ died for the entire creation! Restoration of the original plan is the purpose of redemption!

RECONCILIATION: Reconciliation is the bringing back of every aspect of creation back to the original intent. The prefix "re" means to restore or bring back. "Concile" means to "call into harmony or union." According to 2 Cor. 5:18, we as believers have a calling to reconcile (restore, bring back into harmony) everything back to God. After we ourselves are reconciled, *we* have been given the remarkable "ministry of reconciliation!"

CHRISTIAN: A Christian is legitimately a follower of Christ. This name was first used in Acts 11:26: "And the disciples were called Christians first in Antioch." Please try to separate the word Christian from religion, legalism, unfounded traditions and sectarian beliefs. A true Christian is one who imitates Christ, moves in the spirit of Christ, and has an intimate relationship with God. (See also Acts 26:28, 1 Peter 4:16.)

BELIEVER: I often use the term "believer" to emphasis anyone who believes and has faith in the God of the Scriptures by personal experience. I use this word frequently to define or differentiate one who may be Christian *by name only, but not necessarily by belief deep in one's heart.* In other words, some call themselves Christians because of their *external* country of birth or out of family respect. One becomes a "believer" following a legitimate *internal* personal experience, an *internal* personal commitment, and an ongoing personal practicing of the presence of a personal God. (See Acts 26:28, 1 Peter 4:16.)

CHURCH: Many think of church as a building. In the New Testament, the Greek word *ecclesia*, translated in English as "church," refers to a fellowship of believers. Therefore, the church is a group of believers, not a building! We don't go to church; we *are* the church! The church is made up of "living stones." not cold bricks!

Suggested Reading and Website Resources

Various Resources for Basic Animal, Human, and Soil Information

1. ***Acres USA*** is a monthly magazine voice for "Eco-Agriculture." For the farmer, it has a wide variety of hard-to-find information. This periodical is for those who see themselves as open-minded. Some of the information may require discernment. What else is new! Yet this magazine propagates some dynamic and very cutting edge information. It will challenge you with the insights of others and propose real-life answers. It certainly challenges the status quo and strongly held orthodoxy, if you can accept that challenge. The magazine also sponsors presenters from many walks of life by providing seminars and selling their books. Seminars, books, and tapes reflect everything from backyard farming, goat keeping, beekeeping, and pastured poultry, to large sustainable farms and agricultural practices worldwide. Contact them at 1-800-355-5313 for subscriptions or information, or visit their website: www.acresusa.com

2. ***Natural Care of Pets.*** This spiral-bound book contains over 35 helpful and insightful articles on such subjects as diet and nutrition; home cooking; herbs and supplements; parasite prevention; skin problems; food allergies; cancer helps; stress control; corneal ulcers and "dry eye"; new puppy care; new protocols for vaccinations; importance of food enzymes; and many others. Send $12 plus $3 shipping & handling to: Dr. Roger L. De Haan, Holistic Veterinary Services, 105 Police Club Drive, Kings Mountain, NC 28086. Web: www.aholisticvet.com

3. ***Restoring Health Care as a Ministry.*** This challenging book, authored by Dr. Mark Virkler and Dr. Reuben De Haan, evaluates and integrates healing methodologies according to biblical and spiritual principles. An excitingly new approach to health care, this book comes with my highest recommendation. It is available at the above address or from the authors for $14.95 plus $3.95 shipping and handling. www.cwgministries.org

Creation Mandate Suggested Reading & References

Alternative Medicine, The Definitive Guide. 350 Leading-Edge Physicians Explain Their Treatments...Affordable Self-Help Cures for You and Your Family. (The Burton Goldberg Group, Future Medicine Publishing, 1993).

Angell, Marcia, PhD. *The Truth About Drug Companies—How They Deceive Us and What to Do About It.* (New York: Random House Trade Paperbacks, 2005).

Becker, Robert, MD. *Cross Currents, The Perils of Electropollution, The Promise of Electromedicine.* (New York: St. Martin's Press, 1990).

Becker, Robert, MD, and Gary Selden. *The Body Electric: Electromagnetism and the Foundation of Life.* (New York, Harper Paperbacks, 1998).

Benge, Janet and Benge, Geoff. *George Washington Carver, From Slave to Scientist.* (Seattle, WA: YWAM Publishing, 2001).

Boone, J. Allen. *Kinship With All Life.* (New York: Harper and Row, 1976).

Callahan, Philip, PhD. *Tuning In To Nature: Infrared Radiation and the Insect Communication System,* (Acres USA Publishers, 2001). www.acresusa.com

Dawson, John. *Healing America's Wounds,* (Ventura, CA: Regal Books, 1994).

De Haan, Roger L., DVM. *We Don't Die, We Kill Ourselves, Our Foods are Killing Us!* (Huntsville, AL: Milestones International Publishers, 2006).

Durlacher, James V. *Freedom From Fear Forever: The Acu-Power Way to Overcoming Your Fears, Phobias and Inner Problems.* (Tempe, AZ: Van Ness Publishing, 1997).

Dye, Michael. *Vaccinations: Deception & Tragedy: The Truth about Vaccines and the Dangers They Pose.* (Shelby, NC: Hallelujah Acres Publishing, 1999).

Higa, Teruo. *An Earth Saving Revolution: A Means to Resolve Our World's Problems Through Effective Microorganisms.* (Tokyo, Japan: Sunmark Publishing, 1996).

Huggins, Hal A., DDS, and Thomas E. Levy, MD. *Uninformed Consent: The Hidden Dangers in Dental Care.* (Charlottesville, VA: Hampton Roads Publishing, 1999).

Jensen , Bernard, and Mark Anderson. *Empty Harvest: Understanding the Link Between Our Food, Our Immunity, and Our Planet.* (New York: Avery Publishing Group, 1990).

Johnson, Bill Johnson. *Dreaming With God: Secrets to Redesigning Your World Through God's Creative Flow.* (Shippensburg, PA: Destiny Image Publishers, 2006).

Kendall, R. T. *Total Forgiveness: When Everything in You Wants to Hold a Grudge, Point a Finger and Remember the Pain, God Wants You to Lay It All Aside.* (Lake Mary, FL: Charisma House, 2002).

Lisle, Harvey. *The Enlivened Rock Powders.* (Austin, TX: Acres USA Publishing, 1994).

Lydecker, Beatrice. *Stories the Animals Tell Me.* (New York: Harper and Row, 1977).

Meinig, George, DDS. *Root Canal Cover-up: A Founder of the Association of Root Canal Specialists Discovers Evidence that Root Canals Damage Your Health. Learn What to Do.* (Ojai, CA: Bion Publishing, 1998).

Mittleider, Jacob, and Andrew Nelson. *Food for Everyone: The Mittleider Method: Illustrating the New, Proven Method of Dramatic Food Production as Demonstrated in the United States and the South Pacific.* (Walla Walla, WA: Color Press, 1973).

Oschman, James, and Candace Pert. *Energy Medicine: The Scientific Basis.* (New York: Churchhill Livingstone, 2000).

Pearsall, Paul, PhD. *The Heart's Code: The New Findings About Cellular Memories and Their Role in the Mind/Body/Spirit Connection* (New York: Broadway Books, 1998).

Pottenger, Francis, MD. *Pottenger's Cats: A Study in Nutrition.* (Lemon Grove, CA: Price-Pottenger Nutrition Foundation, 1995).

Pratney, Winkie. *Healing the Land: A Supernatural View of Ecology.* (Grand Rapids, MI: Chosen Books, 1993).

Price, Weston, DDS. *Nutrition and Physical Degeneration.* (Chicago, IL: Keats Publishing, 1989).

Randolph, Larry. *The Coming Shift.* (Fort Mill, SC: MorningStar Publications, 2006).

Ridley, Matt. *Genome: The Autobiography of a Species in 23 Chapters* (New York: Harper Collins, 2006).

Ridley, Matt. *Nature Via Nurture: Genes, Experience and What Makes Us Human.* (New York: Harper Collins, 2003).

Stefanatos, Joanne, DVM. *Animals and Man: A State of Blessedness.* (Minneapolis, MN: Light and Life Publishing Company, 1992).

Stitt, Barbara Reed. *Food & Behavior: A Natural Connection.* (Portland, OR: Natural Press, 1997).

Stitt, Paul. *Beating the Food Giants.* (Portland, OR: Natural Press, 1993).

Dr. Suuqiina. *Can You Feel The Mountains Tremble? A Healing the Land Handbook.* (Portland, TN: Inuit Ministry International, 1999).

Strand, Ray, MD. *What Your Doctor Doesn't Know About Nutrition May Be Killing You.* (Nashville, TN: Thomas Nelson, 2002).

Thrash, Agatha, MD, and Calvin Thrash, MD. *The Animal Connection: The Proven Link Between Cancer and Other Diseases from Animals and Man.* (Seale, AL: New Lifestyle Books, 1983).

Tiner, John Hudson. *For Those Who Dare: 101 Great Christians and How They Changed the World.* (Green Forest, AR: Master Books, 2002).

Tompkins, Peter, and Christopher Bird. *The Secret Life of Plants: A fascinating account of the physical, emotional, and spiritual relations between plants and man.* (New York: Harper and Row, 1973).

Trace, Anne Blake, PhD. *Prozac: Panacea or Pandora? The Rest of the Story.* (West Jordan, UT: Cassia Publications, 2001).

Trudeau, Kevin. *More Natural "Cures" Revealed.* (Birmingham, AL: Alliance Publishing Group, 2006).

Truman, Karol K. *Feelings Buried Alive Never Die...* (Salt Lake City, UT: Olympus Publishing Company, 1991).

Twiss, Richard. *One Church, Many Tribes: Following Jesus the Way God Made You.* (Ventura, CA: Regal Books, 2000).

Van Dyke, Fred, David C. Mahan, Joseph K. Sheldon, and Raymond H. Brand. *Redeeming Creation: The Biblical Basis for Environmental Stewardship.* (Downers Grove, IL: InterVarsity Press, 1996).

Voisin, Andre. *Soil, Grass & Cancer: The Link Between Human and Animal Health and the Mineral Balance of the Soil. Andre Voisin's Classic Text.* (Austin, TX: Acres USA Publishers, 1999).

Walters, Charles. *Minerals for the Genetic Code: An Exposition and Analysis of the Dr. Olree Standard Genetic Periodic Chart and the Physical, Chemical and Biological Connection.* (Austin, TX: Acres USA Publishers, 2006.)

Wheeler, Phil, PhD, and Ron Ward. *The Non-Toxic Farming Handbook.* (Austin, TX: Acres USA Publishers, 2006).

Woodley, Randy. *Mixed Blood, Not Mixed Up: Finding God-given Identity in a Multi-cultural World.* (Scotland, PA: Healing the Land Publishing, 2004). www.eagleswingsministry.com

Websites

www.aholisticvet.com describes Dr. Roger De Haan's unique practice. Newsletter articles may eventually be published monthly on various interesting aspects of animal health care. High quality pet products are currently available for purchase, and some of them may eventually be available on the link-website which follows. Phone consultations are available if desired and time permits. So check us out.

www.mind-bodyministries.com is Dr. De Haan's link website—presently in development. This will include an e-commerce site for various products for people, pets and the land, as well as information and articles of interest. Check out information on Dr. De Haan's first volume in this series: "*We Don't Die, We Kill Ourselves. Our Foods are Killing Us*!"

www.mercola.com is a website authored by natural medical physician, Dr. Joseph Mercola, D.O. It is currently the most popular alternative health newsletter on the web. A traditionally trained but open-minded osteopathic physician, Dr. Mercola has an unusual ability to sift through facts and bring critical insight into today's health problems including: dieting, childhood and adult vaccinations, fads, alternative remedies, diseases, nutritional supplements, and many more. It's free to sign up. Of course, he also has products to sell.

www.hcmionline.com This website shares Health Care Ministry International's (HCMI) approach to health, based on sound natural principles. Authored by Dr. Reuben De Haan, it covers nontraditional health care as it conforms to biblical principles. Seminars and educational materials are offered. This includes a book: *The Foundation, Principles, Concepts and Convictions for Getting Well and Staying Well.* This is book 01 of the TBA Certification Training Program. It is a well-written book explaining 1) Nutrition, 2) Digestion, 3) Elimination, 4) Cleansing, and 5) Detoxification. To order, call: 704-730-9115. If you click on the abstract titled "Death by Medicine" at the bottom of the web "home page," you will probably be shocked by the failure of modern medicine.

www.doctoryourself.com is a privately sponsored website written by Dr. Andrew Saul, PhD, and is a library of natural healing articles with scientific references. www.ncbi.nlm.nih.gov is a government-sponsored website of the National Institute of Health. Type in a question and you will find a wealth of scientific studies and information.

There are hundreds of other websites available with as many approaches. The "Google" and "Yahoo" search engines are other sources of information. For instance, type in "Compost Tea" in a search engine. You wil1 find many sources of information, commercial and homemade compost tea equipment offers, etc. Because you are looking for *truth*, ask God to guide your eyes and your heart in your search, or you could end up in confusion by the mass of conflicting information, facts, ideas and advertising.

Endnotes

1. Dr. Paul Pearsall, *The Heart's Code,* (New York: Broadway Books, a division of Random House, 1998), xi.
2. For challenging information on this subject, read the well-documented book, *The Secret Life of Plants,* by Tompkins & Bird. These authors were the scientists behind the modern lie detector tests used in courts of law. What they found concerning plants will blow your mind! For example, connecting their electrical lie detector instrument to plants helped them solve several mystifying murder cases!
3. Bertrand Russell, *The Impact of Science on Society.* (London: Routledge, 1952, reprint 1998), 116.
4. We must enlarge our concept of farmers and farming! More than a gifted person who cultivates the land and nurtures plants and animals, a true farmer is one who manifests stewardship and guardianship over every part of the creation. Are you gifted in pottery, painting, music, writing or invention? Potters use clay, painters use paint, musicians use instruments, writers use paper and pen, and inventors shape inventions. The farmer is a steward of everything natural within the creation. He accomplishes this by drawing on the resources of his heart and spirit to serve and worship the Creator as well as the creation. The true farmer has his feet on the earth, his hands involved in a worthy endeavor, and his mind, heart and spirit seeking to use every talent and gift in a way that brings honor to the Creator of both heaven and earth!
5. Henry W. Wright, *A More Excellent Way:A Teaching on the Spiritual Roots of Disease.* (New Kensington, PA: Anchor Distributors, 2000).
6. Elden M. Chalmers, Ph.D. Healing the Broken Brain: Science and the Bible Reveal How the Brain Heals, (Coldwater, MI: Remnant Publications, 1999).
7. Francis Pottenger, MD, *Pottengers's Cats—A Study in Nutrition.* Copies of the study may be ordered from the Price-Pottenger Nutrition Foundation, ppnf@aol.com
8. Henry W. Wright, *A More Excellent Way:A Teaching on the Spiritual Roots of Disease, 158.*
9. R. C. Trench, *Trench's Synonyms of the New Testament,* (Peabody, MA: Hendrickson Publishers, 2000), 17-21.
10. Dennis Peacock, from a sermon recorded live in 2005 at "The New Testament Church," Plymouth, MA, Dr. Paul Jehle, senior pastor.
11. Barbara R. Stitt, *Food and Behavior: A Natural Connection*, Revised edition, (Portland, OR: Natural Press, 1997).
12. Samuel Cort and Willis Hackett, *Redeeming Your Mind: Managing Your Mind in Harmony with the Divine Will,* (Coldwater, MI: Remnant Publications, n. d.), 113.
13. Cort and Hackett, *Redeeming Your Mind,* 117.
14. J. Allen Boone, *Kinship with All Life*, (New York: Harper and Row, 1976), 73.
15. Allen Boone, *Kinship with All Life*, 73.
16. Paul Brand, *In His Image*, (Grand Rapids: Zondervan, 1987).
17. Paul A. Stitt, *Beating the Food Giants*, (Portland, OR: Natural Press, 1982).
18. More on good fats. As a society we have been bombarded with statistics to convince us that all fats are bad fats. Advertisements and unscientific data try to convince us to buy non-fat fats(!), hydrogenated margarine, artificial fats, low fat milk and low fat yogurt. It has almost become a religion. This is good for corporate business; but it is *not* good for the consumer!

The truth is finally coming out that we require substantial amounts of *good fats* and *oils*. These include a combination of some animal fats, but mainly fish and cod liver oils; olive, flax, grain and nut oils. The right ratios and amounts of Omega 3, 6 and 9 oils are required at all stages of life. Without these fats and oils the brain and nervous system cannot function properly.

Saturated and hydrogenated fats and oils are solid at room temperature. They are also solid at body temperature! They create inflammation and chronic disorders in the body. Good fats, on the other hand, are liquid at room temperature, and also liquid in the body. They reduce inflammation in the body, and are necessary for many body functions. Brain and nerve tissues are high in fats and oils. The immune and glandular systems require fats and oils in substantial amounts. If you don't have substantial amounts of the good cholesterol, you can't make hormones! This important subject is beyond the purpose of this book, except to bring it to your attention.

My typical recommendation for cats and dogs is for the caretaker to *add* and *rotate* the following oils into the animal's diet: olive oil and ground flax seed or flax oils on a daily basis, and add Omega 3 fish or cod liver oils 2-3 times per week. From what you have read in this book so far, would this principle apply also to you and your family?

Some good brands of fish oils and cod liver oils are: Nordic Naturals (www.nordicnaturals.com), Carlson's, and Dale Alexander's. Be sure to buy and use before the expiration date, and refrigerate all fish oils as they can go rancid.

19. For more information on this subject you can type in those names under the search engine provided by www.mercola.com for some very enlightening information on artificial sweeteners.

20. This is a very brief summary of perhaps 100 pages of guidelines from my first book in this series, *We don't Die, We Kill Ourselves*. Buy your own autographed copy by check or CC from our address provided at the back of this book; or order from our website: www.mindbodyministies.com.

21. Matt Ridley, *Genome*, (Perennial, 2000).

22. Matt Ridley, from back cover of his cassette series titled, *Nature Via Nurture*.

23. In the spring of 2007, some 90 brands were pulled off the shelf in Canada, the US and Mexico—because of kidney failure and death. At this writing the cause had not yet been determined. However aflatoxins, preservatives and contaminated batches have been implicated in similar cases in the past. As the world becomes more contaminated, we suspect this is just the tip of the iceberg.

24. I would also suggest you read Part Five of my book: *We Don't Die, We Kill Ourselves: Our Foods are Killing Us!* Chapter 22 discusses "Emergency Home Remedies." Chapter 24 discusses: "Natural Preparations for an Epidemic or Pandemic Crisis

25. Available from Dr. Starr's office at 4325 Post Road, Jewett, Ohio 43986, 330-739-6025.

26. Dr. Jonathan Wright, "The Vaccine Putting Children at More Risk Than the Disease Itself," *Nutrition and Healing*, October, 2004.

27. Robert Rodale, "Soil Is Better Than Gold," Reprinted by permission of Rodale Inc., all rights reserved.

28. For a complete teaching on this topic, order the Communion With God Study Guide at www.CWGministries.org or call 716-652-6990. Online catalog of 50 books available by

Mark & Patti Virkler as well as 100 college courses through external degree. Email: cwg@cwgministries.org.

29. Kevin Trudeau, *More natural "Cures" Revealed*, (Alliance Publishing Group, 2006), 73.
30. Check out their website at www.bowen.org/index.html.
31. Barbara Levine, *Your Body Believes Every Word You Say*, (Fairfield, CT, Wordswork Press, 2000), 49.
32. Allan Balliett, "Magic Soil of the Lost Amazon," *ACRES U. S. A.*, February, 2007, 17.
33. Allan Balliett, "Magic Soil of the Lost Amazon," 18.
34. John Dawson, *Healing America's Wounds*, (Ventura, CA: Regal Books, 1994), 260.
35. If you are interested in learning more, you can find one version of this prophecy at: www.healingtheland.com/research/prophecy/hopi.html.
36. Statistics based on information in Joshua Elijah Barrett, *Living a God-Glorifying Life Through Good Health*, (Mustang, OK: Tate Publishing, 2007), 175. The pertinent section reads: "In 2003 doctors Gary Null, Carolyn Dean, Martin Feldman, Debora Rasio, and Dorothy Smith released a medical report they titled *Death by Medicine*. This report proves that the number one cause of death in America is not heart disease or lung cancer, but is a result of the medical profession. The number of deaths due to heart disease in 2001 was 699,697; the number of deaths in 2001 from cancer was 553,251. The total number of deaths in America in 2001 which were medical in origin was 783,936! Of this number, 106,000 deaths were the result of adverse drug reactions...Medical error accounted for 98,000 deaths while unnecessary procedures accounted for 37,136. The annual price tag for iatrogenic deaths (deaths from medical causes) is $282 billion."
37. See Appendix 1, endnote 1.

ABOUT THE AUTHOR

Born and raised with an extensive farming background in southern Michigan, Dr. De Haan has always had a drawing toward natural medicine and creative instincts. He has degrees in science and veterinary medicine from Michigan State University, theology from Gordon/Conwell Theological Seminary, and nutrition from Trinity School of Natural Health. In addition, he has taken many advanced courses and obtained various other certifications and postgraduate study degrees. His experience on the mission field included living in the Amazon rainforest for 12 years under the auspices of *Mision de Cristo en Colombia.* In chapter three you will read more about his background in farming, his pilgrimage from disease care to health care, and his years in agricultural missions. You will read about a paradigm change as he faced the challenges of soil management, human and animal nutrition, and the prevention and treatment of disease at all levels of creation.

Presently, Dr. De Haan is involved in teaching and writing, while specializing in part-time health consultations and natural treatments in a clinical setting at his new home office in Kings Mountain, North Carolina.

Dr. De Haan and his wife, Virginia, have been married for 37 years and have three married sons.

Dr. Roger L. De Haan

B.S, D.V.M, M.T.S, C.V.C, C.V.C.P, C.N.H.P & C.H.C

You can get more information on his websites:
www.aholisticvet.com and **www.mind-bodyministries.com**

Contact Information

Dr. Roger L. De Haan
105 Police Club Drive
Kings Mountain, NC 28086
Websites: www.aholisticvet.com • www.mind-bodyministries.com